Language as social
semiotic

Language as social semiotic

The social interpretation of language and meaning

M. A. K. Halliday

Professor of Linguistics, University of Sydney

Edward Arnold

A division of Hodder & Stoughton

LONDON NEW YORK MELBOURNE AUCKLAND

© 1978 M.A.K. Halliday

First published in Great Britain 1978
First published in paperback 1979
Reprinted 1979, 1984, 1986, 1988, 1990, 1992

Distributed in the USA by Routledge, Chapman and Hall, Inc.
29 West 35th Street, New York, NY 10001

British Library Cataloguing in Publication Data

Halliday, Michael Alexander Kirkwood
   Language as social semiotic.
   1. Sociolinguistics
   I. Title
   301.2′1   P40

ISBN 0 7131 6259 7

Printed and bound in Great Britain for Edward Arnold, a division of
Hodder and Stoughton Limited, Mill Road, Dunton Green, Sevenoaks,
Kent TN13 2YA by Athenaeum Press Ltd, Newcastle upon Tyne.

Contents

Introduction 1

I The sociolinguistic perspective
  1 Language and social man (Part 1) 8
  2 A social-functional approach to language 36

II A sociosemiotic interpretation of language
  3 Sociological aspects of semantic change 60
  4 Social dialects and socialization 93
  5 The significance of Bernstein's work for sociolinguistic
    theory 101
  6 Language as social semiotic 108

III The social semantics of text
  7 The sociosemantic nature of discourse 128

IV Language and social structure
  8 Language in urban society 154
  9 Antilanguages 164
  10 An interpretation of the functional relationship between
    language and social structure 183

V Sociolinguistics and education
  11 Sociolinguistic aspects of mathematical education 194
  12 *Breakthrough to literacy*: Foreword to the American edition 205
  13 Language and social man (Part 2) 211

References 236

Index of subjects 245

Index of names 255

Acknowledgements

The publishers' thanks are due to the following for permission to reproduce copyright material:

Chapters 1 and 13: Longman Group Ltd and the Schools Council for 'Language and social man'; Chapter 2: Mouton Publishers, The Hague for an extract from the discussion with M. A. K. Halliday in *Discussing language* by Herman Parret (Janua Linguarum Series Maior **93**); Chapter 3: Società Editrice Il Mulino, Bologna for 'Social aspects of semantic change' from *Proceedings of the 11th International Congress of Linguists* **2** (1972); Chapter 4: Cambridge University Press for the review of *Sociolinguistics: a cross-disciplinary perspective* in *Language in Society* **3** (1974); Chapter 5: Routledge and Kegan Paul Ltd for the Foreword to *Class, Codes and Control* **2**, ed. Basil Bernstein (1973); Chapter 6: Linguistic Association of Canada and the United States for extracts from 'Language as social semiotic' from *The First LACUS Forum*, ed. Adam Makkai and Valerie Becker Makkai, Columbia, South Carolina, Hornbeam Press (1975); Chapter 7: Walter de Gruyter & Co., Berlin for 'Text as semantic choice in social contexts' from *Grammars and descriptions*, ed. Teun A. van Dijk and Janos Petöfi; Hamish Hamilton and Mrs Helen Thurber for 'A Lover and his Lass' by James Thurber, from *Vintage Thurber: the Collection*, © 1963 Hamish Hamilton; Chapter 9: American Anthropological Association for an extract from 'Anti-languages' in *American Anthropologist* **78 (3)** (1976); Chapter 11: UNESCO for an extract from 'Interactions between linguistics and mathematical education', Final Report of the Symposium sponsored by UNESCO, CEDO and ICMI, Nairobi (1974), © 1975 UNESCO; Chapter 12: Bowmar Publishing Corporation, Glendale, California for the Foreword to the American edition of *Breakthrough to literacy: Teachers resource book* by David Mackay, Brian Thompson and Pamela Schaub (1973).

Introduction

The essays in this book, which were written between 1972 and 1976, are linked by a common theme; the title of the collection is an attempt to capture and make explicit what this theme is.

'Language is a social fact', in the frequently-quoted words of Saussure; and to recongize this is, in Saussure's view, a necessary step towards identifying 'language' as the true object of linguistics. Others before him had stressed the social character of language; for example Sweet, who wrote in 1888, 'Language originates spontaneously in the individual, for the imitative and symbolic instinct is inherent in all intelligent beings, whether men or animals; but, like that of poetry and the arts, its development is social'.

Observations such as these can be, and on occasion are, taken as the springboard for a display of exegetical acrobatics which leaves the original writer's intention far behind. In reality, such statements always have a context; they are part of a particular chain of reasoning or interpretative scheme. Saussure is concerned, at this point in his discussion, with the special character of linguistics in relation to other sciences; Sweet is explaining the origin and evolution of dialectal variation in language. It is only at the risk of distortion that we isolate such remarks from their context and fix them in a frame on the wall.

The formulation 'language as social semiotic' says very little by itself; it could mean almost anything, or nothing at all. It belongs to a particular conceptual framework, and is intended to suggest a particular interpretation of language within that framework. This certainly encompasses the view that language is a social fact, though probably not quite in the Saussurean sense, which Firth glossed as 'the language of the community, a function of *la masse parlante*, stored and residing in the *conscience collective*.'

Language arises in the life of the individual through an ongoing exchange of meanings with significant others. A child creates, first his child tongue, then his mother tongue, in interaction with that little coterie of people who constitute his meaning group. In this sense, language is a product of the social process.

A child learning language is at the same time learning other things through language – building up a picture of the reality that is around him and inside him. In this process, which is also a social process, the construal of reality is inseparable from the construal of the semantic system in which the reality is encoded. In this sense, language is a shared meaning potential, at once both a part of experience and an intersubjective interpretation of experience.

There are two fundamental aspects to the social reality that is encoded in language: to paraphrase Lévi-Strauss, it is both 'good to think' and 'good to eat'. Language expresses and symbolizes this dual aspect in its semantic system, which is organized around the twin motifs of reflection and action – language as a means of reflecting on things, and language as a means of acting on things. The former is the 'ideational' component of meaning; the latter is the 'interpersonal' – one can act *symbolically* only on persons, not on objects.

A social reality (or a 'culture') is itself an edifice of meanings – a semiotic construct. In this perspective, language is one of the semiotic systems that constitute a culture; one that is distinctive in that it also serves as an encoding system for many (though not all) of the others.

This in summary terms is what is intended by the formulation 'language as social semiotic'. It means interpreting language within a sociocultural context, in which the culture itself is interpreted in semiotic terms – as an information system, if that terminology is preferred.

At the most concrete level, this means that we take account of the elementary fact that people talk to each other. Language does not consist of sentences; it consists of text, or discourse – the exchange of meanings in interpersonal contexts of one kind or another. The contexts in which meanings are exchanged are not devoid of social value; a context of speech is itself a semiotic construct, having a form (deriving from the culture) that enables the participants to predict features of the prevailing register – and hence to understand one another as they go along.

But they do more than understand each other, in the sense of exchanging information and goods-and-services through the dynamic interplay of speech roles. By their everyday acts of meaning, people act out the social structure, affirming their own statuses and roles, and establishing and transmitting the shared systems of value and of knowledge. In recent years our understanding of these processes has been advanced most of all by Bernstein and Labov, two original thinkers whose ideas, though often presented as conflicting, are in fact strikingly complementary, the one starting from social structure and the other from linguistic structure. Bernstein has shown how the semiotic systems of the culture become differentially accessible to different social groups; Labov has shown how variation in the linguistic system is functional in expressing variation in social status and roles.

Putting these two perspectives together, we begin to see a little way into the rather elusive relation between language and social structure. Variation in language is in a quite direct sense the expression of fundamental attributes of the social system; dialect variation expresses the diversity of social *structures* (social hierarchies of all kinds), while register variation expresses the diversity of social *processes*. And since the two are interconnected – what we do is affected by who we are: in other words, the division of labour is *social* –

dialects become entangled with registers. The registers a person has access to are a function of his place in the social structure; and a switch of register may entail a switch of dialect.

This is how we try to account for the emergence of standard dialects, the correlation of dialects and registers, and the whole complex ideology of language attitudes and value judgements. But these imply more than the simple notion that language 'expresses' social structure and the social system. It would be nearer the point to say that language *actively symbolizes* the social system, representing metaphorically in its patterns of variation the variation that characterizes human cultures. This is what enables people to play with variation in language, using it to create meanings of a social kind: to participate in all forms of verbal contest and verbal display, and in the elaborate rhetoric of ordinary daily conversation. It is this same twofold function of the linguistic system, its function both as expression of and as metaphor for social processes, that lies behind the dynamics of the inter-relation of language and social context; which ensures that, in the micro-encounters of everyday life where meanings are exchanged, language not only serves to facilitate and support other modes of social action that constitute its environment, but also actively creates an environment of its own, so making possible all the imaginative modes of meaning, from back-yard gossip to narrative fiction and epic poetry. The context plays a part in determining what we say; and what we say plays a part in determining the context. As we learn how to mean, we learn to predict each from the other.

The significance of all this for linguistics is that these considerations help to explain the nature of the linguistic system. We shall not come to under-stand the nature of language if we pursue only the kinds of question about language that are formulated by linguists. For linguists, language is object – linguistics is defined, as Saussure and his contemporaries so often felt the need to affirm, by the fact that it has language as its object of study; whereas for others, language is an instrument, a means of illuminating questions about something else. This is a valid and important distinction. But it is a distinction of goals, not one of scope. In the walled gardens in which the disciplines have been sheltered since the early years of this century, each has claimed the right to determine not only what questions it is asking but also what it will take into account in answering them; and in linguistics, this leads to the construction of elegant self-contained systems that are of only limited application to any real issues – since the objects themselves have no such boundary walls. We have to take account of the questions that are raised by others; not simply out of a sense of the social accountability of the discipline (though that would be reason enough), but also out of sheer self-interest – we shall better understand language as an object if we interpret it in the light of the findings and seekings of those for whom language is an instrument, a means towards inquiries of a quite different kind.

In these essays, the attempt is made to look into language from the outside; and specifically, to interpret linguistic processes from the standpoint of the social order. This is in some contrast to the recently prevailing mode, in which the angle of reasoning has been from the language outwards, and the main concern was with the individual mind. For much of the past twenty years linguistics has been dominated by an individualist ideology, having as one of its articles of faith the astonishing dictum, first enunciated by Katz and Fodor in a treatise on semantics which explicitly banished all reference to the social context of language, that 'nearly every sentence uttered is uttered for the first time.' Only in a very special kind of social context could such a claim be taken seriously – that of a highly intellectual and individual conception of language in which the object of study was the idealized sentence of an equally idealized speaker. Even with the breakthrough to a 'sociolinguistic' perspective, it has proved difficult to break away from the ideal individual in whose mind all social knowledge is stored.

The 'grammar' of this kind of linguistics is a set of rules; and the conceptual framework is drawn from logic, whence is derived a model of language in which the organizing concept is that of structure. Since the structural functions are defined by logical relations (e.g. subject and predicate), the linguistic relations are seen as formal relations between classes (e.g. noun and verb). It was Chomsky's immense achievement to show how natural language can be reduced to a formal system; and as long as the twofold idealization of speaker and sentence is maintained intact, language can be represented not only as rules but even as ordered rules. But when social man comes into the picture, the ordering disappears and even the concept of rules is seen to be threatened.

In real life, most sentences that are uttered are not uttered for the first time. A great deal of discourse is more or less routinized; we tell the same stories and express the same opinions over and over again. We do, of course, create new sentences; we also create new clauses, and phrases, and words – the image of language as 'old words in new sentences' is a very superficial and simplistic one. But it really does not matter whether we do this or not; what matters is that we all the time exchange meanings, and the exchange of meanings is a creative process in which language is one symbolic resource – perhaps the principal one we have, but still one among others. When we come to interpret language in this perspective, the conceptual framework is likely to be drawn from rhetoric rather than from logic, and the grammar is likely to be a grammar of choices rather than of rules. The structure of sentences and other units is explained by derivation from their functions – which is doubtless how the structures evolved in the first place. Language is as it is because of the functions it has evolved to serve in people's lives; it is to be expected that linguistic structures could be understood in functional terms. But in order to understand them in this way we have to proceed from the outside inwards, interpreting language by reference to its place in the social process. This is not the same thing as taking an isolated sentence and planting it out in some hothouse that we call a social context. It involves the difficult task of focusing attention simultaneously on the actual and the potential, interpreting both discourse and the linguistic system that lies behind it in terms of the infinitely complex network of meaning potential that is what we call the culture.

If I mention the names of those whose ideas I have borrowed, it is not to claim their authority, but to express indebtedness and to give the reader some hint of what to expect. The present perspective is one which derives from the ethnographic-descriptive tradition in linguistics: from Saussure and Hjelmslev, from Mathesius and the Prague school, from Malinowski and Firth, from Boas, Sapir and Whorf. Among contemporaries, everyone concerned with 'sociolinguistics' is indebted to William Labov; whether or not we accept all of his views, he has uncovered new facts about language (a rare accomplishment) and led the subject along new and rewarding paths. Among all those I have read and, whenever possible, listened to, my personal debt is owed especially to Basil Bernstein and Mary Douglas, to Sydney Lamb and Adam Makkai, to Jeffrey Ellis and Jean Ure, to Trevor Hill, John Sinclair, John Regan, Paddy O'Toole and Robin Fawcett, to my wife Ruqaiya Hasan, and to my former colleagues in Edinburgh and London. Such ideas as I have brought together here are the outcome of the ongoing exchange of meanings that somehow add up to a coherent 'context of situation', that in which language is used reflexively to explore itself.

Beyond these considerations lies an outer context, that of language and the human condition. Put in more prosaic terms, this means that my interest in linguistic questions is ultimately an 'applied' one, a concern with language in relation to the process and experience of education. From working over a number of years with teachers at all levels, primary, secondary and tertiary, in various aspects of language learning and language teaching, including learning to read and write, developing the mother tongue, studying foreign languages and exploring the nature of language, I have become convinced of the importance of the sociolinguistic background to everything that goes on in the classroom. The sociolinguistic patterns of the community, the language of family, neighbourhood and school, and the personal experience of language from earliest infancy are among the most fundamental elements in a child's environment for learning. This emphasis is directly reflected in some of the papers in this volume, for example in the final discussion of topics for further exploration, with the suggestion of the classroom as a centre of sociolinguistic research. But indirectly it is present throughout the book. If some of the argument seems remote from everyday problems of living and learning, this is because these problems are not simple, and no simple account of what happens at the surface of things is likely to be of much help in solving them.

I
The sociolinguistic perspective

1

Language and social man
(Part 1)

1 Language and the environment

If we ever come to look back on the ideology of the 1970s, as suggested by the writer of an imaginary 'retrospect from 1980' published in *The Observer* in the first issue of the decade, we are likely to see one theme clearly standing out, the theme of 'social man'. Not social man in opposition to individual man, but rather the individual in his social environment. What the writer was forecasting – and he seems likely to be proved accurate – was, in effect, that while we should continue to be preoccupied with man in relation to his surroundings, as we were in the 1960s, the 1970s would show a change of emphasis from the purely physical environment to the social environment. This is not a new concern, but it has tended up to now to take second place; we have been more involved over the past twenty years with town planning and urban renewal, with the flow of traffic around us and above our heads, and most recently with the pollution and destruction of our material resources. This inevitably has distracted us from thinking about the other part of our environment, that which consists of people – not people as mere quanta of humanity, so many to the square mile, but other individuals with whom we have dealings of a more or less personal kind.

The 'environment' is social as well as physical, and a state of wellbeing, which depends on harmony with the environment, demands harmony of both kinds. The nature of this state of wellbeing is what environmental studies are about. Ten years ago we first came to hear of 'ergonomics', the study and control of the environment in which people work; many will remember London Transport's advertising slogan 'How big is a bus driver?', announcing the design of new buses 'on ergonomic principles'. This was characteristic of the conception of the environment at that time. Today we would find more emphasis laid on the social aspects of wellbeing. No one would assert that the shape of the bus driver's seat is unimportant; but it no longer seems to be the whole story. There are other aspects of environmental design which seem at least as significant, and which are considerably more difficult to adjust.

Consider for example the problem of pollution, the defensive aspect of environmental design. The rubbish creep, the contamination of air and water, even the most lethal processes of physical pollution appear to be more tractable than the pollution in the social environment that is caused by prejudice and animosity of race, culture and class. These cannot be engineered away. One of the more dangerous of the terms that have been coined in this area is 'social engineering'; dangerous not so much because it suggests manipulating people for evil ends – most people are alert to that danger – but because it implies that the social environment can be fashioned like the physical one, by methods of demolition and construction, if only the plans and the machines are big enough and complicated enough. Some of the unfortunate effects of this kind of thinking have been seen from time to time in the field of language and education. But social wellbeing is not definable, or attainable, in these terms.

'Education' may sound less exciting than social engineering, but it is an older concept and one that is more relevant to our needs. If the engineers and the town planners can mould the physical environment, it is the teachers who exert the most influence on the social environment. They do so not by manipulating the social structure (which would be the engineering approach) but by playing a major part in the process whereby a human being becomes social man. The school is the main line of defence against pollution in the human environment; and we should not perhaps dismiss the notion of 'defence' too lightly, because defensive action is often precisely what is needed. Preventive medicine, after all, is defensive medicine; and what the school has failed to prevent is left to society to cure.

In the development of the child as a social being, language has the central role. Language is the main channel through which the patterns of living are transmitted to him, through which he learns to act as a member of a 'society' – in and through the various social groups, the family, the neighbourhood, and so on – and to adopt its 'culture', its modes of thought and action, its beliefs and its values. This does not happen by instruction, at least not in the pre-school years; nobody teaches him the principles on which social groups are organized, or their systems of beliefs, nor would he understand it if they tried. It happens indirectly, through the accumulated experience of numerous small events, insignificant in themselves, in which his behaviour is guided and controlled, and in the course of which he contracts and develops personal relationships of all kinds. All this takes place through the medium of language. And it is not from the language of the classroom, still less that of courts of law, of moral tracts or of textbooks of sociology, that the child learns about the culture he was born into. The striking fact is that it is the most ordinary everyday uses of language, with parents, brothers and sisters, neighbourhood children, in the home, in the street and the park, in the shops and the trains and the buses, that serve to transmit, to the child, the essential qualities of society and the nature of social being.

This, in brief, is what this chapter is about. It is a general discussion of the relation of language to social man, and in particular language as it impinges on the role of the teacher as a creator of social man – or at least as a midwife in the creation process. That this does not mean simply language in school is already clear. It means, rather, language in the total context of the interaction between an individual and his human environment: between one individual and others, in fact. But the point of view to be adopted will be an educational one, emphasizing those aspects of language and social man that are most relevant to the teacher in the classroom.

It might seem that one could hardly begin to consider language at all without taking account of social man, since language is the means whereby people interact. How else can one look at language *except* in a social context? In the last resort, it is true that the existence of language implies the existence of social man; but this does not by itself determine the point of vantage from which language is being approached. Let us think for a moment of an individual human being, considered as a single organism. Being human, it is also articulate: it can speak and understand language, and perhaps read and write as well. Now the ability to speak and understand arises, and makes sense, only because there are other such organisms around, and it is natural to think of it as an inter-organism phenomenon to be studied from an inter-organism point of view. But it is also possible to investigate language from the standpoint of the internal make-up of that organism: the brain structure, and the cerebral processes that are involved in its speaking and understanding, and also in its learning to speak and to understand. So there is an intra-organism perspective on language as well as an inter-organism one. The two standpoints are complementary; but there tend to be shifts of emphasis between them, trends and fashions in scholarship which lead to concentration on one, for a time, at the expense of the other. In the 1960s the major emphasis was on what we are calling intra-organism studies, on the investigation of language as knowledge, of 'what the speaker knows', running parallel to, and probably occasioned by, the relative neglect of man's social environment. There has now been a move back towards a greater concern with the social aspects of language, a restoring of the balance in linguistic studies, with account once more being taken of the inter-organism factor – that of language as social behaviour, or language in relation to social man.

A diagrammatic representation of the nature of linguistic studies and their relation to other fields of scholarship will serve as a point of reference for the subsequent discussion (figure 1). The diagram shows the domain of language study – of linguistics, to give it its subject title – by a broken line; everything within that line is an aspect or a branch of linguistic studies.

In the centre is a triangle, shown by a solid line, which marks off what is the central area of language study, that of language as a system. One way of saying what is meant by 'central' here is that if a student is taking linguistics as a university subject he will have to cover this area as a compulsory part of his course, whatever other aspects he may choose to take up. There are then certain projections from the triangle, representing special sub-disciplines within this central area: phonetics, historical linguistics and dialectology – the last of these best thought of in broader terms, as the study of language varieties. These sometimes get excluded from the central region, but probably most linguists would agree in placing them within it; if one could give a three-dimensional representation they would not look like excrescences.

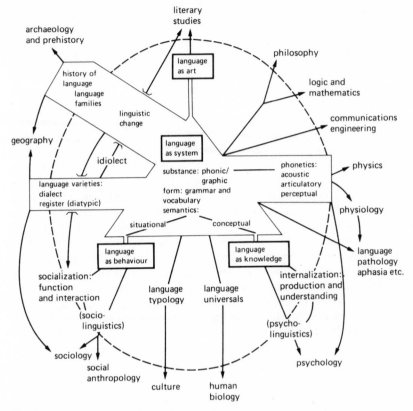

Fig. 1

Then, outside this triangle, are the principal perspectives on language that take us beyond a consideration solely of language as a system, and, in so doing, impinge on other disciplines. Any study of language involves some attention to other disciplines; one cannot draw a boundary round the subject and insulate it from others. The question is whether the aims go beyond the elucidation of language itself; and once one goes outside the central area, one is inquiring not only into language but into language in relation to something else. The diagram summarizes these wider fields under the three headings, 'language as knowledge', 'language as behaviour', 'language as art'.

The last of these takes us into the realm of literature, which is all too often treated as if it was something insulated from and even opposed to language: 'we concentrate mainly on literature here – we don't do much on language', as if 'concentrating on literature' made it possible to ignore the fact that literature is made of language. Similarly the undergraduate is invited to 'choose between lang. and lit.'. In fact the distinction that is being implied is a perfectly meaningful one between two different emphases or orientations, one in which the centre of attention is the linguistic system and the other having a focus elsewhere; but it is wrongly named, and therefore, perhaps, liable to be misinterpreted. One can hardly take literature seriously without taking language seriously; but language here is being looked at from a special point of view.

The other two headings derive from the distinction we have just been drawing between the intra-organism perspective, language as knowledge, and the inter-organism perspective, language as behaviour. These both lead us outward from language as a system, the former into the region of psychological studies, the latter into sociology and related fields. So in putting language into the context of 'language and social man', we are taking up one of the options that are open for the relating of language study to other fields of inquiry. This, broadly, is the sociolinguistic option; and the new subject of sociolinguistics that has come into prominence lately is a recognition of the fact that language and society – or, as we prefer to think of it, language and social man – is a unified conception, and needs to be understood and investigated as a whole. Neither of these exists without the other: there can be no social man without language, and no language without social man. To recognize this is no mere academic exercise; the whole theory and practice of education depends on it, and it is no exaggeration to suggest that much of our failure in recent years – the failure of the schools to come to grips with social pollution – can be traced to a lack of insight into the nature of the relationships between language and society: specifically of the processes, which are very largely linguistic processes, whereby a human organism turns into a social being.

2 Inter-organism and intra-organism perspectives

The diagram in section 1 suggests a context for language study, placing it in the environment of other fields of investigation. It also suggests where 'language and social man' fits into the total picture of language study. The discussion of the diagram will perhaps have made it clear (and this harks back to what was said at the beginning) that when we talk of 'social man' the contrast we are making is not that of social versus individual. The contrast is rather that of social versus psychophysiological, the distinction which we have attempted to draw in terms of inter-organism and intra-organism perspectives.

When we refer to social man, we mean the individual considered as a single entity, rather than as an assemblage of parts. The distinction we are drawing here is that between the behaviour of that individual, his actions and interactions with his environment (especially that part of his environment which consists of other individuals), on the one hand, and on the other hand his biological nature, and in particular the internal structure of his brain. In the first of these perspectives we are regarding the individual as an integral whole, and looking at him from the outside; in the second we are focusing our attention on the parts, and looking on the inside, into the works.

Language can be considered from either of these points of view; the first is what we called on the diagram 'language as behaviour', the second 'language as knowledge'. 'Language and social man' means language as a function of the whole man; hence language man to man (inter-organism), or language as human behaviour.

These are two complementary orientations. The distinction between them is not a difficult one to make; in itself it is rather obvious and simple. But it has become complicated by the fact that it is possible to embed one perspective inside the other: to treat language behaviour as if it were an aspect of our knowledge of language (and hence to see it in terms of the capacity of the human brain), and also, though in a rather different sense, to treat the individual's knowledge of language as a form of behaviour. In other words we can look at social facts from a biological point of view, or at biological facts from a social point of view.

The study of language as knowledge is an attempt to find out what goes on inside the individual's head. The questions being asked are, what are the mechanisms of the brain that are involved in speaking and understanding, and what must the structure of the brain be like in order for the individual to be able to speak and understand language, and to be able to learn to do so?

Now one important fact about speaking and understanding language is that it always takes place in a context. We do not simply 'know' our mother tongue as an abstract system of vocal signals, or as if it was some sort of a grammar book with a dictionary attached. We know it in the sense of knowing how to use it; we know how to communicate with other people, how to choose forms of language that are appropriate to the type of situation we find ourselves in, and so on. All this can be expressed as a form of knowledge: we know how to behave linguistically.

Therefore it is possible, and is in fact quite usual in what is nowadays called 'sociolinguistics', to look at language behaviour as a type of knowledge; so that although one's attention is focused on the social aspects of language – on language as communication between organisms – one is still asking what is essentially an intra-organism kind of question: how does the individual *know how to* behave in this way? We might refer to this as psychosociolinguistics: it is the external behaviour of the organism looked at from the point of view of the internal mechanisms which control it.

We said above that the two perspectives were complementary, and it would be reasonable to conclude that they are really inseparable one from the other. But if so the inseparability holds in both directions. It is true that the individual's potential for linguistic interaction with others implies certain things about the internal make-up of the individual himself. But the converse is also true. The fact that the brain has the capacity to store language and use it for effective communication implies that communication takes place: that the individual has a 'behaviour potential' which characterizes his interaction with other individuals of his species.

Since no doubt the human brain evolved in its present form through the process of human beings communicating with one another, the latter perspective is likely to be highly significant from an evolutionary point of view. But that is not our main point of departure here. There is a more immediate sense in which the individual, considered as one who can speak and understand and read and write, who has a 'mother tongue', needs to be seen in a social perspective. This concerns the part that language has played in his own development as an individual. Let us start with the notion of the individual human organism, the human being as a biological specimen. Like the individual in many other species, he is destined to become one of a group; but unlike those of all other species, he achieves this – not wholly, but critically – through language. It is by means of language that the 'human being' becomes one of a group of 'people'. But 'people', in turn, consist of 'persons'; by virtue of his participation in a group the individual is no longer simply a biological specimen of humanity – he is a person. Again language is the essential element in the process, since it is largely the linguistic inter-change with the group that determines the status of the individuals and shapes them as persons. The picture is as in figure 2:

INDIVIDUAL   GROUP

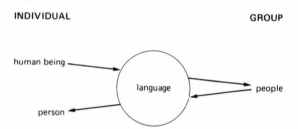

Fig. 2

In other words, instead of looking at the group as a derivation from and extension of the biologically endowed mental power of the individual, we explain the nature of the individual as a derivation from and extension of his participation in the group. Instead of starting inside the organism and looking outwards, we can adopt a Durkheimian perspective and start from outside the organism in order to look inwards.

But when we do adopt this perspective it becomes apparent that we can take the dialectic one stage further, and that when we do so language will still remain the crucial factor. The individual as a 'person' is now a potential 'member': he has the capacity to function within society, and once more it is through language that he achieves this status. How does a society differ from a group, as we conceive it here? A group is a simple structure, a set of participants among whom there are no special relations, only the simple coexistence that is implied by participation in the group. A society, on the other hand, does not consist of participants but of relations, and these relations define social roles. Being a member of society means occupying a social role; and it is again by means of language that a 'person' becomes potentially the occupant of a social role.

   Social roles are combinable, and the individual, as a member of a society, occupies not just one role but many at a time, always through the medium of language. Language is again a necessary condition for this final element in the process of the development of the individual, from human being to person to what we may call 'personality', a personality being interpreted as a role complex. Here the individual is seen as the configuration of a number of roles defined by the social relationships in which he enters; from these roles he synthesizes a personality. Our model now looks like figure 3:

INDIVIDUAL   GROUP

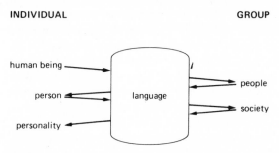

Fig. 3

   Let us now interpret this in terms of a perspective on language. We have gone some way round in order to reach this particular angle of vision, certainly oversimplifying the picture and perhaps seeming to exaggerate the importance of language in the total process. The justification for this is that we have been trying to achieve a perspective that will be most relevant in an educational context. From this point of view, language is the medium through which a human being becomes a personality, in consequence of his membership of society and his occupancy of social roles. The concept of language as behaviour, as a form of interaction between man and man, is turned around, as it were, so that it throws light on the individual: the formation of the personality is itself a social process, or a complex of social processes, and language – by virtue of its social functions – plays the key part in it. Hence just as the view of language as knowledge, which is essentially an individual orientation, can be used to direct attention outwards, through such concepts as the speech act, towards language in society, so the essentially social interpretation of language as behaviour can be used to direct attention onto the individual, placing him in the human environment, as we expressed it earlier, and explaining his linguistic potential, as speaker-hearer and writer-reader, in these terms. This does not presuppose, or preclude, any particular theory about the nature of the mental processes that are involved in his mastery of language, either in how he speaks and understands or in how he learnt to do so in the first place. There are conflicting psychological theories on these questions, as we shall see in the next section; but our present perspective is neutral in this respect.
   The ability to speak and understand, and the development of this ability in

the child, are essential ingredients in the life of social man. To approach these from the outside, as inter-organism phenomena, is to take a functional view of language. The social aspect of language becomes the reference point for the biological aspect, rather than the other way round. In the next two sections we shall consider briefly what this means.

3 A functional approach to language and language development

In the preceding section we outlined a general perspective on language and language learning in which society rather than the individual is at the centre of the picture, and the individual's language potential is interpreted as the means whereby the various social relationships into which he enters are established, developed and maintained. This means that we are taking a functional view of language, in the sense that we are interested in what language can do, or rather in what the speaker, child or adult, can do with it; and that we try to explain the nature of language, its internal organization and patterning, in terms of the functions that it has evolved to serve.

First of all, therefore, we should look briefly into the question of linguistic function, and say a little about it in regard both to what language is and to how it is learnt by a child. Let us take the latter point first, and consider a functional approach to the question of how the child learns his mother tongue. This process, the learning of the mother tongue, is often referred to as 'language acquisition'. This seems rather an unfortunate term because it suggests that language is some kind of a commodity to be acquired, and, although the metaphor is innocent enough in itself, if it is taken too literally the consequences can be rather harmful. The use of this metaphor has led to the belief in what is known as a 'deficit theory' of language learning, as a means of explaining how children come to fail in school: the suggestion that certain children, perhaps because of their social background, have not acquired enough of this commodity called language, and in order to help them we must send relief supplies. The implication is that there is a gap to be filled, and from this derive various compensatory practices that may be largely irrelevant to the children's needs. Now this is a false and misleading view of language and of educational failure; and while one should not make too much of one item of terminology, we prefer to avoid the term 'language acquisition' and return to the earlier and entirely appropriate designation of 'language development'.

In the psychological sphere, there have recently been two alternative lines of approach to the question of language development. These have been referred to as the 'nativist' and the 'environmentalist' positions. Everyone agrees, of course, that human beings are biologically endowed with the ability to learn language, and that this is a uniquely human attribute – no other species has it, however much a chimpanzee or a dolphin may be trained to operate with words or symbols. But the nativist view holds that there is a specific language-learning faculty, distinct from other learning faculties, and that this provides the human infant with a readymade and rather detailed blueprint of the structure of language. Learning his mother tongue consists in fitting the patterns of whatever language he hears around him into the framework which he already possesses. The environmentalist view considers that language learning is not fundamentally distinct from other kinds of learning; it depends on those same mental faculties that are involved in all aspects of the child's learning processes. Rather than having built into his genetic makeup a set of concrete universals of language, what the child has is the ability to process certain highly abstract types of cognitive relation which underlie (among other things) the linguistic system; the very specific properties of language are not innate, and therefore the child is more dependent on his environment – on the language he hears around him, together with the contexts in which it is uttered – for the successful learning of his mother tongue. In a sense, therefore, the difference of views is a recurrence of the old controversy of nature and nurture, or heredity and environment, in a new guise.

Each of these views can be criticized, although the criticisms that are actually made often relate to particular models of the learning process that have no necessary connection with a nativist or environmentalist position. For example, it is sometimes assumed that an environmentalist interpretation implies some form of behaviourist theory, an essentially stimulus-response view of learning; but this is totally untrue. Equally, the nativist view is by no means dependent on the notion that learning proceeds by fitting items into the marked slots which nature provided and running the machine to test whether the match is appropriate. The differences between nativist and environmentalist are differences of emphasis, among other things in their ideas concerning the essential character of language, which stem from two rather different traditions. Broadly speaking, the nativist model reflects the philosophical-logical strand in the history of thinking about language, with its sharp distinction between the ideal and the real (which Chomsky calls 'competence' and 'performance') and its view of language as *rules* – essentially rules of syntax. The environmentalist represents the ethnographic tradition, which rejects the distinction of ideal and real, defines what is grammatical as, by and large, what is acceptable, and sees language as *resource* – resource for meaning, with meaning defined in terms of function. To this extent the two interpretations are complementary rather than contradictory; but they have tended to become associated with conflicting psychological theories and thus to be strongly counterposed.

One argument often put forward in support of a nativist approach must be dismissed as fallacious; this is the theory of the unstructured input, according to which the child cannot be dependent on what he hears around him because what he hears is no more than bits and pieces – unfinished or ungrammatical sentences, full of hesitations, backtracking, unrelated fragments and the like. This idea seems to have arisen because the earliest taperecordings of connected discourse that linguists analysed were usually recordings of intellectual conversations, which do tend to be very scrappy, since the speakers are having to plan as they go along and the premises are constantly shifting, and which are also largely insulated from the immediate situation, so that there are no contextual clues. But it is not in fact true of the ordinary everyday speech that typically surrounds the small child, which is fluent, highly structured, and closely related to the non-verbal context of situation. Moreover it tends to have very few deviations in it; I found myself when observing the language spoken to, and in the presence of, a small child that almost all the sequences were well formed and whole, acceptable even to the sternest grammatical lawgiver. Of course the fact that the notion of unstructured input is unsound does not disprove the nativist theory; it merely removes one of the arguments that has been used to support it.

More important than the grammatical shape of what the child hears, however, is the fact that it is functionally related to observable features of the-situation around him. This consideration allows us to give another account of language development that is not dependent on any particular psycholinguistic theory, an account that is functional and sociological rather than structural and psychological. The two are not in competition; they are about different things. A functional theory is not a theory about the mental processes involved in the learning of the mother tongue; it is a theory about the social processes involved. As we expressed it in the first section, it is concerned with language between people (inter-organism), and therefore learning to speak is interpreted as the individual's mastery of a behaviour potential. In this perspective, language is a form of interaction, and it is learnt through interaction; this, essentially, is what makes it possible for a culture to be transmitted from one generation to the next.

In a functional approach to language development the first question to be asked is, 'what are the functions that language serves in the life of an infant?' This might seem self-contradictory, if an infant is one who does not yet speak; but the paradox is intentional – before he has mastered any recognizable form of his mother tongue the child already has a linguistic system, in the sense that he can express certain meanings through the consistent use of vocal sounds. There are, perhaps, four main reasons for putting the question in this form.

1. We can ask the same question at any stage in the life of the individual, up to and including adulthood; there have in fact been a number of functional theories of adult and adolescent language.

2. It is much easier to answer the question in respect of a very young child; the earlier one starts, the more clearcut the functions are (whereas with an approach based on structure, the opposite is the case; it is in general *harder* to analyse the structure of children's speech than that of adults).

3. We can reasonably assume that the child is functionally motivated; if language is for the child a means of attaining social ends – that is, ends which are important to him as a social being – we need look no further than this for the reasons why he learns it.

4. A functional approach to language, if it includes a developmental

perspective, can throw a great deal of light on the nature of language itself. Language is as it is because of what it has to do.

To these we might add a fifth, though this is not so much a reason for asking the question as an incidental bonus for having done so. One of the problems in studying the language of a very young child is that of knowing what is language and what is not. We can answer that, in a functional context, by saying that any vocal sound (and any gesture, if the definition is made to include gesture) which is interpretable by reference to a recognized function of language is language – provided always that the relationship of sound to meaning is regular and consistent. The production of a sound for the purpose of practising that sound is a means of *learning* language, but is not itself an instance of language. The production of a sound for the purpose of attracting attention *is* language, once we have reason to assert that 'attracting attention' is a meaning that fits in with the functional potential of language at this stage of development.

Looking at the early stages of language development from a functional viewpoint, we can follow the process whereby the child gradually 'learns how to mean' – for this is what first-language learning is. If there is anything which the child can be said to be acquiring, it is a range of potential, which we could refer to as his 'meaning potential'. This consists in the mastery of a small number of elementary functions of language, and of a range of choices in meaning within each one. The choices are very few at first, but they expand rapidly as the functional potential of the system is reinforced by success: the sounds that the child makes do in fact achieve the desired results, at least on a significant number of occasions, and this provides the impetus for taking the process further. As an example, Nigel, whose language I studied in successive six-weekly stages from the age of nine months onwards, started apparently with just two functions and one or two meanings in each. At 10½ months, when he first had a recognizable linguistic system, he could express a total of twelve different meanings; these were derived from four clearly identifiable functions (the first four in the list below) and included, among others, what we might translate as 'do that right now!', 'I want my toy bird down' and 'nice to see you; shall we look at this picture together?' By 16½ months, when he was on the threshold of the second phase of language development, the move into the mother tongue, he had six functions and a total of fifty meanings that he could, and regularly did, express (Halliday 1975a).

In studying Nigel's progress I used as the framework a set of seven initial functions, as follows:

1 Instrumental ('I want'): satisfying material needs
2 Regulatory ('do as I tell you'): controlling the behaviour of others
3 Interactional ('me and you'): getting along with other people
4 Personal ('here I come'): identifying and expressing the self
5 Heuristic ('tell me why'): exploring the world around and inside one

6 Imaginative ('let's pretend'): creating a world of one's own
7 Informative ('I've got something to tell you'): communicating new information.

These headings served as a useful basis for following the developmental progress of an infant whose early speech sounds, although still prelinguistic in the sense that they were not modelled on the English language, were used to convey these kinds of intention – to obtain goods or services that he required (instrumental), to influence the behaviour of those closest to him (regulatory), to maintain his emotional ties with them (interactional), and so on. The meanings that he can express at this stage – the number of different things that he can ask for, for example – are naturally very restricted; but he has internalized the fact that language serves these purposes, and it is significant that for each of them he has one generalized expression, meaning simply, 'I want that' or 'do that!' etc., where the interpretation is given by the situation (e.g. 'I want that spoon' or 'go on singing'), as well as a number of specific expessions, very few at first but soon growing, and soon becoming independent of the presence of the object or other visible sign of his intent.

So by adopting a functional standpoint we can go back to the beginning of the child's language development, reaching beyond the point where he has started to master structures, beyond even his first words, if by 'words' we mean items derived from the adult language; and taking as the foundations of language those early utterances which are not yet English or French or Swahili or Urdu but which every parent recognizes as being meaningful, quite distinct from crying and sneezing and the other nonlinguistic noises the child makes. At this stage, the child's utterances cannot readily be 'translated' into the adult language. Just as we cannot adequately represent the sounds he makes by spelling them, either in the orthography of the mother tongue or even in phonetic script, because the system which these symbols impose is too detailed and specific, so also we cannot adequately represent the meanings the child expresses in terms of adult grammar and vocabulary. The child's experience differs so widely from that of the adult that there is only a very partial correspondence between his meanings and those that the adult is predisposed to recognize. But if his utterances are interpreted in the light of particular functions, which are recognizable to the adult as plausible ways of using language, it becomes possible to bridge the gap between them – and in this way to show why the infant's linguistic system ultimately evolves and develops into that of the adult, which is otherwise the most puzzling aspect of the language development process. By the time he reached the age of 18 months, Nigel could use language effectively in the instrumental, regulatory, intractional and personal functions, and was beginning to use it for pretend-play (the 'imaginative' function), and also heuristically, for the purpose of exploring the environment. Now for the first time he launched into English, making rapid strides in vocabulary and grammar; and it was very clear from a study of his speech that his principal motive for doing so was the use of language as a learning device.

In order for language to be a means of learning, it is essential for the child to be able to encode in language, through words and structures, his experience of processes of the external world and of the people and things that participate in them.

4 Language and social structure

In section 3, we considered the process of learning the mother tongue from a functional point of view, interpreting it as the progressive mastery of a number of basic functions of language and the building up of a 'meaning potential' in respect of each. Here we are adopting a sociolinguistic perspective on language – or rather a perspective which in terms of the earlier discussion would be inter-organism. Language is being regarded as the encoding of a 'behaviour potential' into a 'meaning potential'; that is, as a means of expressing what the human organism 'can do', in interaction with other human organisms, by turning it into what he 'can mean'. What he can mean (the semantic system) is, in turn, encoded into what he 'can say' (the lexicogrammatical system, or grammar and vocabulary); to use our own folk-linguistic terminology, meanings are expressed in wordings. Wordings are, finally, recoded into sounds (it would be nice if we could say 'soundings') or spellings (the phonological and orthographic systems). Terms like *meaning, wording* and *spelling* are so familiar in everyday speech that we are hardly aware of them as ways of talking about language. But every time we say, to a pupil, or to a committee chairman perhaps, 'I think you'll have to alter the wording', we are making systematic assumptions about language, bringing into play what Peter Doughty calls 'a "folk linguistic", a "common sense" about the language we live by' (Doughty *et al.* 1972, 8).

This perspective is valuable to the linguist because it affords an insight into *why* language is as it is. There is no *a priori* reason why human language should have taken just the evolutionary path that it has taken and no other; our brains could have produced a symbolic system of quite a different kind. But if we consider what language is required to do for us, there are certain functions which it must fulfil in all human cultures, regardless of differences in the physical and material environment. These are functions of a very general kind.

1. Language has to interpret the whole of our experience, reducing the indefinitely varied phenomena of the world around us, and also of the world inside us, the processes of our own consciousness, to a manageable number of classes of phenomena: types of processes, events and actions, classes of objects, people and institutions, and the like.

2. Language has to express certain elementary logical relations, like 'and' and 'or' and 'if', as well as those created by language itself such as 'namely', 'says' and 'means'.

3. Language has to express our participation, as speakers, in the speech

situation; the roles we take on ourselves and impose on others; our wishes, feelings, attitudes and judgements.

4. Language has to do all these things simultaneously, in a way which relates what is being said to the context in which it is being said, both to what has been said before and to the 'context of situation'; in other words, it has to be capable of being organized as relevant discourse, not just as words and sentences in a grammar-book or dictionary.

It is the demands posed by the service of these functions which have moulded the shape of language and fixed the course of its evolution. These functions are built into the semantic system of language, and they form the basis of the grammatical organization, since the task of grammar is to encode the meanings deriving from these various functions into articulated structures. Not only are these functions served by all languages, at least in their adult form; they have also determined the way human language has evolved.

So when we study the language development of young children, we are really investigating two questions at once. The first concerns the language they invent for themselves, on the basis of the set of elementary uses or functions of language which reflect the developmental needs, potentialities and achievements of the infant – instrumental, regulatory and so on. The second concerns their transition to the adult language, a language which is still functional in its origins but where the concept of 'function' has undergone a significant change: it is no longer simply synonymous with 'use', but has become much more abstract, a kind of 'metafunction' through which all the innumerable concrete uses of language in which the adult engages are given symbolic expression in a systematic and finite form. To what extent the individual child traces the evolutionary path in moving from one to the other is immaterial; it appears that at a certain point he abandons it, and takes a leap directly into the adult system. Be that as it may, he has to make the transition, and in doing so he carves out for himself a route that reflects the particular circumstances of his own individual history and experience. Geoffrey Thornton expresses this very well when he says that the language which each child learns

> is a unique inheritance. It is an inheritance because he is endowed, as a human being, with the capacity to learn language merely by growing up in an environment in which language is being used around him. It is unique, because . . . no two people occupy identical places in an environment where language learning is taking place, and this must mean that the language learnt is unique to the individual. (Doughty *et al*. 1972, 48).

This takes us back to the perspective outlined in section 2. Biologically we are all alike, in so far as the language-learning capacity is concerned; we have this ability, as a species, just as we have the ability to stand upright and walk, and it is quite independent of the usual measures of 'intelligence' in whatever form. Ecologically, on the other hand, each one of us is unique, since the environmental pattern is never exactly repeated, and one individual's experience is never the same as another's.

However, the uniqueness of the individual, in terms of his personal experience, must be qualified by reference to the culture. Our environment is shaped by the culture, and the conditions under which we learn language are largely culturally determined. This point is significant at two levels, one of which is very obvious, the other less so. It is obviously true in the sense that a child learns the language he hears around him; if he is growing up in an English-speaking society, he learns English. This is a matter of the *linguistic* environment, which is itself part of the culture,' but in a special sense.' Moreover he learns that dialectal variety of English which belongs to his particular socioregional subculture: working-class London, urban middle-class Northern, rural Dorset and so on. (He may of course learn more than one dialect, or more than one language, if the culture is one in which such linguistic diversity is the norm.) It is equally true, but much less obvious, in another sense: namely that the culture shapes our behaviour patterns, and a great deal of our behaviour is mediated through language. The child learns his mother tongue in the context of behavioural settings where the norms of the culture are acted out and enunciated for him, settings of parental control, instruction, personal interaction and the like; and, reciprocally, he is 'socialized' into the value systems and behaviour patterns of the culture through the use of language at the same time as he is learning it.

We can now see the relevance of this to linguistic theories of educational failure, which were referred to briefly in the last section. There has been much discussion of educability lately, and various theories have been put forward. One school of thought has concentrated on the effect of the child's *linguistic* environment – namely, the particular form of language he has grown up to speak. In practice, since educational failure is usually associated with the urban lower working class, this means the particular socioregional dialect; and we find two versions of the 'language failure' theory here, sometimes known as the 'deficit theory' and the 'difference theory'. According to the deficit theory, the whole dialect is simply defective; it lacks some essential elements – it is deficient, perhaps, in sounds, or words, or structures. Now this is not merely nonsense; it is dangerous nonsense. Unfortunately it has rarely been explicitly denied; probably because, as the American educator Joan Baratz put it, 'linguists . . . consider such a view of language so absurd as to make them feel that nobody could possibly believe it and therefore to refute it would be a great waste of time' (Williams 1970a, 13). There is no such thing as a deficient social dialect. But, on the other hand, if a teacher believes that there is, and that some or all of his pupils speak one, then, as Frederick Williams has very convincingly shown in his investigations in American schools, he thereby predisposes the children to linguistic failure. This is known as the 'stereotype hypothesis': children, no less than adults, will come to behave like the stereotype to which they are consigned (Williams 1970a, ch. 18).

This then leads us into the 'difference' version of the theory, according to which the problem is not that the child's speech is deficient but that it is different – different, in implication, from some received standard or norm.

This would obviously be important if it meant that the child did not understand the language in which he was being taught (as happens with many
immigrant children). But for the native English-speaking child, this is not the
problem. Wherever he comes from, and whatever section of society he
comes from, the speech differences are relatively slight and superficial, and
in any case he has heard the teacher's language frequently on television and
elsewhere, so that he never has more than very temporary difficulty in
understanding it, and in fact is usually rather competent at imitating it – an
activity, however, which he tends to consider more appropriate to the
playground than to the classroom. So the difference theory resolves itself
into a question of prejudice: if the child fails as a result of differences
between his language and that of the school, it is not because there are
difficulties of understanding but because the child's variety of English
carries a social stigma: it is regarded by society as inferior. If 'society' here
includes the teacher, the child is, effectively, condemned to failure from the
start.

To that extent, then, the difference theory, unlike the deficit theory, is at
least partially true: there *are* prejudices against certain varieties of English,
and they *are* shared by some teachers. But they are by no means shared by all
teachers; and it is difficult to believe that this factor by itself could be
sufficient explanation of the full extent of educational failure, especially
since children have a great capacity for adaptation – if one form of behaviour
does not pay off they will usually switch to another, and they are quite
capable of doing so where language is concerned. Moreover the prejudices
are getting less, whereas the general view is that educational failure is
increasing.

We return to this discussion in chapter 5 below, with reference to the
work of Basil Bernstein. Educational failure is really a social problem,
not a linguistic one; but it has a linguistic aspect, which we can begin to
understand if we consider the cultural environment in the second of the two
senses mentioned above. It is not the linguistic environment, in the sense of
which language or dialect the child learns to speak, that matters so much as
the cultural or subcultural environment as this is embodied in and transmitted through the language. In other words, the 'language difference' may
be significant, but if so it is a difference of function rather than of form.

It is this fundamental insight which lies behind Professor Bernstein's
theoretical and empirical work in the field of language and society; together
with a further insight, namely that what determines the actual cultural-
linguistic configuration is, essentially, the social structure, the system of
social relations, in the family and other key social groups, which is characteristic of the particular subculture. Bernstein (1971, 122) writes:

> A number of fashions of speaking, frames of consistency, are possible in any
> given language and . . . these fashions of speaking, linguistic forms or codes, are
> themselves a function of the form social relations take. According to this view,
> the form of the social relation or, more generally, the social structure generates

distinct linguistic forms or codes and *these codes essentially transmit the culture and so constrain behaviour.* [His italics.]

If we accept that, as the American sociological linguist William Stewart expressed it, 'so much of human behaviour is socially conditioned rather than genetically determined', it is not difficult to suppose an intimate connection between language on the one hand and modes of thought and behaviour on the other.

This view is associated first and foremost with the work of the great American linguist Benjamin Lee Whorf, who wrote 'An accepted pattern of using words is often prior to certain lines of thinking and modes of behaviour.' Whorf emphasized that it is not so much in 'special uses of language' (technical terms, political discourse etc.) as 'in its constant ways of arranging data and its most ordinary everyday analysis of phenomena that we need to recognize the influence [language] has on other activities, cultural and personal' (1956, 134–5). Bernstein (1971, 123) points out that, in Whorf's thinking, 'the link between language, culture and habitual thought is *not* mediated through the social structure', whereas his own theory

> places the emphasis on changes in the social structure as major factors in shaping or changing a given culture through their effect on the consequences of fashions of speaking. It shares with Whorf the controlling influence on experience ascribed to 'frames of consistency' involved in fashions of speaking. It differs [from] Whorf by asserting that, in the context of a common language in the sense of a general code, there will arise distinct linguistic forms, fashions of speaking, which induce in their speakers *different* ways of relating to objects and persons.

Bernstein has investigated *how* this connection is made, and suggests that it is through linguistic codes, or fashions of speaking, which arise as a consequence of the social structure and the types of social relation associated with it. As Mary Douglas put it, 'The control [of thought] is not in the speech forms but in the set of human relations which generate thought and speech' (1972, 312).

What are these linguistic codes, or fashions of speaking? They relate, essentially, to a functional interpretation of language. It is not the words and the sentence structures – still less the pronunciation or 'accent' – which make the differer.ce between one type of code and another; it is the relative emphasis placed on the different functions of language, or, to put it more accurately, the kinds of meaning that are typically associated with them. The 'fashions of speaking' are sociosemantic in nature; they are patterns of meaning that emerge more or less strongly, in particular contexts, especially those relating to the socialization of the child in the family. Hence, although each child's language-learning environment is unique, he also shares certain common features with other children of a similar social background; not merely in the superficial sense that the material environments may well be alike – in fact they may not – but in the deeper sense that the forms of social relation and the role systems surrounding him have their effect on the kind of choices in meaning which will be highlighted and given prominence in different types of situation. Peter Doughty comments: 'the terms *elaborated* and *restricted* refer to characteristic ways of using language to interact with other human beings; they do not suggest that there are two kinds of "meaning potential"' (Doughty *et al*. 1972, 104–5).

This dependence on social structure is not merely unavoidable, it is essential to the child's development; he can develop only as *social* man, and therefore his experience must be shaped in ways which make him a member of society and his particular section of it. It becomes restrictive only where the social structure orients the child's thinking *away from* the modes of experience that the school requires. To quote Bernstein again, 'the different focusing of experience . . . creates a major problem of educability only where the school produces discontinuity between its symbolic orders and those of the child' (1971, 183–4). In other words, the processes of becoming educated require that the child's meaning potential should have developed along certain lines in certain types of context, especially in relation to the exploration of the environment and of his own part in it. To what extent this requirement is inherent in the very concept of education, and to what extent it is merely a feature of education as it is at present organized in Britain and other highly urbanized societies, we do not know; but as things are, certain ways of organizing experience through language, and of participating and interacting with people and things, are necessary to success in school. The child who is not predisposed to this type of verbal exploration in this type of experiential and interpersonal context 'is not at home in the educational world', as Bernstein puts it. Whether a child is so predisposed or not turns out not to be any innate property of the child as an individual, an inherent limitation on his mental powers, as used to be generally assumed; it is merely the result of a mismatch between his own symbolic orders of meaning and those of the school, a mismatch that results from the different patterns of socialization that characterize different sections of society, or subcultures, and which are in turn a function of the underlying social relations in the family and elsewhere. Mary Douglas says of Bernstein that he asks 'what structuring in society itself calls for its own appropriate structures of speech' (1972, 5); and she goes on to add 'A common speech form transmits much more than words; it transmits a hidden baggage of shared assumptions', a 'collective consciousness that constitutes the social bond'.

It is all too easy to be aware of subcultural differences in speech forms, because we are all sensitive to differences of dialect and accent. Unfortunately this is precisely where we go wrong, because differences of dialect and accent are in themselves irrelevant; in Bernstein's words, 'There is nothing, but nothing, in the dialect as such, which prevents a child from internalizing and learning to use universalistic meanings' (1971, 199), and dialect is a problem only if it is *made* a problem artificially by the prejudice and ignorance of others. It is much harder to become aware of the *significant* differences, which are masked by dialectal variation (and which by no means always correspond to dialect distinctions), and which do not appear in the obvious form of differences in vocabulary or grammatical structure. We are still far from being able to give a comprehensive or systematic account of the linguistic realizations of Bernstein's codes or of the ways in which language operates in the transmission of culture. But the perspective is that of language and social man, and the functional investigation of language and language development provides the basis for understanding.

In essence, what seems to happen is this. The child first constructs a language in the form of a range of meanings that relate directly to certain of his basic needs. As time goes on, the meanings become more complex, and he replaces this by a symbolic system – a semantic system with structural realizations – based on the language he hears around him; this is what we call this 'mother tongue'. Since this is learnt, and has in fact evolved, in the service of the same basic functions, it is, essentially, a functional system; but its functionality is now built in at a very abstract level. This is what was referred to at the beginning of this section, when I said that the adult linguistic system has, in effect, the four generalized functional components, or 'metafunctions', experiential, logical, interpersonal and textual. These form the basis for the organization of meaning when the child moves from his original protolanguage into language proper.

But he does not abandon the original concrete functional elements of the system as he invented it. These still define the purposes for which language is used; and out of them evolve the social contexts and situation types that make up the patterns of use of language in daily life – including those contexts that Bernstein has shown to be critical in the socialization process. Herein lies the basis of the significant subcultural variation that we have been looking at. In *which* particular contexts of use will the child bring to bear *which* portions of the functional resources of the system? Seen from a linguistic point of view, the different 'codes', as Bernstein calls them, are different strategies of language use. All human beings put language to certain types of use, and all of them learn a linguistic system which has evolved in that context; but what aspects of the system are typically deployed and emphasized in one type of use or another is to a significant extent determined by the culture – by the systems of social relations in which the child grows up, including the roles he himself learns to recognize and to adopt. All children have access to the meaning potential of the system; but they may differ, because social groups differ, in their interpretation of what the situation demands.

5 Language and situation

Children grow up, and their language grows up with them. By the age of two and a half or even earlier, the child has mastered the adult language *system*; the framework is all there. He will spend the rest of his childhood – the rest of his life, even – mastering the adult *language*.

Language, as we have stressed, is a potential: it is what the speaker can do. What a person can do in the linguistic sense, that is what he can do as speaker/hearer, is equivalent to what he 'can mean'; hence the description of language as a 'meaning potential'.

To describe language as a potential does not mean we are not interested in the actual, in what the speaker does. But in order to make sense of what he does, we have to know what he can do. This is true whatever our particular angle on language, whether we are looking at it as behaviour, or as knowledge (Chomsky's 'competence'), or as art: what *is*, the actual sentences and words that constitute our direct experience of language, derives its significance from what *could be*. But it is in the social perspective that we are best able to explain what *is*, because we can pay attention to situations of language use, taking account of the nonlinguistic factors which serve as the controlling environment. It is at least theoretically possible to look at the 'actual' in isolation from the social context (so-called 'theories of performance'), but it has not yet been shown to be very fruitful.

When we come to examine the adult language in its contexts of use, we at once run up against the difficulty that the one thing we cannot specify is the 'use' of any given utterance. Nor can we enumerate the total set of possible uses for language as a whole. We cannot draw up a general list setting out the adult's uses of language, in the way that we were able to do for the developmental functions in the language of the very small child. Or rather – which amounts to the same thing – we could draw up a hundred and one such lists, and there would be no means of preferring one list over another. Then when we came to consider actual instances we should have to recognize that in any particular utterance the speaker was in fact using language in a number of different ways, for a variety of different purposes, all at the same time. The use of language is not a simple concept.

Nevertheless it is a very helpful one, without which we cannot explain either the variation we find within a language – the different styles, levels of formality and so on – or the nature of language itself. The latter is outside our scope here, although we referred in the preceding section to the inherently functional organization of the linguistic system. But the former is fundamental to any consideration of language in an educational context. The ability to control the varieties of one's language that are appropriate to different uses is one of the cornerstones of linguistic success, not least for the school pupil. (For an excellent discussion of 'differences according to use', see Doughty *et al.* 1972, ch. 11, 'Diversity in written English' by John Pearce.)

The basic concept here is that of 'context of situation', originally suggested by Malinowski (1923) and subsequently elaborated by Firth in his 1950 paper 'Personality and language in society' (see Firth 1957, ch. 14). Essentially what this implies is that language comes to life only when functioning in some environment. We do not experience language in isolation – if we did we would not recognize it as language – but always in relation to a scenario, some background of persons and actions and events from which the things which are said derive their meaning. This is referred to as the 'situation', so language is said to function in 'contexts of situation' and any account of language which fails to build in the situation as an essential ingredient is likely to be artificial and unrewarding.

It is important to qualify the notion of 'situation' by adding the word 'relevant.' The 'context of situation' does not refer to all the bits and pieces of the material environment such as might appear if we had an audio and video recording of a speech event with all the sights and sounds surrounding the utterances. It refers to those features which are relevant to the speech that is taking place. Such features may be very concrete and immediate, as they tend to be with young children whose remarks often bear a direct pragmatic relation to the environment, e.g. *some more!* 'I want some more of what I've just been eating.' But they may be quite abstract and remote, as in a technical discussion among experts, where the 'situation' would include such things as the particular problem they were trying to solve and their own training and experience, while the immediate surroundings of objects and events would probably contain nothing of relevance at all. Even where the speech does relate to the immediate environment, it is likely that only certain features of it will be relevant; for example, is it the presence of a particular individual that matters, or is it a certain role relationship, no matter who is occupying the roles in question? If John says *I love you*, it presumably does matter that it was said to Mary and not Jane; but if he says *Can you put up a prescription for me?*, what is relevant in that situation is the *role* of dispensing chemist, and not the identity of the individual who happens to be occupying it at that particular time and place.

In general, the ability to use language in abstract and indirect contexts of situation is what distinguishes the speech of adults from that of children. Learning language consists in part in learning to free it from the constraints of the immediate environment. This process *begins* very early in life, when the child first learns to ask for things that are not visible and to recall objects and events which he has observed earlier. But it is a gradual process, which takes place in different ways with different children; this is one of the variables which Bernstein has found to be significant – which *types* of situation serve as the gateway to more abstract and generalized contextual meanings. As he says, 'certain groups of children, through the forms of their socialization, are oriented towards receiving and offering universalistic meanings in *certain contexts*' (1971, 196). This in itself is not important; but it becomes important if there are certain *types* of situation which play a central part in the child's total development, since these are the ones where he will need to use language in ways that are least dependent on the here and now.

This leads us to the notion of a situation type. Looking at how people actually use language in daily life, we find that the apparently infinite number of different possible situations represents in reality a very much smaller number of general *types* of situation, which we can describe in such terms as 'players instructing novice in a game', 'mother reading bedtime story to child', 'customer ordering goods over the telephone', 'teacher guiding pupils' discussion of a poem' and the like. Not all these situation types are equally interesting, and some are obviously very trivial; but in the last resort the importance of any abstract category of this kind depends on what we are going to make of it, and the significance of the notion of 'context of situation' for the present discussion is that some situation types play a crucial role in the child's move into the adult language. For example, if a mother or father is playing with a child with some constructional toy, such as a set of building bricks, this type of situation is likely to contain some remarks of guidance and explanation, with utterances like *I don't think that one will go on there; it's too wide*. The context of situation for this utterance is one in which the child is gaining instruction relating to his handling of objects, and although any one instance is not by itself going to make much difference, an accumulation of experiences of this kind may be highly significant. And if it regularly happens that the remarks relate not just to *this particular* tower that is being built with *these particular* bricks, but to tower-building in general – in other words, if the context of situation is not limited to the actual physical surroundings, but extends to more general and less immediate environments, as would be implied by a remark such as *the smaller ones have to go at the top* – then language is now serving a primary function in this aspect of the child's development. Hence he will have a strong sense of *this* use of language, of language as a means of learning about the physical environment and about his own ability to interact with it and control it.

The types of situation which seem to be most central to the child's socialization have been identified by Bernstein in the most general terms. He refers to them as 'critical socializing contexts', using 'context' in the sense of a generalized situation type. He identifies the 'regulative' context, 'where the child is made aware of the rules of the moral order, and their various backings'; the 'instructional' context, 'where the child learns about the objective nature of objects and persons, and acquires skills of various kinds'; the 'imaginative or innovating' contexts, 'where the child is encouraged to experiment and re-create his world on his own terms'; and the 'inter-personal' context, 'where the child is made aware of affective states – his own, and others' (Bernstein 1971, 181, 198). These turn out to be already anticipated in the developmental functions through which the child has first started to build up a linguistic system of his own: the instrumental, regulatory and so on, described in section 3 above. For example, those types of situation which involve explanation and instruction, Bernstein's 'instructional context', typically pick up the developmental thread that first appeared in the form of a 'heuristic' function, the child's early use of language to explore his environment. They are therefore critical also in the child's learning of *language*, since it is through using language in situations of these types that he builds on and expands his meaning potential.

This is where the notions of context of situation, and situation type, become important for the school. The school requires that the child should be able to use language in certain ways: first of all, most obviously, that he should be able to use language to learn. The teacher operates in contexts of situation where it simply has to be taken for granted that for every child, by the time he arrives in school, language is a means of learning; and this is an assumption that is basic to the educational process. Less obvious, but perhaps no less fundamental, is the assumption that language is a means of personal expression and participation: that the child is at home, linguistically, in interpersonal contexts, where his early use of language to interact with those emotionally important to him, and to express and develop his own uniqueness as an individual (the interactional and personal functions), has in the same way been taken up and extended into new realms of meaning. No doubt both these assumptions are true, as they stand: every normal child has mastered the use of language both for entering into personal relationships and for exploring his environment. But the *kind* of meanings that one child expects to be associated with any particular context of situation may differ widely from what is expected by another. Here we are back to Bernstein's codes again, which we have now approached from another angle, seeing them as differences in the meaning potential which may be typically associated with given situation types. As we have seen, these differences have their origin in the social structure. In Ruqaiya Hasan's words, 'the "code" is defined by reference to its semantic properties' and 'the semantic properties of the codes can be predicted from the elements of social structure which, in fact, give rise to them' (Berstein 1973, 258).

Now the very young child, in his first ventures with language, keeps the functions of language fairly clearly apart; when he speaks, he is doing only one thing at a time – asking for some object, responding to a greeting, expressing interest or whatever it is. When he starts learning his mother tongue, however, the contexts of situation in which he uses it are already complex and manysided, with a number of threads of meaning running simultaneously. To vary the metaphor, we could say that all speech other than the protolanguage of infancy is polyphonic: different melodies are kept going side by side, and each element in the sentence is like a chord which contributes something to all of them. This is perhaps the most striking characteristic of human language, and one which distinguishes it from all other symbolic communication systems.

6 Register

This last point is a reflection of the contexts of situation in which language is used, and the ways in which one type of situation may differ from another. Types of linguistic situation differ from one another, broadly speaking, in three respects: first, what is actually taking place; secondly, who is taking part; and thirdly, what part the language is playing. These three variables, taken together, determine the range within which meanings are selected and the forms which are used for their expression. In other words, they determine the 'register'. (See table 1, p. 35.)

The notion of register is at once very simple and very powerful. It refers to the fact that the language we speak or write varies according to the type of situation. This in itself is no more than stating the obvious. What the theory of register does is to attempt to uncover the general principles which govern this variation, so that we can begin to understand *what* situational factors determine *what* linguistic features. It is a fundamental property of all languages that they display variation according to use; but surprisingly little is yet known about the nature of the variation involved, largely because of the difficulty of identifying the controlling factors.

An excellent example of register variation (and of how to investigate and describe it) is provided by Jean Ure in a paper entitled 'Lexical density and register differentiation' (1971). Here Jean Ure shows that, at least in English, the lexical density of a text, which means the proportion of lexical items (content words) to words as a whole, is a function first of the medium (that is, whether it is spoken or written – written language has a higher lexical density than speech) and, within that, of the social function (pragmatic language, or 'language of action', has the lowest lexical density of all). This is probably true of all languages; but whether it is or not, it is a basic fact about English and a very good illustration of the relation between the actual and the potential that we referred to at the beginning of this section. We could say, following Dell Hymes, that it is part of the speaker's 'communicative competence' that he knows how to distribute lexical items in a text according to different kinds of language use; but there is really no need to introduce here the artificial concept of 'competence', or 'what the speaker knows', which merely adds an extra level of psychological interpretation to what can be explained more simply in direct sociolinguistic or functional terms.

It is easy to be misled here by posing the question the wrong way, as a number of writers on the subject have done. They have asked, in effect, 'what features of language are determined by register?', and then come up with instances of near-synonymy where one word differs from another in level of formality, rhetoric or technicality, like 'chips' and 'French-fried potatoes', or 'deciduous dentition' and 'milk teeth'. But these are commonplaces which lie at the fringe of register variation, and which in themselves would hardly need any linguistic or other kind of 'theory' to explain them. Asked in this way, the question can lead only to trivial answers; but it is the wrong question to ask. *All* language functions in contexts of situation, and is relatable to those contexts. The question is not what peculiarities of vocabulary, or grammar or pronunciation, can be directly accounted for by reference to the situation. It is *which* kinds of situational factor determine *which* kinds of selection in the linguistic system. The notion of register is thus a form of prediction: given that we know the situation, the social context of language use, we can predict a great deal about the language that will occur, with reasonable probability of being right. The important theoretical question then is: what exactly do we need to know about the social context in order to make such predictions?

Let us make this more concrete. If I am talking about gardening, I may be more likely to use words that are the names of plants and others words referring to processes of cultivation; and this is one aspect of the relation of language to situation – the subject matter of gardening is part of the social context. But, in fact, the probability of such terms occurring in the discourse is also dependent on what I and my interlocutor are doing at the time. If we are actually engaged in gardening while we are talking, there may be very few words of this kind. Jean Ure quotes an amusing example from some Russian research on register: 'The recording was of people frying potatoes, and frying potatoes was what they were talking about; but since, it seems, neither frying nor potatoes were represented lexically in the text, the recording was a mystification to all who had not been in the kitchen at the time.' The image of language as merely the direct reflection of subject matter is simplistic and unsound, as Malinowski pointed out fifty years ago; there is much more to it than that, and this is what the notion of register is all about.

What we need to know about a context of situation in order to predict the linguistic features that are likely to be associated with it has been summarized under three headings: we need to know the 'field of discourse', the 'tenor of discourse' and the 'mode of discourse'. (See Halliday *et al.* 1964, where the term 'style of discourse' was used instead of 'tenor'. Here I shall prefer the term 'tenor', introduced by Spencer and Gregory (Enkvist *et al.* 1964). A number of other, more or less related, schemata have been proposed; see especially Ellis 1965, 1966; Gregory 1967.) John Pearce summarizes these as follows (Doughty *et al.* 1972, 185–6):

> Field refers to the institutional setting in which a piece of language occurs, and embraces not only the subject-matter in hand but the whole activity of the speaker or participant in a setting [we might add: 'and of the other participants']. . . .
> Tenor . . . refers to the relationship between participants . . . not merely variation in formality . . . but . . . such questions as the permanence or otherwise of the relationship and the degree of emotional charge in it. . . .
> Mode refers to the channel of communication adopted: not only the choice between spoken and written medium, but much more detailed choices [we might add: 'and other choices relating to the role of language in the situation']. . . .

These are the general concepts needed for describing what is linguistically significant in the context of situation. They include the subject-matter, as an aspect of the 'field of discourse' – of the whole setting of relevant actions and events within which the language is functioning – for this is where subject-matter belongs. We do not, in fact, first decide what we want to say, independently of the setting, and then dress it up in a garb that is appropriate to it in the context, as some writers on language and language events seem to assume. The 'content' is part of the total planning that takes place. There is no clear line between the 'what' and the 'how'; all language is language-in-use, in a context of situation, and all of it relates to the situation, in the abstract sense in which I am using the term here.

I should here make a passing reference to dialects, which are part of the picture of language and social man, although not primarily relevant in the educational context except as the focus of linguistic attitudes. Our language is also determined by who we are; that is the basis of dialect, and in principle a dialect is with us all our lives – it is not subject to choice. In practice, however, this is less and less true, and the phenomenon of 'dialect switching' is widespread. Many speakers learn two or more dialects, either in succession, dropping the first when they learn the second, or in coordination, switching them according to the context of situation. Hence the dialect comes to be an aspect of the register. If for example the standard dialect is used in formal contexts and the neighbourhood one in informal contexts, then one part of the contextual determination of linguistic features is the determination of choice of dialect. When dialects come to have different meanings for us, the choice of dialect becomes a choice of meaning, or a choice between different areas of our meaning potential.

Like the language of the child, the language of the adult is a set of socially-contextualized resources of behaviour, a 'meaning potential' that is related to situations of use. Being 'appropriate to the situation' is not some optional extra in language; it is an essential element in the ability to mean. Of course, we are all aware of occasions when we feel about something said or written that it might have been expressed in a way that was more appropriate to the task in hand; we want to 'keep the meaning but change the wording.' But these are the special cases, in which we are reacting to purely conventional features of register variation. In the last resort, it is impossible to draw a line between 'what he said' and 'how he said it', since this is based on a conception of language in isolation from any context. The distinction between one register and another is a distinction of *what* is said as much as of *how* it is said, without any enforced separation between the two. If a seven-year-old insists on using slang when you think he should be using more formal language, this is a dispute about registers; but if he insists on talking about his football hero when you want him to talk about a picture he has been painting, then this is equally a dispute over registers, and one which is probably much more interesting and far-reaching for both teacher and pupil concerned.

Thus our functional picture of the adult linguistic system is of a culturally specific and situationally sensitive range of meaning potential. Language is the ability to 'mean' in the situation types, or social contexts, that are generated by the culture. When we talk about 'uses of language', we are concerned with the meaning potential that is associated with particular situation types; and we are likely to be especially interested in those which are of some social and cultural significance, in the light of a sociological theory of language such as Bernstein's. This last point is perhaps worth stressing. The way that we have envisaged the study of language and social man, through the concept of 'meaning potential', might be referred to as a kind of 'sociosemantics', in the sense that it is the study of meaning in a social or sociological framework. But there is a difference between 'social' and 'sociological' here. If we describe the context of situation in terms of *ad hoc* observations about the settings in which language is used, this could be said to be a 'social' account of language but hardly a 'sociological' one, since the concepts on which we are drawing are not referred to any kind of general social theory. Such an account can be very illuminating, as demonstrated in a brilliant paper published twenty years ago by T. F. Mitchell, called 'The language of buying and selling in Cyrenaica' – though since the language studied was Cyrenaican Arabic and the paper was published in a learned journal in Morocco, it was not at first widely known (Mitchell 1957). But for research of this kind to be relevant to a teacher who is professionally concerned with his pupils' success in language, it has to relate to social contexts that are themselves of significance, in the sort of way that Bernstein's 'critical contexts' are significant for the socialization of the child. The criteria would then be sociological rather than simply social – based on some theory of social structure and social change. In this respect, the earlier terms like Firth's 'sociological linguistics', or 'sociology of language' as used by Bernstein, are perhaps more pointed than the currently fashionable label 'sociolinguistics'.

Table 1   Varieties in language

Dialect ('dialectal variety') = variety 'according to the user'	**Register** ('diatypic variety') = variety 'according to the use'
A dialect is: 　what you speak (habitually) 　determined by who you are (socio-region of origin and/or adoption), and 　expressing diversity of social structure (patterns of social hierarchy)	A register is: 　what you are speaking (at the time) 　determined by what you are doing (nature of social activity being engaged in), and 　expressing diversity of social process (social division of labour)
So in principle dialects are: 　different ways of saying the same thing and tend to differ in: 　phonetics, phonology, lexicogrammar (but not in semantics)	So in principle registers are: 　ways of saying different things and tend to differ in: 　semantics (and hence in lexicogrammar, and sometimes phonology, as realization of this)
Extreme cases: 　antilanguages, mother-in-law languages	Extreme cases: 　restricted languages, languages for special purposes
Typical instances: 　subcultural varieties (standard/nonstandard)	Typical instances: 　occupational varieties (technical, semi-technical)
Principal controlling variables: 　social class, caste; provenance (rural/urban); generation; age; sex	Principal controlling variables: 　field (type of social action); tenor (role relationships); mode (symbolic organization)
Characterized by: 　strongly-held attitudes towards dialects as symbol of social diversity	Characterized by: 　major distinctions of spoken/written; language in action/language in reflection

2

A social-functional approach to language*

(Parret) *Do you stress the instrumentality of linguistics rather than its autonomy?*

(Halliday) These are not really contradictory. But there are two different issues involved when you talk about autonomy. One is : 'To what extent *is* the subject self-sufficient?' My answer is: 'It isn't.' (But then what subject is?) The second is: 'To what extent *are we studying* language for the purpose of throwing light on language, and to what extent for the purpose of throwing light on something else?' This is a question of goals; it is the question why you are doing it. In this sense the two perspectives are complementary. Probably most people who have looked at language in functional terms have had a predominantly instrumental approach; they have not been concerned so much with the nature of language as such as with the use of language to explore something else. But I would say that in order to understand the nature of language itself we also have to approach it functionally. So I would have both perspectives at once. It seems to me that we have to recognize different purposes for which language may be studied. An autonomous linguistics is the study of language for the sake of understanding the linguistic system. An instrumental linguistics is the study of language for understanding something else – the social system, for example.

One needs for a relevant linguistic theory other larger theories, behavioural and sociological theories. One can find in your publications many allusions to Bernstein's sociology. What does Bernstein mean for you?

If you are interested in inter-organism linguistics, in language as interaction, then you are inevitably led to a consideration of language in the perspective of the social system. What interests me about Bernstein is that he is a theoretical sociologist who builds language into his theory not as an optional extra but as an essential component (Bernstein 1971, esp. chs. 7–10). In Bernstein's view, in order to understand the social system, how it persists and changes in the course of the transmission of culture from one generation to another, you have to understand the key role that language plays in this. He approaches this first of all through the role that language plays in the socialization process; he then moves on towards a much more general social theory of cultural transmission and the maintenance of the social

---

* From a discussion with Herman Parret (Herman Parret, *Discussing language* (The Hague: Mouton 1974)).

system, still with language playing a key role. To me as a linguist this is crucial for two reasons, one instrumental and one autonomous if you like. Speaking 'instrumentally', it means that you have in Bernstein's work a theory of the social system with language embedded in it, so that anyone who is asking, as I am, questions such as 'What is the role of language in the transmission of culture? how is it that the ordinary everyday use of the language, in the home, in the neighbourhood and so on, acts as an effective channel for communicating the social system?' finds in Bernstein's work a social theory in the context of which one can ask these questions. In the second place, speaking 'autonomously', this then feeds back into our study of the linguistic system, so that we can use the insights we get from Bernstein's work to answer the question: why is language as it is? Language has evolved in a certain way because of its function in the social system.

Why this privileged position of language in the socialization process, for Bernstein and for you?

I suppose because, in the processes by which the child becomes a member of society, language does in fact play the central part. Even if you take the most fundamental type of personal relationship, that of the child and its mother, this is largely mediated through language. Bernstein has the notion of *critical socializing contexts*; there are a small number of situation types, like the regulative context (control of the child's behaviour by the parent), which are critical in the socialization of the child. The behaviour that takes place within these contexts is largely linguistic behaviour. It is the linguistic activity which carries the culture with it.

You and Bernstein mean by language vocalized language and not other systems of signs?

Yes, although we would of course agree on the important role of para-linguistic systems like gesture. Clearly the more that one can bring these into the total picture, the more insight one will gain. But nevertheless language, in the sense of speech, natural language in its spoken form, is the key system.

Other linguists working in the field of sociolinguistics are Hymes and Labov. Is there again solidarity with these researchers?

Hymes has adopted, in some of his work at least, an intra-organism perspective on what are essentially inter-organism questions (see for example Hymes 1971). This is a complex point. Let me put it this way: suppose you are studying language as interaction, you can still embed this in the perspective of language as knowledge. This is what is lying behind Hymes's notion of *communicative competence*, or competence in use. To link this up with the recent history of the subject, we should mention Chomsky first. The great thing Chomsky achieved was that he was the first to show that natural language could be brought within the scope of formalization; that you could in fact study natural language as a formal system. The cost of this was a very high degree of idealization; obviously, he had to leave out of consideration a great many of those variations and those distinctions that precisely interest those of us who are concerned with the sociological study of language. From this point of view Chomskyan linguistics is a form of reductionism, it is so highly idealized. Now, Chomsky's idealization is expressed in the distinction he draws between competence and performance. Competence (in its original sense) refers to the natural language in its idealized form; performance refers to everything else – it is a ragbag including physiological side-effects, mental blocks, statistical properties of the system, subtle nuances of meaning and various other things all totally unrelated to each other, as Hymes himself has pointed out. If you are interested in linguistic *interaction*, you don't want the high level of idealization that is involved in the notion of competence; you can't use it, because most of the distinctions that are important to you are idealized out of the picture.

What can you do about this? You can do one of two things. You can say, in effect, 'I accept the distinction, but I will study performance'; you then set up 'theories of performance', in which case it is necessary to formulate some concept (which is Hymes's communicative competence) to take account of the speaker's ability to use language in ways that are appropriate to the situation. In other words, you say there is a 'sociolinguistic competence' as well as a linguistic competence. Or you can do what I would do, which is to reject the distinction altogether on the grounds that we cannot operate with this degree and this *kind* of idealization. We accept a much lower level of formalization; instead of rejecting what is messy, we accept the mess and build it into the theory (as Labov does with variation). To put it another way, we don't try to draw a distinction between what is grammatical and what is acceptable. So in an inter-organism perspective there is no place for the dichotomy of competence and performance, opposing what the speaker knows to what he does. There is no need to bring in the question of what the speaker knows; the background to what he does is what he could do – a potential, which is objective, not a competence, which is subjective. Now Hymes is taking the intra-organism ticket to what is actually an inter-organism destination; he is doing 'psycho-sociolinguistics', if you like. There's no reason why he shouldn't; but I find it an unnecessary complication.

That is an interesting point here. What according to you is the role of psychology as a background theory of linguistic theory? I am thinking here of Saussure's and Chomsky's view that linguistics is a subpart of psychology.

I would reject that absolutely; not because I would insist on the autonomy of linguistics, nor because I would reject the psychological perspective as one of the meaningful perspectives on language, but because this is an arbitrary selection. If someone is interested in certain particular questions, then for him linguistics is a branch of psychology; fine, I accept that as a statement of his own interests and purposes. But if he tries to tell me that all linguistics has to be a branch of psychology, then I would say no. I am not really interested in the boundaries between disciplines; but if you pressed me for one specific answer, I would have to say that for me linguistics is a branch of sociology. Language is a part of the social system, and there is no need to interpose a psychological level of interpretation. I am not saying this is not a relevant perspective, but it is not a necessary one for the exploration of language.

We are now coming to one of the key points: your opinion about the relation between grammar and semantics, and also about that between behavioural potential, meaning potential and grammar. Can you say that there is a progression between 'to do', 'to mean' and 'to say', in your perspective?

Yes. First let me say that I adopt the general perspective on the linguistic system you find in Hjelmslev, in the Prague school, with Firth in the London school, with Lamb, and to a certain extent with Pike – language as a basically tristratal system: semantics, grammar, phonology. (Grammar means lexicogrammar; that is, it includes vocabulary.) Now, it is very important to say that each of these systems, semantics, grammar and phonology, is a system of potential, a range of alternatives. If we take the grammatical (lexicogrammatical) system, this is the system of what the speaker *can say*. This relates back to the previous point we were discussing – it seems to me unnecessary to talk about what the speaker knows; we don't need to be concerned with what is going on in his head, we simply talk about an abstract potential. What the speaker can say, i.e., the lexicogrammatical system as a whole, operates as the realization of the semantic system, which is what the speaker *can mean* – what I refer to as the 'meaning potential'. I see language essentially as a system of meaning potential. Now, once we go outside the language, then we see that this semantic system is itself the realization of something beyond, which is what the speaker *can do* – I have referred to that as the 'behaviour potential'. I want to insist here that there are many different ways of going outside language; this is only one of them. Perhaps it would be better at this point to talk in terms of a general semiotic level: the semantic system, which is the meaning potential embodied in language, is itself the realization of a higher-level semiotic which we may define as a behavioural system or more generally as a social semiotic. So when I say *can do*, I am specifically referring to the behaviour potential as a semiotic which can be encoded in language, or of course in other things too.

One of your statements is that 'can mean' is a form of 'can do'.

Yes, and that could be confusing, because it is trying to say two things at once in an abbreviated form. To my mind, the key concept is that of *realization*, language as multiple coding. Just as there is a relation of realization between the semantic system and the lexicogrammatical system, so that *can say* is the *realization* of *can mean*, so also there is a relation of realization between the semantic system and some higher-level semiotic which we can represent if you like as a behavioural system. It would be better to say that *can mean* is 'a realization of *can do*', or rather 'is one form of the realization of *can do*'.

Now, in the early sixties those of us who were interested in what people do linguistically were labelled 'taxonomic' by the transformationalists, who criticized us for being data-oriented, for looking at instances, for dealing with corpuses, and so on. To my knowledge, no linguist has ever simply described a corpus; this is a fiction invented for polemic purposes. The question is, what status do you give to instances of language behaviour? There are many purposes for which we may be interested in the *text*, in what people actually *do* and *mean* and *say*, in real situations. But in order to make sense of the text, what the speaker actually says, we have to interpret it against the background of what he 'can say'. In other words, we see the text as actualized potential; it is the actual seen against the background of the potential. But note that the actual and the potential are at the same level of abstraction. This is what makes it possible to relate the one to the other. They are at the same level of coding within the system, so that any text represents an actualization (a path through the system) at each level: the level of *meaning*, the level of *saying* (or *wording*, to use the folk-linguistic term for the lexicogrammatical system), and of course the level of *sounding* or *writing*.

The key notion is that of 'realization', in the Hjelmslevian sense: each level is the realization of the lower level?
Rather of the *higher* level. The earlier tradition usually had the meaning at the top, not at the bottom!

If you can speak of a teleology of your whole description, can you say that semantics or sociosemantics is the key to the whole system?
Well, yes. If I was forced to choose a key, it would be that.

This semantic level is structured – you use the term 'network'. Can you explain this term 'semantic network' here?
I would use the term *network* for all levels, in fact: semantic network, grammatical network, phonological network. It refers simply to a representation of the potential at that level. A network is a network of options, of choices; so for example the semantic system is regarded as a set of options. If we go back to the Hjelmslevian (originally Saussurean) distinction of paradigmatic and syntagmatic, most of modern linguistic theory has given priority to the syntagmatic form of organization. *Structure* means (abstract) *constituency*, which is a syntagmatic concept. Lamb treats the two axes together: for him a linguistic stratum is a network embodying both syntagmatic and paradigmatic relations all mixed up together, in patterns of what he calls AND nodes and OR nodes. I take out the paradigmatic relations (Firth's *system*) and give priority to these; for me the underlying organization at each level is paradigmatic. Each level is a network of paradigmatic relations, of ORs – a range of alternatives, in the sociological sense. This is what I mean by a *potential*: the semantic system is a network of meaning potential. The network consists very simply of a set of interrelated systems, the *system* being used here in the Firthian sense, though perhaps slightly more abstract, and making fuller use of his own 'polysystemic' principle. Let me just define it: a system is a set of options, a set of

possibilities A, B or C, together with a condition of entry. The entry condition states the environment: 'in the environment X, there is a choice among A, B and C'. The choice is obligatory; if the conditions obtain, a choice must be made. The environment is, in fact, another choice (and here I depart from Firth, for whom the environment of a system was a place in structure – the entry condition was syntagmatic, whereas mine is again paradigmatic). It is equivalent to saying 'if you have selected X (out of X and Y), then you must go on to select either A, B or C.' The 'then' expresses logical dependence – there is no real time here – it is a purely abstract model of language as choice, as sets of interrelated choices. Hudson's recent book (1971) gives an excellent account of system networks in grammar.

Now this is what is represented in the network. The network is a representation of options, more particularly of the interrelations among options. Hence, a semantic network is a representation of semantic options, or choices in meaning.

Is there any difference between a semantic structure and a grammatical structure?

We may have some confusion here through the use of the term *structure*. May I use it in the Firthian sense: just as the system is the form of representation of paradigmatic relations, the structure is the form of representation of syntagmatic relations. The output of any path through the network of systems is a structure. In other words, the structure is the expression of a set of choices made in the system network. We know more or less what the nature of grammatical structures is. We know that constituent structure in some form or other is an adequate form of representation of the structures that are the output of the lexicogrammatical level. It is much less clear what is the nature of the structures that are the output of the semantic level. Lamb used to draw a distinction here: he used to say that the semantic structures were networks, while lexicosyntactic structures were trees and morphological structures were strings. I don't think he holds to this any more. If you take the sort of work that Geoffrey Turner has been doing, of the investigation of language development in young children, where we have been using the notion of meaning potential in the form of semantic system networks, in this situation it has been possible to bypass the level of semantic structure and go straight into lexicogrammatical constituent structure (Turner 1973). That's all right for certain limited purposes. But there is obviously a limitation here, and when we attempt semantic representation for anything other than these highly restricted fields, it is almost certainly going to be necessary to build in some concept of semantic structure. But what it will look like exactly I don't know. I don't think we can tell yet. Probably some form of relational network on the lines that Lamb and Peter Reich are working on (Reich 1970).

The input of the semantic network is sociological and particular, and the output is linguistic and general. What do you mean by 'particular' on the one hand and 'general' on the other hand?

Let me take an example. Suppose you are interested, in a context of cultural transmission, in the way in which a mother controls the behaviour of the child. She is expressing, through the use of language, certain abstract behavioural options, which we then characterize in terms which relate them to some model of the social system. In other words, she may be choosing among different forms of control – a simple imperative mode, a positional appeal, a personal appeal or the like, as in Bernstein's work; and when we show how this choice is encoded in language, what we are doing is deriving a set of linguistic categories from options in the social system. Now these will be very general categories, in the linguistic system: forms of transitivity, or forms of modification within the noun phrase, for example. But in order to get to them, we have to go through a network of behavioural options which become highly specific. A linguistic category such as 'clause type: material process, benefactive' appears (among other things) as the expression of some behavioural option that is highly specific in terms of the social theory, such as 'threat of loss of privilege'. The sociological categories which these linguistic ones realize will in relation to the social system be very particular, deriving from particular social contexts. You can relate this to the well-known problem of getting from the 'macro' scale of society to the 'micro' scale of language. This is wrongly posed, in my view; the problem is not one of size, but of level of abstraction. What are, for language, highly abstract and general categories have to be seen as realizing highly concrete and specific notions in the social structure.

The whole difficulty is to define the relation on the one hand between the behavioural potential and the meaning potential and on the other hand between the meaning potential and the grammar. These two relations, that is what your linguistic theory has to define. What are the different conditions for a semantic network in connection with the other two levels of the whole theory?

I would see both these relations as defined by the concept of realization. The semantic network is one level in a system of multiple coding. There are two main trends in thinking about language, aren't there? There is the *realizational* view, language seen as one system coded in another and then recoded in another; and the *combinatorial* view, where language is seen as larger units made up of smaller units. Of course both these relations are found in language, but people assign them very varying statuses. If we adopt the first emphasis, which is the Hjelmslevian view, we can extend the realizational concept outside language, so that just as the lexicogrammatical system realizes the semantic system, the semantic system realizes the behavioural system, or the social semiotic. If we then consider any specific part of the semantic system, there are three conditions which our representation must meet. One is that it must associate this part of the system with other parts of the same system on the same level. In other words, we must be able to show what is the total semantic potential within which the particular set of options that we are dealing with operates. But at the same time, we must be able to relate it to the other systems in both directions: both upward and downward. That is, if we claim that we have identified a set of options in meaning, not only do we have to relate these to other sets of options in meaning in a systematic way, but we have also to show, first, how this set of options in meaning realizes an aspect of the social system and, secondly, how it is in turn realized in the lexicogrammatical system. This is a very strong demand, in a sense, because if one says that there is a significant choice in meaning in social-control situations between, say, moral disapprobation and other forms of disapprobation, as Geoffrey Turner does, or between imperative and obligative types of rule-giving, then one must be able to specify three things: one, exactly how this relates to the other options in meaning that have been set up; two, how this expresses higher-level behavioural options; three, how this is in turn realized in the grammar. If we claim that a child can interpret the social system by listening to what his mother says, then presumably a linguist should be able to do the same.

How can one define the dissimilarity of realization between the semantics and the grammar then? In other words, what is the definition of grammar?

Well, I am not very clear on the boundaries here, between lexicogrammar and semantics. I tend to operate with rather fluid boundaries. But it can be defined theoretically, in that the lexicogrammatical system is the level of internal organization of language, the network of relations of linguistic form. And it is related outside language only indirectly, through an interface. I would also want to define it functionally, in terms of the metafunctions; we haven't come to that yet. Let us just say that it is the purely internal level of organization, the core of the linguistic system.

With a 'grammatical' and a 'lexical' part?

Yes, but – at least in my perspective; one might conceive differently for other purposes – the two are not really different. The lexical system is not something that is fitted in afterwards to a set of slots defined by the grammar. The lexicon – if I may go back to a definition I used many years ago – is simply the most delicate grammar. In other words, there is only one network of lexicogrammatical options. And as these become more and more specific, they tend more and more to be realized by the choice of a lexical item rather than by the choice of a grammatical structure. But it is all part of a single grammatical system.

Is 'syntax' also a component of the grammar?

You notice I am avoiding the term *syntax*; only for this reason – that it has come into present-day linguistics from two different sources and so it has two different meanings. On the one hand you have syntax in the context of semantics-syntactics-pragmatics, where it is defined in terms of a general theory of signs, on criteria which are drawn from outside language. On the other hand, there is the context in which you have semantics-grammar-phonetics, and then within grammar you have the division into syntax-morphology. This is a different sense of the term, where the criteria are within language itself; syntax is that part of the grammatical system which deals with the combination of words into sentences, or phrases into sentences. But I myself am not convinced of the traditional linguistic distinction between syntax and morphology, at least as a general phenomenon; I think it applies to certain languages only, and so I don't feel the need to use syntax in that sense. But I am avoiding using it in the other sense because of the confusion between the two meanings of the term.

I would like to come back to the relation between semantics and grammar. Is it possible that a semantic option has more than one realization in the grammar?

Yes. Well, that's a very good and open question, to my mind. Let me start by saying that I think we must admit theoretically that it is possible. We may have what Lamb calls *diversification* between levels. What this means is that, in addition to one-to-one relations in the coding system, where one element on one level is realized by one element on another level, you may also have many-to-one and one-to-many. Now here we are talking about one-to-many; in other words, the phenomenon where one element in the semantic system is realized by more than one in the lexicogrammatical system. First, then, we must admit theoretically that this happens, that there is free variation in the grammatical system, with one meaning realized by two or more forms. But then I would add that we should always be suspicious when we find this, because it usually turns out that the distinction in the lexicogrammatical system does in fact express a more delicate distinction in the semantic system that we haven't yet got round to. In other words, let us not go so far as to deny free variation, but let us be highly suspicious of any actual instances of it, because very often it turns out that there is a more subtle or more 'delicate' distinction in the semantic system which is being expressed in this way.

Can we go so far as to say that the grammatical system is 'arbitrary' in connection with the meaning differences?

What do you mean by arbitrary?

In the Saussurean sense the relation between 'signifiant/signifié' is arbitrary. There is no isomorphism between the two levels. This seems to be important because in generative semantics each syntactic difference means at the same time a semantic difference. There is no arbitrary relation between syntax and semantics there.

Well, I would tend to agree with this. When we talk about the arbitrariness of the sign, we are referring to the Saussurean content/expression relation. I believe every linguist must agree that there is arbitrariness at this point. But there is I think just this one point in the whole linguistic system where we can talk about arbitrariness – that is, at the line that is drawn by Hjelmslev between content and expression. The relations across this line are arbitrary; this we must accept. But if we are considering the relation between semantics and grammar, which is all within Hjelmslev's content, then I would say it is not arbitrary. Consider a grammatical structure. A grammatical structure is a configuration of roles, or functions if you like, each of which derives from some option in the semantic system – not one to one, but as a whole. Let us take an example from child language. The child says *water on*, meaning 'I want the water tap turned on.' We relate this to some general meaning or function for which the child is using language: in this case, the satisfaction of a material desire. We can see that the grammatical structure represents this very clearly. It consists of two elements, one identifying the object of the desire, i.e. *water*, and the other specifying the nature of the request, i.e. *on*. We express this by means of structural labels. It is clear that the grammatical structure here is a non-arbitrary configuration of elements which, taken as a whole, represent the function for which language is being used, and each of which constitutes a particular role within that function. Let me say in passing that this was said by Malinowski (1923) when he pointed out that the elementary structures of the child's language represented very clearly the functions that language served for it. I agree with this, but I would go further and say that it is also a property of adult language: if you take a grammatical structure, for example a transitivity structure that we represent in terms of categories like agent, process and goal, or a modal structure, in terms of a modal element, consisting of subject plus finiteness, and a residual or 'propositional' element, each of these grammatical structures represents a configuration that is derived as a whole from the semantic level of which it is the realization. So, in that sense, I would consider that the linguistic system at that point is non-arbitrary. The arbitrariness comes in simply in the relation between the content and the expression.

Is it possible to relate all that you said about the scope of linguistics, and about the relationships between behaviour, meaning and grammar, to the 'functional' aspect of your theory of language?

Yes. I would accept the label 'functional' and I think the point that we have just been discussing provides an excellent illustration of this. Consider any sentence of the adult language, for example in English 'Balbus built a wall'. Taking up what I said just now, this represents a configuration of roles, or syntactic functions, a configuration which is not arbitrary since it represents very clearly the meaning of the sentence as a set of options in the semantic system.

We can now go on to say that this sentence embodies a number of structures all at the same time; there are represented in that sentence at least three – let us confine ourselves to three – different structural configurations, each one of which corresponds to a different function of language. On the one hand, there is a transitivity structure involved in it; we could characterize this as Agent + Process + Goal of result. Now this configuration represents the function of language expressing a content, what I prefer to call the *ideational* function: language as expressing the speaker's experience of the external world, and of his own internal world, that of his own consciousness. But on the other hand that clause has structure also in the modal sense, representing what I would call the *interpersonal* function of language, language as expressing relations among participants in the situation, and the speaker's own intrusion into it. So the clause consists simultaneously of a *modal* element plus a *residual* element. The modal element expresses the particular role that the speaker has chosen to adopt in the situation and the role or role options that he has chosen to assign to the hearer. At the same time the clause has a third structural configuration, that in terms of a *theme* and a *rheme*, which is its structure as a message in relation to the total communication process – expressing its operational relevance, if you like. The point I want to make is this: in my opinion all these three – and I would be prepared to add one or two more – structural configurations are equally semantic; they are all representations of the meaning of that clause in respect of its different functions, the functions which I have referred to as *ideational*, *interpersonal* and *textual*. So in all these cases the structure is not arbitrary, to link up with what we were saying before.

Is there any difference between the typology of the 'uses' of language and the typology of the 'functions' of language? I believe that you define the 'function' as a discrete area of formalized meaning potential.

Right. I would like to make a distinction between *function* and *use*, just as you suggest, and somewhat in these terms. As far as the adult language is concerned, it is possible to talk about the *uses* of language, by which I would understand simply the selection of options within the linguistic system in the context of actual situation types: *use* in its informal everyday sense. In that sense, *use* is a valuable concept; but we can't really enumerate the uses of language in a very systematic way – the nearest we can come to that is some concept of situation types, of which Bernstein's critical socializing contexts would be an example. Now I would distinguish that from *function*, because the whole of the adult language system is organized around a small number of functional components. The linguistic system, that is to say, is made up of a few very large sets of options, each set having strong internal constraints but weak external constraints. By 'strong internal constraints' I mean that there is strong environmental conditioning on choice: if you make a certain selection in one system within that set of options, this will determine up to a point the selection you make in other systems within the same set. Whereas the external constraints are weak; that is to say, the selection does not affect the choices that you make in the other sets of options.

Take for instance the structure of the clause. There is one set of options in *transitivity* representing the type of process you are talking about, the participant roles in this process and so on. This is a tightly-organized set of systems, each one interlocking with all the others. And there is another set of options, those of *mood*, relating to the speaker's assignment of speech roles to himself and to the hearer, and so on; there systems are again tightly organized internally. But there is little mutual constraint between transitivity and mood. What you select in transitivity hardly affects what you select in mood, or vice versa. Now what are these components? Fundamentally, they are the components of the language system which correspond to the abstract functions of language – to what I have called *metafunctions*, areas of meaning potential which are inherently involved in all uses of language. These are what I am referring to as ideational, interpersonal and textual; generalized functions which have as it were become built into language, so that they form the basis of the organization of the entire linguistic system.

Would you identify the 'function' of language with the 'structure' of language?

May I make a distinction here between two uses of the term *structure*?

Structure can be used in a sense which is more or less synonymous with *system*, where *structure of language* means, in effect, the linguistic system. I have been avoiding using the term *structure* in that sense, in order to avoid confusion; so let me comment on *function* and *system* first. The linguistic system is functional in origin and in orientation, so that in order to understand the nature of the linguistic system we have to explain it as having evolved in the context of this set of basic functions. System is not identical with function, but rather the linguistic system is organized around the set of abstract functions of language. I think that is true in the phylogenetic sense in the evolution of language; I am sure it is true in the ontogenetic sense, in the development of language by a child. In other words, the nature of the linguistic system is such that it has to be explained in functional terms.

The other sense of *structure* is the stricter, Firthian sense, where structure is the abstract category for the representation of syntagmatic relations in language. Here I would say that *function* and *structure* are also different concepts, and in order to relate them we have to think of *function* in its other sense of structural functions or roles, like Agent, Actor, Subject, Theme and the rest. A linguistic structure is then a configuration of functions. But this is *function* in a different sense, though the two are ultimately related.

Isn't it the case that you use an extrinsic definition of 'function'? There is also another definition in the Hjelmslevian sense where 'function' is nothing else than intersystematic relationship. Your definition is an extrinsic definition of 'function'.

Yes; in the first sense I am defining *function* extrinsically. I am not using the term in its technical Hjelmslevian sense. But I think there is an important connection between this extrinsic sense and the second sense I referred to just now, *function* used in the meaning of grammatical functions as distinct from grammatical classes or categories. That notion of function refers to an element of structure considered as a role in the total structural configuration. There is a relationship between this meaning of function and the extrinsic sense in which I am using the term: the grammatical functions, in the sense of roles, are derivable from the extrinsic functions of language.

The category of function is a very classic one in linguistic theory and has been used since Saussure and Hjelmslev. I assume that the Prague school was inspired and fascinated by Bühler's scheme of the different functions of language (Bühler 1934; Vachek 1966). *Do you believe that the Bühler scheme is still valuable, or that Bühler's definition of the expressive, conative and referential functions of language is still valid?*

I think to a certain extent it is; but remember that Bühler is not attempting to explain the nature *of the linguistic system* in functional terms. He is using language to investigate something else. His interest is, if you like, psycholinguistic; and one might compare for example Malinowski's functional theory of language, which is also aimed outside language although in another direction, ethnographic or sociolinguistic as it would be called now. I would consider both these views entirely valid in terms of their own purposes, but I would want myself to adopt a somewhat different (though related) system of functions in order to direct it inwards to explain the nature of the linguistic system. The definition is still extrinsic but the purpose is an intrinsic one. I can explain very simply the relation between the functional framework that I use and that of Bühler. My own *ideational* corresponds very closely to Bühler's *representational*, except that I want to introduce the further distinction within it between *experiential* and *logical*, which corresponds to a fundamental distinction within language itself. My own *interpersonal* corresponds more or less to the sum of Bühler's *conative* and *expressive*, because in the linguistic system these two are not distinguished. Then I need to add a third function, namely the *textual* function, which you will not find in Malinowski or Bühler or anywhere else, because it is intrinsic to language: it is the function that language has of creating text, of relating itself to the context – to the situation and the preceding text. So we have the *observer* function, the *intruder* function, and the *relevance* function, to use another terminological framework that I sometimes find helpful as an explanation. To me the significance of a functional system of this kind is that you can use it to explain the nature of language, because you find that language is in fact structured along these three dimensions. So the system is as it were both extrinsic and intrinsic at the same time. It is designed to explain the internal nature of language in such a way as to relate it to its external environment.

Could you give a brief description of what you mean by the 'logical' and 'experiential' functions of language?

Within the ideational function, the lexicogrammatical system embodies a clear distinction between an experiential and a logical component in terms of the types of structure by which these are realized. The *experiential* function, as the name implies, is the 'content' function of language; it is language as the expression of the processes and other phenomena of the external world, including the world of the speaker's own consciousness, the world of thoughts, feelings and so on. The *logical* component is distinguished in the linguistic system by the fact that it is expressed through recursive structures, whereas all the other functions are expressed through nonrecursive structures. In other words, the logical component is that which is represented in the linguistic system in the form of parataxis and hypotaxis, including such relations as coordination, apposition, condition and reported speech. These are the relations which constitute the logic of natural language; including those which derive from the nature of language itself – reported speech is obviously one example of this, and another is apposition, the 'namely' relation. I think it is necessary to distinguish the logical from the experiential, partly because logical meanings are clearly distinct in their realization, having exclusively this linear recursive mode of expression, and partly because one can show that the logical element in the linguistic system, while it is ideational in origin, in that it derives from the speaker's experience of the external world, once it is built into language becomes neutral with respect to the other functions, such that all structures whatever their functional origin can have built into them inner structures of a logical kind.

Is the 'ideational' function identical with the 'referential' function of language?

Well, I think it includes the referential function, but it is wider. It depends how widely one is using the term *referential*. It is certainly wider than the strict definition of referential, but it might be considered as equivalent to referential in the sense in which Hymes uses the term, provided one points out that it has these two subcomponents of experiential and logical – I am not sure where Hymes would put the logical element in the linguistic system. Hymes (1969) has a basic distinction between referential and socioexpressive; as I understand it, this would correspond pretty closely, his *referential* to my *ideational*, noting this query about the logical, and his *socioexpressive* to my *interpersonal*.

Is it possible in your linguistic theory to elaborate a 'hierarchy' of functions, or is it sufficient to make up the 'taxonomy' of functions?

Yes, the latter. I would not like to impose a hierarchy of functions, because I believe that there can be hierarchy only for the purpose of given investigations. It is noticeable that those whose orientation is primarily psycholinguistic tend to give priority to the ideational function, whereas for those whose orientation is primarily sociolinguistic the priorities are at least equal and possibly the other way – priority might be given to the interpersonal function. This could be reflected in the direction of derivation. If, let us say, one was working with a functionally-based generative semantics, it might well be that for sociological, or rather 'inter-organism', purposes one's generative component would be the interpersonal function, whereas for a more psychologically-oriented, 'intra-organism' semantics the generative component would be, as it usually is in generative semantics, the ideational one.

I believe that this question of hierarchy of functions is very important in linguistic discussion nowadays. I think for example of the Chomskyan sophistication of the 'expressive' function of language. Chomsky defines language as

expression of thought and he wouldn't like to see stressed the more com-
municative features of the semantic structure of language. What do you think
of the stress on the expressive function of language?

I find it unhelpful to isolate any one function as fundamental. I have very
much a goal-oriented view, and I can see that for certain types of inquiry it
may be useful to single out one function rather than another as fundamental,
but I don't find this useful myself. It seems to me important to give equal
status in the linguistic system to all functions. And I would point out that our
traditional approach to grammar is not nearly as one-sidedly oriented
towards the ideational function as sometimes seems to be assumed. For
instance, the whole of the mood system in grammar, the distinction between
indicative and imperative and, within indicative, between declarative and
interrogative – this whole area of grammar has nothing whatever to do with
the ideational component. It is not referential at all; it is purely interpersonal, concerned with the social-interactional function of language. It is
the speaker taking on a certain role in the speech situation. This has been
built into our interpretation of grammar, and I see no reason for departing
from this and treating the social meaning of language as some kind of
optional extra.

Would you say it is very peripheral?

I don't think it is peripheral at all. I don't think we can talk about the
functions in these terms of *central* and *peripheral*. If you want a model of the
production of discourse, I would say that meanings in all functions are
generated simultaneously and mapped onto one another; not that we first of
all decide on a content and then run it through an interaction machine to
decide whether to make it a statement or a question. (I avoid using the term
expressive in this discussion simply because there is a confusion here between *expressive* meaning the expression of thought and *expressive* in the
more usual Bühler sense which is non-representational and corresponds to
Hymes's use in *socio-expressive*.)

Can one say that the communicative function is a kind of super-function or
macro-function, and that the other functions that you mentioned are sub-
functions of the communicative function?

Again I would be unhappy with that. I would want to insist – though
always pointing out that it is simply for the purposes of the kinds of investigation I personally am interested in – on the ideational and interpersonal
having equal status. The textual function can be distinguished from these
two in that it is an enabling function which is intrinsic to language; but as
between the first two, I can't see either being more all-embracing than the
other. All three could be called *metafunctions* – *meta-* rather than *macro-*,
the point being that they are *abstract*; they represent functions of language *as*
incorporated into the linguistic system. You notice I am hedging slightly on
your question, because I am not quite sure how to relate these to what you
are calling 'the communicative function'.

But that depends on the definition that you give of the nature of language. Do you see language first of all as 'communication' or as an isomorphic system of logical relations?

Certainly not as an isomorphic system of logical relations. I suppose therefore I see it as communication, though I would rather say that I see language as a *meaning potential*. It is a form of *human semiotic*, in fact the main form of human semiotic; and as such I want to characterize it in terms of the part that it plays in the life of social man. Or, what is the same thing in more abstract terms, I see the linguistic system as a component – an essential component – of the social system.

I believe that it is necessary to say that the speaker and the hearer have a certain 'knowledge' of the functions of language. Can you specify this?

I think that is certainly implied by what I say, but I would make no use of that formulation.

Why?

Because it is introducing a level of discourse which is unnecessary in this context. It is certainly true that for a speaker and a hearer to interact linguistically they must have this knowledge; but we only know that they have this knowledge because we see them interact. If therefore it is possible to describe the interaction in the form that I mentioned earlier, that is as the actualization of a system of potentials, then it becomes unnecessary to introduce another level, that of knowledge. This would not be true for example in relation to Lamb's work – I mention Lamb because what he does is entirely compatible with my own. We have very much the same premises about language, but we differ precisely in that he is primarily looking at language intra-organistically and I the other way. For Lamb, of course, the whole point is to find out what it is that the speaker has in his head; therefore he is trying to characterize the knowledge that you have just mentioned (Lamb 1971, 1974). But I am not. I am trying to characterize human interaction, and it is unnecessary to attempt to interpose a component of what the speaker-hearer knows into the total descriptive framework.

Is a functional theory of language such as yours a theory of language as 'language system', as the Saussurean 'langue'? I believe that your theory of language is a step against the very classic dichotomies of 'langue'/'parole' or 'competence'/'performance' and so on.

Yes. It is true that I find little use for these dichotomies – though I should point out that this thought is far from being original to me. My former teacher, Firth, himself criticized these very cogently in some of his own writings (Firth 1957, esp. ch. 16). He said that he found it unnecessary to operate with mind/body, mentalism/mechanism, word/idea and 'such dualisms'. I would agree with Firth – again, always saying that it depends on the purpose for which you are looking at language. I mentioned earlier that, for what we are going to call sociolinguistic purposes for the moment, it is necessary to minimize the distinction between what is *grammatical* and what is *acceptable*. If I put this another way I think it will clarify the point here. There will always be *idealization* in any study of language, or indeed in any systematic inquiry. The point is here that we need to reduce the level of idealization, to make it as low as possible, in order that we can understand the processes of interaction, the sort of phenomena studied from an ethnomethodological standpoint by Sacks, Schegloff and others (e.g. Schegloff 1971; Sacks *et al*. 1974). We have to impose as low a degree of idealization on the facts as is compatible with a systematic inquiry. This means, in other words, that what is grammatical is defined as what is acceptable. There is no distinction between these two, from which it also follows that there is no place for a distinction between competence and performance or between *langue* and *parole*, because the only distinction that remains is that between the *actual* and the *potential* of which it is an actualization.

What is the meaning of one of your statements: 'In order to understand the nature of language, it is necessary to start from considerations of its use?'
Oh yes, this is a very closely-related point, and comes back to what I was saying earlier. I think that the use of language can be defined in precisely these terms, namely as the actualization of a potential. Now we want to understand *language in use*. Why? Partly in order to approach this question of how it is that ordinary everyday language transmits the essential patterns of the culture: systems of knowledge, value systems, the social structure and much else besides. How do we try to understand language in use? By looking at what the speaker says against the background of what he might have said but did not, as an actual in the *environment* of a potential. Hence the environment is defined paradigmatically: using language means making choices in the environment of other choices. I would then take the next step of saying that, when we investigate the nature of the linguistic system by looking at how these choices that the speaker makes are interrelated to each other in the system, we find that this internal structure is in its turn determined by the functions for which language is used – hence the functional components we were talking about. We then have to take one more step and ask how is it that the linguistic system has evolved in this way since, as we have seen, the abstract functional components are, although related to, yet different from the set of concrete uses of language that we actually find in given situations. This can best be approached through studies of language development, through the study of how it is that the child learns the linguistic system. I think when we look at that from a functional point of view, we find some kind of an answer to the question how it is that the linguistic system evolved in contexts of use.

Is the study of the acquisition of language in the child not a kind of diachronic linguistics?
Yes, I think in a sense it is, though I think one has got to be careful here. I have been interested in language development in the child from a functional point of view, and I think that one gets a great deal of insight here into the

nature of the linguistic *system* and how it may have evolved. But I think one has to be careful and say simply how it 'may' have evolved. We cannot know for certain that ontogeny reflects phylogeny. All we can say is that when we examine how a child learns the linguistic system from the functional standpoint, we get a picture which *could* be a picture of how human language evolved. One very interesting thing that happens, or at least did in the case of the child I was studying, is that you first of all find him creating his own language on what is presumably a phylogenetic model. Then there comes a very sudden discontinuity – at least a discontinuity in the expression, and, more important, in the nature of the system itself – when the child as it were shrugs his shoulders and says, look, this is just too much work creating the whole of human language again from the start; why don't I settle for the readymade language that I hear around me? And he moves into the adult system.

One way of studying linguistics could be to see how people learn to mean. Learning how to mean is exactly the title of one of your papers. It is a study of the child's language, and language development and acquisition, topics which are very much at stake nowadays. Can you tell me what this study of learning how to mean has to offer to general linguistics?
I see this again from a functional perspective. There has been a great deal of study of language development in the past ten or fifteen years, but mainly on the acquisition of syntax seen from a psycholinguistic point of view – which is complementary, again, to a 'sociosemantic' perspective. To me there seem to be two aspects to be stressed here. One is: what is the *ontogenesis* of the system, in the initial stage before the child takes over the mother tongue? The other is: what are the strategies through which a child moves into the mother tongue and becomes linguistically adult? I would simply make two points here. I think by studying child language you get a very good insight into function and use (which for the very young child, as I said, are synonymous). We can postulate a very small set of uses, or functions, for which the child first creates a semiotic system. I have tried this out in relation to one subject, and you can see the child creating a meaning potential from his own vocal resources in which the meanings relate quite specifically to a certain set of functions which we presume to be general to all cultures. He learns for instance that language can be used in a regulatory function, to get people to do what he wants; and within that function he learns to express a small number of meanings, building up a system of content/expression pairs where the expression is derived entirely from his own resources. He creates a language, in functional terms. Then at a certain point he gives up this trail. In the case that I studied, the child dropped the language-creating process at the stage where he had a potential of about four or five functions with some fifty meanings altogether, roughly fifty elements in the system. Anyway the stage comes when he switches and starts taking over the adult system. So there is a discontinuity in the expression; but there is no discontinuity in the content, because to start with he maps the expres-

sions of the adult system on to his own functional framework. He does this, it seems to me, by a gradual separation of the two notions of function and use; on the one hand the original uses of language go on expanding, as he goes on using language in new and other ways, but at the same time he builds this functional framework into the linguistic system itself. I have tried to describe how he does this; basically I think he does it through internalizing a fundamental distinction between pragmatic uses of language, those which demand a response, and represent a way of participating in the situation, and what I call 'mathetic' uses of language, those which do not demand a response but represent rather a way of observing and of learning as one observes. Now these two come out of his original set of very concrete functions, but they turn into functional components of the linguistic system itself, the interpersonal and the ideational that we were talking about earlier.

Are the causes for this change environmental?
I assume them to be environmental with a biological foundation. The biological conditions must be met, the level of maturation must have been reached. Given that level of maturation, then I would look for environmental causes in the social system. I don't want to get into arguments about the psycholinguistic mechanisms involved, because I don't think this assumes any particular psycholinguistic perspective.

Is your point of view not too behaviouristic here?
No, I would say that it is emphatically not behaviouristic. It has always seemed to me, and again here I am simply following Firth, that behaviourist models will not account for linguistic interaction or for language development. There is a very curious notion that if you are assigning a significant role to the cultural environment in language learning you are a behaviourist. There is no logical connection here at all. We should perhaps demolish the fallacy of the *unstructured input*. There has been a myth around over the past few years that the child must have a specific innate language-learning capacity, a built-in grammar, because the data to which he is exposed are insufficient to account for the result. Now that is not true. The language around him is fantastically rich and highly structured; Labov (1970a) has said this and he is quite right. It is quite unnecessary to postulate a learning device having these highly specific linguistic properties. That doesn't mean it is wrong; it means it isn't necessary. I want to distinguish very sharply here between the particular psychological model which you use and the functional conditions on language learning. These do not presuppose each other in any way. What I am doing is simply studying the child's language development in an interactional perspective, and this has got nothing whatever to do with behaviourist theories of psychology.

How does this viewpoint on language development in the child lead us into a sociosemantic approach to language?
First, it points up the fact that a child who is learning language is learning 'how to mean'; that is, he is developing a semantic potential, in respect of a

set of functions in language that are in the last resort social functions. They represent modes of interaction between the child and others. So the child learns how to interact linguistically; and language becomes for him a primary channel of socialization, because these functions are defined by social contexts, in Bernstein's sense as I mentioned earlier. The child's semantics therefore is functionally specific; what he is developing is a 'social semantics', in the sense that it is a meaning potential related to a particular set of primary social functions. And second – though it's a closely related point – it is above all through a developmental approach that we can make concrete the notion of language as part of the social semiotic: the concept of the culture as a system of meaning, with language as one of its realizations.

Could you explain more concretely your hypothesis about the functional origin of language? What does the system of functions look like in this first phase of the development of language in the child?

In this first phase I suggested that the child learns: the *instrumental* function, which is the 'I want' function of language, language used to satisfy a material need; the *regulatory* function, which is the 'do as I tell you' function, language used to order people about; the *interactional* function, 'me and you', which is language used to interact with other people; the *personal* function, 'here I come', which is language used as the expression of the child's own uniqueness; the *heuristic* function comes a little while behind, and is language as a means of exploring the environment, the 'tell me why' function of language; and finally the *imaginative* function, 'let's pretend', which is really language for the creation of an environment of one's own. In the case of the particular subject I worked with, these six functions had all appeared in his protolanguage: he had developed a semiotic system in respect of all these six functions without making any demand on the adult language at all. The elements of the system were entirely his own invention.

Then there came a point at which he switched, and as it were gave up his own special system in favour of that of English. Simultaneously with this switch, he generalized out of his original range of functions this very general functional opposition between what I referred to as the *pragmatic* and the *mathetic*. With this child the distinction was very clear, because he developed an interesting strategy of his own, which was absolutely consistent: he used a rising intonation for all pragmatic utterances, and a falling one for all mathetic ones. So he knew exactly what he was doing: either he was using language as an intruder, requiring a response ('I want something', 'do something', etc.), which he did on a rising tone; or he was using language as an observer, requiring no response (in the meanings of observation, recall or prediction), and with these there was a falling tone. The pragmatic function evolved here clearly out of the instrumental and regulatory uses of language. The mathetic function evolved in a way that was much less clear; it required a lot of time to trace the history of this, but I think it arises out of the personal and heuristic functions. Language is first used to identify the self, in contradistinction to the environment; it is then used to explore the environment, and by the same token then to explore the self. This child made a beautiful distinction between the rising tone for the pragmatic or 'doing' function and the falling tone for the mathetic or 'learning' function.

Next stage, the adult language, unlike the child's protolanguage, gives him the possibility of meaning more than one thing at once. There comes the moment when these functions are incorporated into the linguistic system itself, in the highly abstract form of the metafunctions I mentioned earlier: the pragmatic function into the interpersonal function in the linguistic system and the mathetic function into the ideational function in the linguistic system. Whereas, in the first stage, the functions stand in an 'either . . . or' relationship – the child is using language *either* to do this *or* to do that – the beauty of the adult linguistic system is that he can do more than one thing at once. In fact he *must* do more than one thing at once, because now, in the adult stage, every time he opens his mouth he is both observer and intruder at the same time. And this is why human language evolved by putting between the meaning and the sound a formal level of grammatical structure, because it is the grammatical structure which allows the different functions to be mapped onto one another in a sort of *polyphony*. I use this metaphor because in polyphonic music the different melodies are mapped onto one another so that any particular chord is at one and the same time an element in a number of different melodies. In the same way, in adult language any element in the syntagm – say a word – is at one and the same time filling a role in a number of different structures. Now you can't do this without a grammar. The child's system is a two-level system: it has a content and an expression. The adult system is a three-level system, of content, form and expression.

So this functional plurality makes the difference between adult language and child language?

Yes; this is what I mean by functional plurality – that any utterance in the adult language operates on more than one level of meaning at once. This is the crucial difference between the adult language and the child's language.

Everything you have said up till now proves that your view of the scope of linguistics differs widely from the views we are acquainted with in various other trends. This is perhaps a good occasion to turn back to our starting-point. I would like to ask you to redefine what you mean by 'linguistics' and by 'sociolinguistics', and what you mean by saying that 'a good linguist has to go outside linguistics'.

Well, I hope I didn't quite put it that way, that a good linguist *has* to go outside linguistics! Let's go back to the observation that there are two main perspectives on language: one is the intra-organism perspective, the other is the inter-organism perspective. In the intra-organism perspective we see language as what goes on in the head; in the inter-organism perspective it is what goes on between people. Now these two perspectives are com-plementary, and in my opinion linguistics is in the most healthy state when both are taken seriously. The past ten or fifteen years have been characterized by a very large concentration on intra-organism linguistics, largely under the influence of Chomsky and his 'language as knowledge' or psycholinguistic perspective. I am personally glad to see that there is now a return to the inter-organism perspective in which we take account of the fact that people not only speak, but that they speak to each other. This is the fact that interests me. People often ask, must you make a choice whether you are going to study intra- or inter-organism linguistics, can't you just study language? I would say, up to a point you can. If you are studying the inner areas of the linguistic system, linguistic form in Hjelmslev's sense – the phonological and lexicogrammatical systems – you can be neutral up to a point; but the moment you go into semantics, your criteria of idealization depend on your making a selection. You either say with Chomsky that linguistics is a branch of theoretical psychology, or – which is equally valid – that linguistics is a branch of theoretical sociology. For that matter you could say that linguistics is a branch of theoretical aesthetics.

What are the implications of your view for the problem of language teaching?

The type of perspective I have on language naturally relates to my own interests. My interests are primarily in language and the social system and then, related to this, in the two areas of language and education, and language and literature. All these have something in common. They make it necessary to be interested in what the speaker does; in the *text*. Now in order to make sense of 'what the speaker does', you have to be able to embed this in the context of 'what the speaker can do'. You've got to see the text as an actualized potential; which means that you have got to study the potential. As regards language teaching – could I rather say 'language in education', because I am not so much concerned with pedagogical linguistics as with educational linguistics, and with the kinds of presupposition that are made about language in the educational system at present? – here again you need a functional perspective. Let me take one example. Consider the question of literacy, teaching reading and writing: what is learning to read and to write? Fundamentally it is an extension of the functional potential of language. Those children who don't learn to read and write, by and large, are children to whom it doesn't make sense; to whom the functional extension that these media provide has not been made clear, or does not match up with their own expectations of what language is for. Hence if the child has not been oriented towards the types of meaning which the teacher sees as those which are proper to the writing system, then the learning of writing and reading would be out of context, because fundamentally, as in the history of the human race, reading and writing are an extension of the functions of language. This is what they must be for the child equally well. Here is just one instance of a perspective on language in the context of the educational system.

In stylistics too the emphasis is on the study of the text, and again there is a functional basis to this. We are interested in what a particular writer has written, against the background of what he might have written – including comparatively, against the background of other things he has written, or that other people have written. If we are interested in what it is about the language of a particular work of literature that has its effect on us as readers, then we shall want to look not simply at the effects of linguistic prominence, which by themselves are rather trivial, but the effects of linguistic prominence in respect of those functions of language which are highlighted in the particular work. I am thinking here of Zumthor's point (1972) where he has said that the various genres of literature in different epochs are characterized by differences of emphasis on the different functions of language. I think this is very true. It seems to me that you can only understand the linguistic properties of the text in relation to the orientation of the whole of which it is a part to certain patterns of linguistic function. I have tried to illustrate this in my (1971) study of the language of Golding's *The Inheritors*, where it is very clearly the transitivity system that is at work. The whole book is about transitivity, in a certain sense. There is a highlighting of man's interpretation of the processes of the external world; and therefore it is no accident that there is a highlighting in the language, in the grammar, of certain aspects of the transitivity system. This illustrates once again the same perspective on language. A central position is accorded to the study of the text; no sharp separation is made between competence and performance; the text is seen as an actualization of the total potential, in the context of a functional theory for the interpretation of the potential. I see this as the thread which links the social, the educational and the literary perspectives on language.

II

A sociosemiotic interpretation of language

3

Sociological aspects of semantic change

1 Text, situation and register

1.1 Let us start with the concept of a text, with particular reference to the text-in-situation, which may be regarded as the basic unit of semantic structure – that is, of the semantic process. The concept 'text' has no connotations of size; it may refer to speech act, speech event, topic unit, exchange, episode, narrative and so on.

Now from one point of view, the main interest of the text is what it leaves out. For example, the participants in an encounter accord each other certain statuses and roles, and they do so partly by means of attention to the text, the meanings that are exchanged. Yet, as Cicourel has pointed out, we know very little about how they do it; we have no real theory of linguistic interaction. Somehow, symbolic behaviour is interpreted, and meanings are assigned. Cicourel suggests (1969, 186–9) that the individual operates with four interpretative principles or assumptions, which he calls 'reciprocity of perspectives', 'normal forms', 'the etcetera principle' and 'descriptive vocabulary as indexical expressions'. In any exchange of meanings, the individual assumes (i) that interpretations of experience are shared (others see things the same way); (ii) that there are principles of selection and organization of meaning, and therefore also (iii) of reconstituting and supplementing omissions (we agree on what to leave out, and the other fills it in – these are I think encodings rather than omissions, with shared 'key' or unscrambling procedures), and (iv) that words, or rather words-in-structures, linguistic forms, are referred identically to past experience. These principles act as 'instructions for the speaker-hearer for assigning infinitely possible meanings to unfolding social scenes.' The speaker-hearer relies heavily on the social system for the decoding of text.

Cicourel argues for a 'generative semantics' 'that begins with the member's everyday world as the basic source for assigning meaning to objects and events' (1969, 197); and this kind of approach to the nature and function of text is a characteristic of ethnomethodological linguistic studies such as those of Sacks and Schegloff. An example is Schegloff's (1971) account of how people refer to location, which reveals some of the general principles on which the speaker-hearer relies in the production and understanding of discourse relating to the identification of places and of persons. It is clear from his account that when participants select, from among a number of 'correct' designations (such as those involving geographical or personal reference points), the adequate or, as he puts it, 'right' semantic options, they are making use of the relevant particulars of the context of situation: in Schegloff's own formulation, 'interactants are context-sensitive.' This is another instance of the general principle of presupposition that is embodied in the text-forming potential of the linguistic system. Just as the speaker selects the appropriate information focus, distributing the meanings of the text into information that he decides to treat as recoverable to the hearer (given) and information that he decides to treat as non-recoverable (new), so in Schegloff's example the speaker selects the appropriate coordinates, and their degree of accuracy, in specifying where things are. Schegloff appears, however, to leave out the important component of 'rightness' that consists in the participant's option of being 'wrong': that is, of selecting a semantic configuration that violates the situational-contextual restraints, with a specific communicative effect – an option which, at least in the case of information focus, participants very readily take up. (Cf. the discussion of information structure, and information focus, in Halliday 1967b.)

1.2 From a sociolinguistic standpoint, a text is meaningful not so much because the hearer does *not* know what the speaker is going to say, as in a mathematical model of communication, but because he *does* know. He has abundant evidence, both from his knowledge of the general (including statistical) properties of the linguistic system and from his sensibility to the particular cultural, situational and verbal context; and this enables him to make informed guesses about the meanings that are coming his way.

The selection of semantic options by the speaker in the production of text (in other words, what the speaker decides to mean) is regulated by what Hymes (1967) calls the 'native theory and system of speaking'. The member of the community possesses a 'communicative competence' that 'enables [him] to know when to speak and when to remain silent, which code to use, when, where and to whom, etc.'; in other words, to know the 'rules of speaking', defined by Grimshaw (1971, 136) as 'generalizations about relationships among components' of the speech situation. Hymes has given a list, now very familiar, of the eight components of speech, which may be summarized, and to a certain extent paraphrased, as follows: form and content, setting, participants, ends (intent and effect), key, medium, genre, and interactional norms. We may compare this with various earlier lists, such as that of Firth (1950) which comprised the participants (statuses and roles), relevant features of the setting, verbal and nonverbal action, and effective result.

One of the difficulties with such lists is to know what theoretical status to assign to them in relation to the text. Hymes includes 'form and content of message', i.e. the text itself, as one of the components; compare Firth's 'verbal action of the participants'. An alternative approach is to consider the situational factors as determinants of the text. This is exemplified in the triadic formula used by Halliday, McIntosh and Strevens (1964), with its categories of field, tenor and mode. These are categories at a more abstract level which are regarded as determining rather than as including the text; they represent the situation in its generative aspect. Field refers to the ongoing activity and the particular purposes that the use of language is serving within the context of that activity; tenor refers to the interrelations among the participants (status and role relationships); and mode covers roughly Hymes' channel, key and genre. There are some theoretical advantages to be gained from working with a triadic construct, advantages which relate to the nature of the linguistic system, as suggested in chapter 7.

The categories of field, tenor and mode are thus determinants and not components of speaking; collectively they serve to predict text, via the intermediary of the code, or (since 'code' has been used in a number of different senses) to predict what is called the register (Ure and Ellis 1972). These concepts are intended to make explicit the means whereby the observer can derive, from the speech situation, not the text itself, of course, but certain systematic norms governing the particulars of the text. These norms, taken together, constitute the register. In other words, the various subcategories of field, tenor and mode have associated with them typical semantic patterns – on the assumption, that is, of what Fishman calls congruence (1971a, 244–5); so that if for a given instance of language use the situational features are specified, in appropriate terms, typical linguistic features can be specified by derivation from them. (Note that we are concerned with the semantic properties of the text and not with the ritual lexicogrammatical variants that are associated with levels of formality and the like, although these form one part of the total picture.) If the observer can predict the text from the situation, then it is not surprising if the participant, or 'interactant', who has the same information available to him, can derive the situation from the text; in other words, he can supply the relevant information that is lacking. Thus the 'register' concept provides a means of investigating the linguistic foundations of everyday social interaction, from an angle that is complementary to the ethnomethodological one; it takes account of the processes which link the features of the text, considered as the realization of semantic patterns, to the abstract categories of the speech situation. It is these processes which embody the 'native theory and system of speaking'.

How far are such concepts relatable to the linguistic system? The literature of sociolinguistics abounds with references to the linguist's practice of treating the linguistic system as an invariant, by contrast with the sociolinguist's interest in variation; but all linguists are interested in variation, and the distinction is a largely artificial one. The underlying question is that of the nature of linguistic choice; specifically, of the various types of choice, and their accommodation and interaction in the linguistic system. The distinction is unfortunate since it implies that 'code choice' – in the sense of ritual variation, the choice of appropriate levels of formality etc. – is to be isolated from other aspects of choice. Sociolinguistic discussions have often rested on the tacit assumption that there was nothing at all to be said about the choice between *cat* and *dog* – that is a matter of the system – whereas a distinct theory was needed to account for the choice between *cat* and *mog* [*mog* being a slang term for 'cat' in certain British dialects]. But both these choices are choices that are made within the linguistic system; what is needed is a theory which accounts for both.

This points in the direction of a functional semantics, towards a further elaboration of the theories of the Prague school, who have always explicitly concerned themselves with variation. Hymes (1969, 113) recognizes two types of meaning, 'social meaning' and 'referential meaning': 'Languages have conventional units, structures and relations . . . that are what I shall call "stylistic" (serving social meaning) as well as referential.' Elsewhere he uses the term 'socio-expressive' for the former. In my own work I have used a triadic system, with ideational, interpersonal and textual components (the first two probably equivalent to Hymes's referential and social), the ideational being then further resoluble into experiential and logical (Halliday 1967c, 1972). If we assume for the moment that the linguistic system is in fact essentially trimodal at the semantic level (and there is strong internal evidence for this), then on the basis of the three-way categorization of the situational determinants of text into field, tenor and mode, we can make a tentative correlation between the situation, the text, and the semantic system; by and large, it is the ideational component of the system that is activated by the choice of field, the interpersonal by the tenor, and the textual by the mode. There is, in other words, a general tendency whereby the speaker, in encoding the role relationships in the situation (the tenor; Hymes's 'participants' and 'key'), draws on the interpersonal component in the semantic system, realized for example by mood; in encoding the activity, including subject-matter (the field; Hymes's 'setting' and 'ends'), draws on the ideational component, realized for example by transitivity; and in encoding the features of the channel, the rhetorical mode and so on (the mode; Hymes's 'instrumentalities' and 'genre') draws on the textual component, realized for example by the information focus. These are approximations only; but they are suggestive given that the two sets of categories, the components of the speech situation on the one hand and those of the semantic system on the other, are established independently of each other. The following passage provides an illustration of this point; Nigel, at 1 year 11 months, is exchanging meanings with his mother (Halliday 1975c):

> *Mother* [in bathroom, Nigel sitting on chair]: Now you wait there till I get your facecloth. Keep sitting there. [But Nigel is already standing up on the chair.]
> *Nigel* [in exact imitation of mother's intonation pattern, not in correcting intonation]: Keep standing thére. Put the mug on the flóor.
> *Mother*: Put the mug on the floor? What do you want?
> *Nigel*: Daddy tòothbrush.
> *Mother*: Oh you want Daddy's toothbrush do you?
> *Nigel*: Yés . . . you [= I] want to put the fròg in the múg.
> *Mother*: I think the frog is too big for the mug.
> *Nigel*: Yes you can put the dùck in the múg . . . make búbble . . . make búbble.

Mother: Tomorrow. Nearly all the water's run out.
Nigel: You want Mummy red tóothbrush . . . yes you can have Mummy old red tóothbrush.

We might identify the situational features in some such terms as the following:

Field: Personal toilet, assisted [mother washing child]; concurrently [child] exploring (i) container principle (i.e. putting things in things) and (ii) ownership and acquisition of property (i.e. getting things that belong to other people)

Tenor: Mother and small child interaction; mother determining course of action; child pursuing own interests, seeking permission; mother granting permission and sharing child's interests, but keeping her own course in view

Mode: Spoken dialogue; pragmatic speech ('language-in-action'), the mother's guiding, the child's furthering (accompanying or immediately preceding) the actions to which it is appropriate; cooperative, without conflict of goals

Looking at the text, we find that the *field* tends to determine the transitivity patterns – the types of process, e.g. relational clauses, possessive (*get, have*) and circumstantial: locative (*put*), material process clauses, spatial: posture (*sit, stand*); also the minor processes, e.g. circumstantial; locative (*in*); perhaps the tenses (*simple present*); and the *content* aspect of the vocabulary, e.g. naming of objects. All these belong to the ideational component of the semantic system.

The *tenor* tends to determine the patterns of mood, e.g. [mother] imperative (*you wait, keep sitting*) and of modality, e.g. [child] permission (*want to, can*, and nonfinite forms such as *make bubble* meaning 'I want to be allowed to . . .'); also of person, e.g. [mother] 'second person' (*you*), [child] 'first person' (*you* [= *I*]), and of key, represented by the system of intonation (pitch contour, e.g. child's systematic opposition of rising, demanding a response, versus falling, not demanding a response). These are all part of the interpersonal component.

The *mode* tends to determine the forms of cohesion, e.g. question-and-answer with the associated type of ellipsis (*What do you want? – Daddy toothbrush*); the patterns of voice and theme, e.g. active voice with child as subject/theme; the forms of deixis, e.g. exophoric [situation-referring] *the*; and the lexical continuity, e.g. repetition of *mug, toothbrush, put in*. All these fall within the textual component of the semantics.

1.3 Thus one main strand in the sociolinguistic fabric consists in interrelations among the three levels of (i) social interaction, represented linguistically by the text; (ii) the speech situation; and (iii) the linguistic system. This interrelationship constitutes the systematic aspect of everyday speech. From the sociological point of view, the focus of attention here is on the 'micro' level. By contrast, the 'macro' level involves a further classifying of speech situations, a situational typology such as is embodied in Fishman's notion of 'domain', defined (1971a, 248) as 'the large-scale aggregative regularities that obtain between variables and societally recognized functions.' A macro-level sociology of language pays attention to a 'more generalized description of sociolinguistic variation', in which there is association between a domain, on the one hand, and a specific variety or language on the other. A domain may be defined in terms of any of the components of speech situation: for example, in Paraguay it is found that Guarani is used in settings which are rural, and, among the nonrural, in those which are (the intersection of) nonformal, intimate and nonserious. Spanish is used in settings which are (the intersection of) urban and either formal or, if nonformal, non-intimate. If the setting is nonrural, nonformal, intimate and serious, the choice of language depends on other variables: language order (i.e. which was the mother tongue), language proficiency and sex (Rubin 1968). Here the situational criteria are extremely mixed. Generalizations of this kind involve the relating of situation types 'upward' to the general 'context of culture', in the sense in which that term was used by Malinowski (1923).

Typically in such 'macro-level' descriptions the concern is with communities where there is bilingualism or multilingualism, or at least some form of diglossia. The shift that takes place is between languages, or between 'high' and 'low' (classical and colloquial) varieties of the same language; and this is seen to reflect certain broad categories of situational variable. The situational features that determine 'code shift' may themselves be highly specific in nature; for example Gorman, studying the use of English, Swahili and the vernacular by speakers of eight of Kenya's major languages, found that 'Swahili is characteristically used more frequently than English in conversations with fathers and less frequently in conversations with siblings, although there are exceptions . . .' (1971, 213) – exceptions which were in turn partly relatable to the topic of the conversation.

It is the relative impermanence of these situational factors which leads to the phenomenon of 'code-switching', which is code shift actualized as a process within the individual: the speaker moves from one code to another, and back, more or less rapidly, in the course of daily life, and often in the course of a single sentence. Gumperz (1971) describes code shift and code-switching as the expression of social hierarchy in its various forms, notably caste and social class. The verbal repertoire of the speaker, his code potential, is a function of the social hierarchy and of his own place in it; while the particular context of interaction, the social-hierarchical properties of the situation, determine, within limits set by other variables (and always allowing for the individual's role discretion; there is personal as well as transactional switching, in Gumperz's terms), the selection that he makes from within that repertoire.

Hence this particular concept of a 'code', in the sense of a language or language variety coexisting with other languages or language varieties in a (multilingual and multidialectal) society, such that the individual typically controls more than one code, extends naturally and without discontinuity to that of code as social dialect – dialectal variety in language that is related to social structure and specifically to social hierarchy. The situation may determine which code one selects, but the social structure determines which codes one controls. The limiting case would be an ideal diglossia in which every member has access to both the superposed or 'high' variety and one regional or 'low' variety. In general, however, the speaker's social dialect repertoire is a function of his personal caste or class history.

Theoretically a social dialect is like a regional dialect, in that it can be treated as invariant in the life history of the speaker. This in fact used to be regarded as the norm. In practice, however, it is misleading; as Labov remarks in this connection (1970a, 170): 'As far as we can see, there are no single-style speakers.' Labov refers to 'style shift' rather than 'code shift', understanding by this a shift in respect of certain specified variables that is governed by one particular situational restraint, namely the level of formality. The variables he finds are grammatical and phonological ones, such as the presence or absence of *be* in copular constructions, e.g. *he [is] wild*; negative concord, as displayed in the music-hall Cockney sentence *I don't suppose you don't know nobody what don't want to buy no dog*, or its absence; θ v. $t\theta$ v. t in initial position, e.g. in *think*; plus or minus postvocalic *r*, etc. Labov's work has shown that one cannot define a social dialect, at least in an urban context, except by having recourse to variable rules as well as categorical rules; in other words, variation must be seen as inherent in the system. Labov's own earlier definition of an urban speech community, as a group of speakers sharing the same linguistic attitudes, which he arrived at after finding that speech attitudes were more consistent than speech habits, could therefore, in the light of his own studies of variation, be revised to read 'a group of speakers showing the same patterns of variation' – which means, in turn, reinstating its original definition as a group of speakers who share the same social dialect, since social dialect is now defined so as to include such variation (cf. Wolfram 1971).

However, as Labov remarks, although 'there are a great many styles and stylistic dimensions . . . *all such styles can be ranged along a single dimension, measured by the amount of attention paid to speech*' (1970a). Hence, for example, the five stylistic levels that are postulated in order to show up variation in postvocalic *r*: casual speech, careful speech, reading, word lists and minimal pairs. In other words the type of linguistic variation that is associated with these contexts, through the 'amount of attention paid to speech', is itself largely homogeneous; it can be represented in the form of points along a scale of deviation from an implied norm, the norm in this case being a prestige or 'standard' form. The speaker is not switching between alternative forms that are equally deviant and thus neutral with regard to prestige norms (contrasting in this respect with rural speakers in dialect boundary areas). He is switching between variants that are value-charged: they have differential values in the social system. This by no means necessarily implies that the so-called 'prestige' forms are most highly valued for all groups in all contexts (Labov 1970a, 204), but simply that the effect of such variation on linguistic change cannot be studied in isolation from the social system which determines the sets of values underlying the variation.

1.4 Discussion of language and social structure usually centres around the influence of social structure on language; but in Labov's perspective any such effect is marginal, in terms of the linguistic system as a whole. 'The great majority of linguistic rules are quite remote from any social value'; 'social values are attributed to linguistic rules only when there is variation' (1970a, 204–5). In other words, there is interaction between social hierarchy and certain features of the dialectal varieties that it gives rise to, such that these features are the object of variation; but no general principles relating language and language variety to the social order.

Such principles are to be found, in a very different perspective, in the work of Bernstein. Here the social structure, and social hierarchy, is shown to be related to variety in language; not to social dialect, however, but to register. This distinction is a fundamental one. Whereas social dialects are different grammatical and phonological representations of a semantic system, registers are different semantic configurations (leaving open the question whether they are derived from identical semantic systems or not). Hence Bernstein's focus of attention is the relation of social structure to meaning – that is, to the meanings that are typically expressed by the members.

Bernstein (1971) has drawn attention to principles of semiotic organization governing the choice of meanings by the speaker and their interpretation by the hearer. These he refers to as 'codes'; and there is a considerable source of confusion here, as the same term 'code' is being used in radically different senses. The codes control the meanings the speaker-hearer attends to (cf. Cicourel's 'socially distributed meanings'). In terms of our general picture, the codes act as determinants of register, operating on the selection of meanings within situation types: when the systemics of language – the ordered sets of options that constitute the linguistic system – are activated by the situational determinants of text (the field, tenor and mode, or whatever conceptual framework we are using), this process is regulated by the codes.

. A unique feature of Bernstein's work is that it suggests how the social structure is represented in linguistic interaction. According to Bernstein, the essential element governing access to the codes is the family role system, the system of role relationships within the family; and he finds two main types, the positional role system, and the personal role system. In the former, the part played by the member (for example in decisionmaking) is largely a function of his position in the family: role corresponds to ascribed status. In the latter, it is more a function of his psychological qualities as an individual; here status is achieved, and typically there are ambiguities of role. The two types are found in all social classes, but sections of the middle class favour the person-oriented types, and strongly positional families are found mainly in the lower working class; thus there is a mechanism for the effect of social class on language, via the interrelation of class and family type.

Bernstein postulates two variables within the code: elaborated versus restricted, and person-oriented versus object-oriented. The idealized sociolinguistic speaker-hearer would control equally all varieties of code; there is of course no such individual, but the processes of socialization of the child do demand – and normally lead to – some degree of access to all. It appears however that some extreme family types tend to limit access to certain parts of the code system in certain critical socializing contexts: a strongly positional family, for example, may orient its members away from the personal, elaborated system in precisely those contexts in which this type of code is demanded by the processes of formal education, as education is at present constituted – which may be a contributory factor in the strongly social-class-linked pattern of educational failure that is found in Britain, the USA and elsewhere.

It is important to avoid reifying the codes, which are not varieties of language in the sense that registers and social dialects are varieties of language. The relation of code to these other concepts has been discussed by Ruqaiya Hasan, who points out that the codes are located 'above' the linguistic system, at the semiotic level (1973, 258):

> While social dialect is defined by reference to its distinctive formal properties, the code is defined by reference to its semantic properties . . . the semantic properties of the codes can be predicted from the elements of social structure which, in fact, give rise to them. This raises the concept 'code' to a more general level than that of language variety; indeed there are advantages in regarding the restricted and the elaborated codes as codes of behaviour, where the word 'behaviour' covers both verbal and nonverbal behaviour.

The code is actualized in language through register, the clustering of semantic features according to situation type. (Bernstein in fact uses the term 'variant', e.g. 'elaborated variant', to refer to those characteristics of a register which derive from the choice of code.) But the codes themselves are types of social semiotic, symbolic orders of meaning generated by the social system. Hence they transmit, or rather control the transmission of, the underlying patterns of a culture and subculture, acting through the primary socializing agencies of family, peer group and school.

At this point we can perhaps set up some sort of a model in which the linguistic system, and the social system in its restricted sense of social structure, are represented as integral parts of the wider reality of the social system in the more all-embracing sense of the term. For analytical purposes we will add a third component, that of 'culture' in the sense of the ideological and material culture, to serve as the source of speech situations and situation types. Malinowski's context of culture (and context of situation) is the product of the social structure together with the culture in this limited sense; so are Fishman's domains. Figure 4 (above the line) attempts to present in schematic form the analytic relations that we have set up.

1.5 Naturally there are other components of a sociolinguistic theory which are not included in this summary. Among other things, a sociolinguistic theory implies a theory of text: not merely a methodology of text description, but a means of relating the text to its various levels of meaning. In van Dijk's (1972) account of a 'text grammar', text is regarded as 'continuous discourse' having a deep or macro-structure 'as a whole' and a surface or micro-structure as a sequence of sentences; a set of transformation rules relates macro- to micro-structures. In other words, text is the basic linguistic unit, manifested at the surface as discourse. It cannot be described by means of sentence grammars.

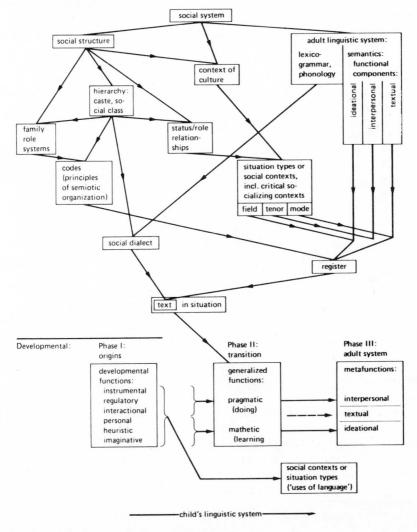

Fig. 4   Schematic representation of language as social semiotic, and child's mode of access to it

Now the last point is worth underlining. The notion of the text as a super-sentence is essentially comparable to that of the sentence as a super-phoneme; it ignores the essential fact that the two are related by realization, not by size. We have adopted here the view of the text as a semantic unit, irrespective of size, with sentences (and other grammatical units) as the realization of it. The essential problem, then, is that of relating, not 'macro' to 'micro' structures (which differ in size), but one level (stratum) to another: of relating the text not only 'downwards' to the sentences which realize it but also 'upwards' to a higher level of meaning, of which it is itself the realization or projection. Typically, in a sociolinguistic context, this refers to the sociological meanings that are realized by texts of everyday conversation, perhaps especially those involving the text in its role in cultural transmission; but these are not essentially different in kind from others such as narratives (van Dijk 1972, 273ff; cf. Labov and Waletzky 1967; Greimas 1971), including children's narratives, and even literary texts.

To say that sociolinguistics implies a theory of text is to say no more than that it implies a linguistic theory, one which meets the usual requirement of specifying both system and process, in Hjelmslev's sense of the terms, at all levels (cf. Dixon 1965). The sentences, clauses and so on which form the material of everyday linguistic interaction (material that is already, of course, highly processed, once it can be referred to in these terms) are to be interpreted both as realizations and as instances: as the realization of meanings which are instances of the meaning potential. The meaning potential is a functional potential; the analysis of text is in the last resort also functional, being such as to relate the text to the functional components of the semantic system, ideational, interpersonal and textual (or other such frame of reference). These functional components provide the channel whereby the underlying meanings are projected onto the text, via the semantic configurations that we are calling registers. I shall not complicate the exposition further by trying to include in it specific reference to the various other orders of meaning, literary, psychological and so forth, that are projected onto the semantic system and thereby onto the text.[1] But I should like to add one more dimension to the picture. This concerns the learning of language by the child, as this process appears in the light of a sociolinguistic interpretation of language development (Halliday 1975a).

1.6 A child learning his mother tongue is constructing a meaning potential: that is, he is constructing a semantic system, together with its realizations. This process seems to take place in three phases, of which the middle one is functionally transitional. The child begins (Phase I) by developing a semiotic of his own, which is not derived from the adult linguistic system that surrounds him; it is a language whose elements are simple con-

---

[1] See in this connection Zumthor's characterization of medieval poetry (1972, 171): 'Nombreuses sont les textes où l'une des deux fonctions, idéationnelle ou interpersonnelle, domine absolument, au point d'estomper, parfois d'effacer presque, les effets de l'autre. C'est là, me semble-t-il, un trait fondamental de la poésie médiévale.'

tent/expression pairs, having meaning in certain culturally defined and possibly universal functions. These functions can be enumerated tentatively as follows: instrumental, regulatory, interactional, personal, heuristic, imaginative. Figure 5 shows Nigel's protolanguage at $10\frac{1}{2}$ months (Halliday 1975a). Such expressions owe nothing to the mother tongue; this is the stage at which, in many folklores, the child can talk to animals and to spirits, but adults cannot join in.

Then comes a discontinuity, round about 18 months: a point where the child ceases to recapitulate phylogeny and begins to adopt the adult model. From now on the speech around him, the text-in-situation which is a more or less constant feature of his waking environment, comes to determine his language development. He is embarked on a mastery of the adult system, which has an additional level of coding in it: a grammar (including a vocabulary), intermediate between its meanings and its sounds.

Functionally, however, there is no discontinuity; language continues to function for the child in the same contexts as before. But the interpolation of a grammatical system, besides vastly increasing the number of possible meanings which the system is capable of storing, also at the same time opens up a new possibility, that of functional combination: it becomes possible to mean more than one thing at once. How does the child help himself over this stage? Nigel did it by generalizing from his function set an opposition between language as doing and language as learning: the pragmatic function versus the mathetic function, as I called it. In situational terms, the pragmatic is that which demands some (verbal or nonverbal) response; the mathetic is self-sufficient and does not require a response. Nigel happened to make this distinction totally explicit by means of intonation, producing all pragmatic utterances on a rising tone and all mathetic ones on a falling tone; that was his particular strategy. But the image of language as having a pragmatic and a mathetic potential may represent every child's operational model of the system at this stage.

Probably most children enter Phase II of the language-learning process with some such two-way functional orientation, or grid; and this functional grid, we may assume, acts selectively on the input of text-in-situation, as a semantic filter, rejecting those particulars that are not interpretable in terms of itself, and accepting those which as it were resonate at its own functional frequencies. It is perhaps worth stressing here, in view of the prevailing notion of unstructured or degenerate input, that the utterances the child hears around him are typically both richly structured and highly grammatical, as well as being situationally relevant (cf. Labov 1970a); the child does not lack for evidence on which to build up his meaning potential.

In Phase II the child is in transition to the adult system. He has mastered the principle of an intermediate, lexicogrammatical level of coding; and he has also mastered the principle of dialogue, namely the adoption, assignment and acceptance (or non-acceptance) of communicative roles, which are social roles of a special kind, those that come into being only through language. The semiotic substance of the pragmatic/mathetic distinction, between language as doing and language as learning, has now been incorporated into the grammar, in the form of the functional distinction between interpersonal and ideational in the adult system. These latter are the 'metafunctions' of the adult language: the abstract components of the semantic system which correspond to the two basic extrinsic functions of language (those which Hymes calls 'social' and 'referential'; cf. above). At the same time the child begins to build in the third component, the 'textual' one; this is what makes it possible to create text, language that is structured in relation to the context of its use (the 'context of situation'). These three components are clearly distinct in the system, as sets of options having strong internal but weak external constraints.

Here is the source of the complex nature of linguistic 'function', which causes some difficulty in the interpretation of functional theories of language, yet which is a major characteristic of the adult semiotic. On the one hand, 'function' refers to the social meaning of speech acts, in contexts of language use; on the other hand, it refers to components of meaning in the language system, determining the internal organization of the system itself. But the two are related simply as actual to potential; the system is a potential for use. The linguistic system is a sociolinguistic system.

At this stage, then, the generalized functions which serve as the basis for various strategies whereby a child can learn the meanings of the adult language gradually evolve through three stages. At first, they are alternatives: at (say) 18 months, every utterance is either one or the other (*either* mathetic *or* pragmatic). Then they become differences of emphasis: at (say) 21 months, every utterance is predominantly one or the other (*mainly* mathetic/ideational *but also* pragmatic/interpersonal; or vice versa). Finally they come to be combined: at (say) 24 months, every utterance is both (*both* ideational *and* interpersonal). What makes this possible is that both come to be expressed through the lexicogrammatical system; the 'functions' have changed their character, to become abstract components of the semantics, simultaneous modes of meaning each of which presupposes the presence of the other. And this apparently is what enables the child to structure the input which he receives so that any one text comes to be interpreted as a combination of the same kind. To put this another way, being himself (at first) on any one occasion either observer or intruder, he can grasp the fact that the adult language allows the speaker – indeed obliges him – to be both observer and intruder at the same time. When these processes of functional development are completed, the child has effectively entered the adult language system; the final phase, Phase III, consists in mastering the adult language. Phase III, of course, continues throughout life.

I have attempted to incorporate the developmental components of the sociolinguistic universe of discourse into figure 4 (p. 69); this is the part below the horizontal line. The double vertical bar crosscutting this line, towards the left, represents the point of discontinuity in the expression, where the child begins to take over the grammar and phonology of the adult

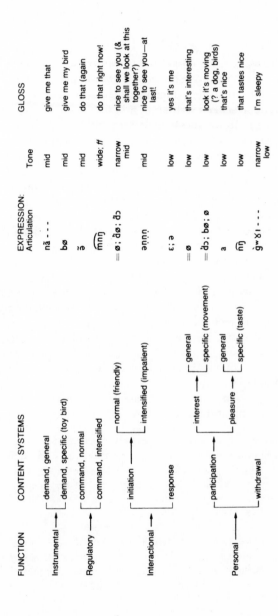

FUNCTION	CONTENT SYSTEMS	EXPRESSION: Articulation	Tone	GLOSS
Instrumental	demand, general	nã - - -	mid	give me that
	demand, specific (toy bird)	bø	mid	give me my bird
Regulatory	command, normal	ĩə̃	mid	do that (again
	command, intensified	m̃n̩ŋ̍	wide: ff	do that right now!
Interactional	initiation — normal (friendly)	= ø ; dø ; dɔ	narrow mid	nice to see you (& shall we look at this together?)
	initiation — intensified (impatient)	ə̃n̩n̩	mid	nice to see you—at last!
	response	e ; ɛ	low	yes it's me
	participation — interest — general	= ø	low	that's interesting
	participation — interest — specific (movement)	= dɔ ; bø ; ø	low	look it's moving (? a dog, birds)
	participation — pleasure — general	a	low	that's nice
	participation — pleasure — specific (taste)	n̩n̩	low	that tastes nice
Personal	withdrawal	ġʷɤ̃ɪ - - - -	narrow low	I'm sleepy

Note: *All tones are falling.* = indicates items related in both meaning and sound.

Fig. 5 Nigel at 0;9 to 0;10½

language. In the content, there is a rapid expansion from this point on – but no essential discontinuity.

2 Variation and change

2.1 Much of the work referred to above embodies a concept of variation. Typically, this refers to variation between different forms of language within a speech community: between languages or major sublanguages, between dialects, and between speech styles (i.e. minor dialectal variants, in Labov's sense of the term). If we distinguish terminologically between variety, meaning the existence of (dialectal, etc.) varieties, and variation, meaning the movement between varieties (i.e. variety as the state, variation as the process), then the individual speaker displays variation (that is, switches) under certain sociolinguistic conditions; in the typical instance, these conditions relate to the level of formality (degree of attention paid to speech, in Labov's formulation), role relationships, topic of discourse and so on. But there may be variety without variation: this would be the idealized form of the situation studied in rural dialectology, where dialects exist but members do not switch between them.

Just as there may be variety without variation, so also there may be variation without change. Labov has demonstrated the existence of this kind of stable variation, where the variants either are not charged with social value or else are the object of conflicting values which, as it were, cancel each other out – a low-prestige form may also have solidarity function, perhaps. But while variation does not always imply change, it is usually presumed to be a feature of sociolinguistic change – change that is related to social phenomena – that it is preceded by, and arises out of, variation, such variation being a product of the interaction of language with the social system. Labov's formulation is as follows (1970a, 205):

> In the course of change, there are inevitably variable rules, and these areas of variability tend to travel through the system in a wave-like motion. The leading edge of a particular linguistic change is usually within a single group, and with successive generations the newer form moves out in wider circles to other groups. Linguistic *indicators* which show social distribution but no style shift [i.e. variety without variation] represent early stages of this process. *Markers* which show both stylistic and social stratification represent the development of social reaction to the change and the attribution of social value to the variants concerned. *Stereotypes*, which have risen to full social consciousness, may represent older cases of variation which may in fact have gone to completion; or they may actually represent stable oppositions of linguistic forms supported by two opposing sets of underlying social values.

Taken as a whole, linguistic change involves, in Labov's words, 'oscillation between internal pressures and interaction with the social system'; it includes, but is not limited to, change of a 'sociolinguistic' kind. The internal pressures Labov sees. as other linguists have done, as a 'process of structural

generalization', to be explained as a kind of grammatico-semantic equilib-
rium in which 'there is inevitably some other structural change to compensate for the loss of information involved' (1970a, 183). An example
given is that, in Trinidad English, the past tense *gave* was replaced by the
present form *give*, and therefore the form *do give* was introduced to distinguish present from past: instead of *I give/I gave*, the same system is
realized as *I do give/I give*.

The assumption appears to be that, while sociolinguistic change takes
place in the expression, at the grammatical and phonological levels, it cannot
affect the content: the semantic system remains unchanged. (Sociolinguistic
changes in the expression are usually presented not as changes in the system
but as microscopic changes affecting certain elements of the system, the
implication being that it is the purely internal mechanisms that bring about
change in the system – including the change that is required to regulate the
balance which has been impaired by socially conditioned changes affecting
its elements. But, as Labov himself has pointed out elsewhere (1971), it is
difficult to make a very clearcut distinction between the system and its
elements.) If this is to be understood in the limited sense that semantic
changes are not brought about by accidental instances of morphological or
phonological syncretism, it presumably applies whether or not such
instances are interpreted as the outcome of social processes; this question is
clearly beyond our present scope. But if it is taken more generally to mean
that there are no other forms of linguistic change involving relations between the social system and the linguistic system, this would seem open to
challenge, since it excludes the possibility of changes of a sociosemantic
kind.

Semantic change is an area in which no very clear boundary can be
maintained between change that is internal and change that is socially
conditioned, although the two are in principle distinguishable; it bears out
Hoenigswald's observation (1971, 473) that 'The internal and the external
factors in linguistic change are densely intertwined, but not . . . inextricably
so.' The existence of semantic variety is traditionally taken for granted in
language and culture studies; but the instances that can be cited of culturally
conditioned semantic change are quite limited in their scope. These changes
are typically fairly microscopic, affecting specific subsystems, especially
those concerned with the linguistic expression of social status and role; a
well-known example is Friedrich's (1966) study of Russian kin terms, relating the changes in the number and kind of kinship terms in general use to
changes in the structure of social relationships in Russian society. Semantic
field theory, which takes the *champ de signification* as the constant and
examines the changes in the meaning of the elements of the subsystem
within it, also lends itself to sociocultural explanations (Trier's classic example of the field of 'knowing' in medieval German). But it seems unlikely
that we should expect to find, at the semantic level, 'sociolinguistic' changes
of a more general or macroscopic kind.

However, it is not so much major shifts in the linguistic system that are in question, as linguistic changes which relate to general features of the social system, or to sociological constructs that have their own validity apart from being merely a form of the explanation of linguistic phenomena. There are two types of fairly pervasive semantic change, the one well recognized, the other more problematical, that come to mind here. The first is the large-scale introduction of new vocabulary, as in periods of rapid technical innovation; the other is change in what Whorf called 'fashions of speaking', or semantic styles.

The first of these processes is characterized by the appearance in the language of a large number of previously non-existent thing-meanings: objects, processes, relations and so forth, realized by a variety of means in the lexicogrammatical structure including – but not limited to – the creation of vocabulary. (To call this process 'introduction of new vocabulary' is a misleading formulation; rather it is the introduction of new thing-meanings, which may or may not be expressed by new lexical elements.) One major source of insight into this process is planned sociolinguistic change, in the general context of language planning. The key concept in language planning is that of 'developing a language'. It is not entirely clear in which sense 'develop' is being used here: does it imply that there are underdeveloped languages (in which case no doubt they should be referred to as 'developing' languages – but the linguistic distinction between developed languages and others is a very dubious one), or should the term be interpreted rather in the sense of developing a film, bringing out what is already latently there? However that may be, 'developing a language' typically refers to vocabulary extension, the creation of new terms by some agency such as a commission on terminology, or at least in the course of some officially sponsored activity such as the production of reference works and textbooks.

What is the essential nature of such change, when viewed from a linguistic standpoint? Haugen (1966) refers to it as 'elaboration of function', and the relevant concept is, presumably, a functional one: the language is to function in new settings, types of situation to which it has previously been unadapted. This is certainly a true perspective. But it is remarkable how little is yet known about the processes involved, especially about the natural processes of functional adaptation in non-western languages. There is a fairly extensive literature on technical innovation in European languages, tracing the development of industrial and other terminologies (e.g. Wexler 1955, on the evolution of French railway terminology); and on technical vocabularies as they are found in existence in languages everywhere (folk taxonomies; e.g. Frake 1961; Conklin 1968; Basso 1967). But studies of innovation in non-European languages are rare. A notable example is Bh. Krishnamurthi's (1962) work on Telugu, investigating how the members of farming, fishing and weaving communities incorporate new thing-meanings – new techniques, new apparatus and equipment – into their own linguistic resources.

2.2 This leads us into the second heading, that of fashions of speaking. It is often held, at least implicitly, that the semantic styles associated with the various registers of the 'world languages', such as technical English or Russian, or political French, are inseparable from the terminologies, and have to be introduced along with them wherever they travel. Certainly it is a common reproach against speakers and writers using a newly created terminology that they tend to develop a kind of 'translationese', a way of meaning that is derived from English or whatever second language is the main source of innovation, rather than from the language they are using. No doubt it is easier to imitate than to create in the developing language semantic configurations which incorporate the new terminological matter into existing semantic styles. But this is not exactly the point at issue. There is no reason to expect all ideologies to be modelled on the semiotic structure of Standard Average European; there are other modes of meaning in literature than the poetry and the drama of Renaissance Europe, and it will not be surprising to find differences in other genres also, including the various fields of intellectual activity. This is not to suggest that the semantic styles remain static. The alternative in the development of a language is not that of either becoming European or staying as it is; it is that of becoming European or becoming something else, more closely following its own existing patterns of evolution.

It is very unlikely that one part of the semantic system would remain totally isolated from another; when new meanings are being created on a large scale, we should expect some changes in the fashions of speaking. It is far from clear how these take place; but it is certainly quite inadequate to interpret the innovations simply as changes in subject matter. The changes that are brought about in this way involve media, genres, participants and participant relations, all the components of the situation. New registers are created, which activate new alignments and configurations in the functional components of the semantic system. It is through the intermediary of the social structure that the semantic change is brought about. Semantic style is a function of social relationships and situation types generated by the social structure. If it changes, this is not so much because of what people are now speaking about as because of who they are speaking to, in what circumstances, through what media and so on. A shift in the fashions of speaking will be better understood by reference to changing patterns of social interaction and social relationships than by the search for a direct link between the language and the material culture.

2.3 One phenomenon that shows up the existence of an external or 'sociolinguistic' factor in semantic change is that of areal affinity. Abdulaziz (1971) has drawn attention to the areal semantic effect whereby speakers of East African languages, whether these are related to Swahili or not, find Swahili easier to handle than English because of the very high degree of intertranslatability between Swahili and their own language. Gumperz and Wilson's account (1971) of the semantic identity of Marathi, Kannada and Urdu as spoken in a region of South India along the Marathi-Kannada border is especially revealing in this respect. Since such instances are typically also characterized by a high degree of phonological affinity, the idealized case of areal affinity may be characterized in Hjelmslevian terms as one in which the content systems are identical and the expression systems are identical; what differs is simply the encoding of the one in the other, the one point of arbitrariness in the linguistic system.

It seems possible that the key to some of the problems of areal affinity may be found in a deeper understanding of creolization, in the light of recent studies. The development of areas of affinity is itself presumably the effect of a creolization process, and hence it is not essentially different from historical contact processes in general, but rather is a natural consequence of them. In the same way the large-scale semantic innovation referred to above can also be seen as an instance of creolization, one leading to the development of new lines of semantic affinity which no longer follow areal (regional) patterns. Neustupný (1971), in an interesting discussion of linguistic distance in which he attempts to isolate the notion of 'sociolinguistic distance', proposed to define the condition of 'contiguity' in social rather than in geographical terms. It is not easy to see exactly what this means; it cannot be maintained that a requirement for the development of an area of affinity is a common social structure, since, quite apart from the phenomenon of large-scale technical borrowing (which is typically associated with the opposite situation, but might be excluded from consideration here), in fact the most diverse social structures are to be found within regions of established linguistic affinity. Yet some concept of a common social system, at some very abstract level, is presumably what is implied by the more usual but vague assertion of a 'common culture' as a concomitant of areal resemblances.

At any rate, areal affinity is a fact, which demonstrates, even though it does not explain, that the semantic systems of different languages may be alike – and therefore that they may be less alike. There is often difficulty enough of mutual comprehension within one language, for example between rural and urban speakers, simply because one is rural and the other urban. The diachronic analogue to this areal affinity is presumably generational affinity; the generation gap is certainly a semiotic one, and is probably reflected in the semantic system. We do not have the same system as our grandfathers, or as ourselves when young. Linguists are accustomed to leaving such questions in the hands of specialists in communication, mass media, pop culture and the like; but they have implications for the linguistic system, and for linguistic change. New forms of music, and new contexts of musical performance, demand new instruments, though these are never of course totally new.

3 Meaning and social structure

3.1 As with other levels of the linguistic system, the normal condition of the semantic system is one of change. The specific nature of the changes that take place, and their relation to external factors, may be more readily understood if we regard the semantic system as being itself the projection (encoding, realization) of some higher level of extralinguistic meaning.

From a sociolinguistic viewpoint, the semantic system can be defined as a functional or function-oriented meaning potential; a network of options for the encoding of some extralinguistic semiotic system or systems in terms of the two basic components of meaning that we have called the ideational and the interpersonal. In principle this higher-level semiotic may be viewed in the tradition of humanist thought as a conceptual or cognitive system, one of information about the real world. But it may equally be viewed as a semiotic of some other type, logical, ideological, aesthetic or social. Here it is the social perspective that is relevant, the semantic system as realization of a social semiotic; in the words of Mary Douglas (1971, 389),

> If we ask of any form of communication the simple question what is being communicated? the answer is: information from the social system. The exchanges which are being communicated constitute the social system.

Information from the social system has this property, that it is, typically, presented in highly context-specific doses. Whereas a logical semantics may be a monosystem, a social semantics is and must be a polysystem, a set of sets of options in meaning, each of which is referable to a given social context, situation type or domain.

The semantic system is an interface, between the (rest of the) linguistic system and some higher-order symbolic system. It is a projection, or realization, of the social system; at the same time it is projected onto, or realized by, the lexicogrammatical system. It is in this perspective that the sociolinguistic conditions of semantic change may become accessible.

Let us illustrate the notion of a context-specific semantics from two recent studies. In both cases for the sake of simplicity I will choose very small sets of options, sets which, moreover, form a simple taxonomy. The first is from Turner (1973), somewhat modified. Turner, on the basis of a number of investigations by Bernstein and his colleagues in London, constructs a semantic network for a certain type of regulative context within the family, involving general categories of parental control strategy: 'imperative', 'positional' and 'personal'. Each of these is then further subcategorized, 'imperative' into 'threat of loss of privilege' and 'threat of punishment', 'positional' into 'disapprobation', 'rule-giving', 'reparation-seeking' and 'positional explanation', 'personal' into 'recognition of intent' and 'personal explanation'. Figure 6 shows the system under 'threat of loss of privilege'; these are the options that have been shown to be available to the mother who selects this form of control behaviour.

In order to show how these options are typically realized in the lexicogrammatical system, we indicate the contribution that each makes to the final structure of the sentence (references are to paragraphs in Roget's *Thesaurus*):

rejection: material process, Roget § 293 Departure or § 287 Recession:
             Hearer *you* = Affected; positive

command: 'middle' type; imperative, jussive, exclusive

decision: either 'middle' type, or (rarer) 'non-middle' (active, Speaker
             I = Agent); indicative, declarative

resolution: future tense

obligation: modulation, necessity

deprivation: material process, benefactive, Roget § 784 Giving; 'non-
             middle' type; (optional) Speaker *I* = Agent; Hearer *you* =
             Beneficiary; indicative, declarative; future tense; negative

Examples:

(1)   you go on outside
(2)   you're going upstairs in a minute
(3)   I'll have to take you up to bed
(4)   you're not going to be given a sweet/I shan't buy you anything

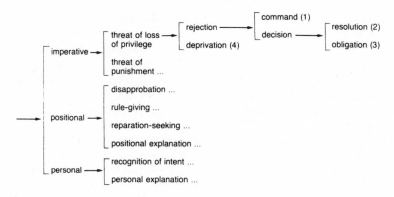

Fig. 6

Taken as a whole the system reveals correlation at a number of points with social class, as well as with other social factors; for example, in the investigation from which this is taken, significantly more middle-class mothers than working-class mothers selected the 'rule-giving' type of positional control.

The second example is taken from Coulthard *et al.* 1972. For a fuller representation of this semantic network, see figure 7 (pp. 82–3) from Halliday 1975c; see Sinclair *et al.* 1972 for a fuller report. This is a study of semantics in the classroom. The socializing agent is the school, where presumably regulative and instructional contexts are inseparably associated. The authors investigated the options open to the teacher for the initiation of discourse: he may select 'direct', which is predominantly regulative in intent, or he may select 'inform' or 'elicit', which are predominantly instructional. Figure 8 (p. 85) shows some of the options under the 'directive' heading; the form of presentation is adapted to match that of Turner.

The unmarked modal realization of the 'directive' category is the imperative; but there are marked options in which the other moods occur. 'Proscribed action' (1) is a behavioural directive which may be realized through imperative, declarative or interrogative clause types. Directives relating to non-proscribed actions may be (2) isolated exchanges (behavioural) or (3) parts of interactions (procedural); they may be (4) requests, encoded in the various modal forms, or (5) references to an action which ought to have been performed but has not been, typically in past tense interrogative. (Cf. Ervin-Tripp 1969, 56ff.)
Examples:

(1)   don't rattle / what are you laughing at / someone is still whistling
(2,4) will you open the door? / I want you to stop talking now
(2,5) did you open that door?
(3,4) you must all stop writing now
(3,5) have you finished?

These illustrations are, of course, very specific in their scope; but they bring out the general point that, in order to relate the linguistic realization of social meanings to the linguistic system, it is necessary to depart from the traditional monolithic conception of that system, at least at the semantic level, and to consider instead the particular networks of meanings that are operative in particular social contexts. How these various semantic systems combine and reinforce each other to produce a coherent, or reasonably coherent, world view is a problem in what Berger and Kellner call the 'microsociology of knowledge'. In their analysis of the sociology of marriage, they interpret the marriage relation as a continuing conversation, and observe (1970, 61), 'In the marital conversation, a world is not only built, but it is kept in a state of repair and ongoingly refurnished.' This is achieved through the cumulative effect of innumerable microsemiotic encounters, in the course of which all the various semantic subsystems are brought into play.

3.2 Hymes made the point several years ago that 'the role of language may differ from community to community' (1966, 116). Hymes was making a distinction between what he called two types of linguistic relativity: crosscultural variation in the system (the fashions of speaking, or 'cognitive styles' as he called them) and crosscultural variation in its uses.

But we should not press this distinction too hard. The system is merely the user's potential, or the potential for use; it is what the speaker-hearer 'can mean'. This semantic potential we are regarding as one form of the projection of his symbolic behaviour potential: the 'sociosemiotic' system, to use Greimas's (1969) term. In any given context of use – a given situation type, in a given social structure – the member disposes of networks of options, sets of

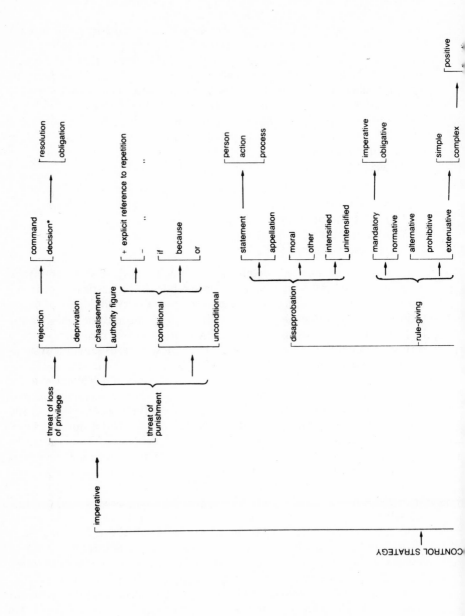

CONTROL STRATEGY

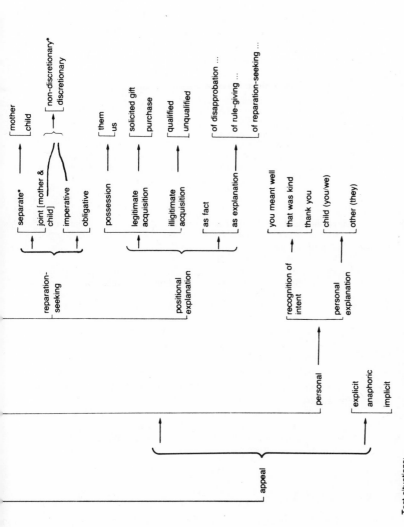

Test situations:
What would you do if — brought you a bunch of flowers and you found out that he/she had got them from a neighbour's garden?

Imagine — had been out shopping with you and when you got home you found he/she'd picked some little thing from one of the counters without you noticing. What would you say or do?

Fig. 7 Semantic system for a class of regulative [social control] situations

Threat of loss of privilege

Rejection:	material process ('Departure', R 293; 'Recession', R 297); Hearer *you* = Medium; positive
Deprivation:	material process: benefactive ('Giving', R 784); Hearer *you* = Beneficiary (Recipient/Client); negative
Command:	middle; imperative: jussive: exclusive. Ex: you go on upstairs; go up to bed now
Decision:	indicative: declarative [*either* middle *or* non-middle: active/passive, Speaker *I* = Agent (optional in passive); middle* if rejection, non-middle* if deprivation]
Resolution:	future /: in present / present in present Ex: you're going upstairs; I'll take / I'm taking you upstairs [rejection]; I'm not going to buy you anything; you're not going to be given a sweet [deprivation]
Obligation:	modulation: passive: necessary Ex: I'll have to take you upstairs; you'll have to go upstairs [rejection]; you won't have to have a sweet; I shan't be able to give you a sweet; next time you won't be able to go shopping with me [deprivation]

Threat of punishment

Chastisement:	material process ('Punishment', R 972; Hearer *you* = Medium; non-middle: active,* Speaker *I* = Agent; indicative: declarative; future /: in present; positive Ex: I'll smack you; you'll get smacked
Authority figure:	material process ('Punishment', R 972; 'Disapprobation', R 932 [paras. beginning *reprehend* . . ., sense of 'verbal punishment']; Hearer *you* = Medium; non-middle; 3rd person (father,* policeman*) = Agent; indicative: declarative; future /: in present; positive Ex: the policeman will tell you off; Daddy'll smack you
Conditional:	'you do that'
'if':	hypotactic; condition in dependent clause, threat in main clause Ex: if you do that, . . .
'because':	hypotactic; condition in main clause, threat in dependent clause Ex: don't / you mustn't do that because . . .
'or':	paratactic; condition in clause 1, threat in clause 2 Ex: don't / you mustn't do that or . . .
explicit reference to repetition:	*again* in condition [/ *next time* = *if* . . . *again*] Ex: if you do that again, . . . ; next time you do that . . . ; don't do that again because / or . . .

Lexicogrammatical realizations of some categories of 'Control Strategy' (see fig. 7, 'imperative')

Numbers following R refer to numbered paragraphs in *Roget's Thesaurus*.
* = typical form

semiotic alternatives, and these are realized through the semantic system. From this point of view, as suggested in the last section, the semantic system appears as a set of subsystems each associated with a particular domain, or context of use. What we refer to as 'the system' is an abstract conceptualization of the totality of the user's potential in actually occurring situation types.

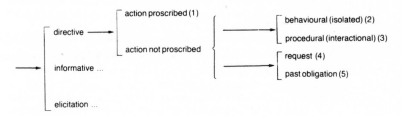

Fig. 8

In other words, different groups of people tend to mean different things. Hymes is undoubtedly right in recognizing crosscultural variation in the system, and it would not be surprising if we also find intracultural (i.e. cross-subcultural) variation. One may choose to separate this observation from the observation that different groups of people tend to use language in different ways, using the one observation to explain the other; but in any case, the fact has to be accounted for, and cannot readily be accommodated in a conceptual framework which imposes a rigid boundary between competence and performance and reduces the system to an idealized competence which is invariable and insulated from the environment.

Labov has shown how, under conditions of social hierarchy, social pressures act selectively on phonological and grammatical variables, leading to variation and change. How far do such pressures also operate in the case of semantic change? Although Labov himself does not consider the semantic level, his work on non-standard varieties of English has important implications for this question.

In a recent paper (1970b), Labov gives a lively discussion of Negro Non-Standard English for the purpose of demonstrating that it is just as grammatical and just as 'logical' as any of the 'standard' forms of the language. This is not news to linguists, for whom it has always been a cardinal axiom of their subject; this is why, as Joan Baratz once pointed out, linguists have rarely taken the trouble to deny the various myths and folk-beliefs about the illogicality of non-standard forms. There is no doubting the logic of all linguistic systems. But although all linguistic systems are equally 'logical', they may differ in their semantic organization; and there have been serious discussions about the possibility of 'deep structure' differences – which we may interpret as semantic differences – among the different varieties of English (Loflin 1969).

It may be tempting to take it for granted that all varieties of a language must be semantically identical, since as we know there are many people who misinterpret variety in evaluative terms: if two systems differ, they hold, then one must be better than the other. It has been difficult enough to persuade the layman to accept forms of English which differ phonologically from the received norm, and still more so those which differ grammatically; there would probably be even greater resistance to the notion of semantic differences. But one should not be browbeaten by these attitudes into rejecting the possibility of subcultural variety in the semantic system. In the words of Louis Dumont (1970, 289),

> The oneness of the human species . . . does not demand the arbitrary reduction of diversity to unity; it only demands that it should be possible to pass from one particularity to another, and that no effort should be spared in order to elaborate a common language in which each particularity can be adequately described.

It is not too difficult to interpret this possibility of subcultural differences at the semantic level on the basis of a combination of Labov's theories with those of Bernstein. Labov, presumably, is using the term 'logic' in his title in imitation of those who assert that non-standard English 'has no logic'; the meaning is 'logicalness', the property of being logical, rather than the kind of logic that it displays. There is no reason to believe that one language or language variety has a different logic from another. But this does not mean their semantic systems must be identical. Labov's findings could, with enough contrivance, be reduced to differences of grammar – thereby robbing them of any significance. What they in fact display are differences of semantic style, code-regulated habits of meaning, presumably transmitted through social and family structure, that distinguish one subculture from another. Bernstein's work provides a theoretical basis for the understanding of this kind of semantic variety, making it possible to envisage a social semiotic of a sufficiently general kind. Some such theory of language and social structure is a prerequisite for the interpretation of sociolinguistic phenomena, including Labov's own findings and the principles he derives from them. It is all the more to be regretted, therefore, that Labov included in his valuable polemic some ill-founded and undocumented criticisms of Bernstein's work; e.g. 'The notion is first drawn from Bernstein's writings that . . .', followed by a quotation from somebody else which is diametrically opposed to Bernstein's ideas. (Because of his misunderstanding of Bernstein, Labov assumes – one must assume that he assumes it, since otherwise his criticism would lose its point – that the speech which quotes from Larry is an example of restricted code; in other words, Labov appears to confuse Bernstein's 'code' with social dialect, despite Bernstein's explicit distinction between the two (1971, 199, but clear already in 1971, 128, first published in 1965; cf. again Hasan 1973). It is my impression that in Larry's speech as Labov represents it the controlling code is predominantly an elaborated one, although it is impossible to categorize such small speech samples with any real significance; but in any case, as Bernstein has been at pains to establish, differences of code are relative – they are tendencies, or orientations, within which each individual displays considerable variation: a fact which helps to explain some of Labov's own findings.[2] Bernstein would, I have no doubt, agree with the points that Labov purports to make against him; but more important than that, Bernstein's work provides the necessary theoretical support for Labov's own ideas. Since this work has been misunderstood in some quarters it may be helpful to attempt a brief recapitulation of it here.

3.3 We can, I think, identify three stages in the development of Bernstein's theoretical ideas. In the first stage, roughly prior to 1960, Bernstein examined the pattern of educational failure in Britain, and attempted an explanation of it in terms of certain nonlinguistic projections of the social system, particularly modes of perception. In the second stage, roughly 1960–65, he came to grips not only with language but also with linguistics, and came up with certain linguistic findings, of considerable interest but still of a rather unsystematic kind. In the third stage he combined his two previous insights and sought explanations in terms of a social semiotic, with the linguistic semiotic, i.e. semantics, as its focal point. This has meant a major step towards a genuinely 'sociolinguistic' theory – one that is at once both a theory of language and a theory of society.

Bernstein had begun with the observation that educational failure was not distributed randomly in the population, tending to correlate with social class; the lower the family in the social scale, the greater the child's chances of failure. Clearly there was some incompatibility between lower-working-class social norms and the middle-class ethos and the educational system based on it. The pattern emerged most starkly as a discrepancy between measures of verbal and nonverbal intelligence; the discrepancy was significantly greater in the lower working class – and it tended to increase with age. There was obviously, therefore, a linguistic element in the process, and Bernstein developed his first version of the 'code' theory to try to account for it: 'elaborated code' represented the more verbally explicit, context-independent type of language, one which maintained social distance, demanded individuated responses, and made no assumptions about the hearer's intent; while the 'restricted code' was the more verbally implicit, context-dependent, socially intimate form in which the hearer's intent could be taken for granted and hence responses could be based on communalized norms. Education as at present organized demanded elaborated code; therefore, if any social group had, by virtue of its patterns of socialization,

---

[2] It is astonishing that Labov finds in Bernstein a 'bias against all forms of working-class behavior'; if anything, Bernstein's sympathies would seem to be the other way. As Mary Douglas puts it, 'As far as the family is concerned, Basil Bernstein betrays a preference for "positional" control rather than for "personal" appeals . . . [His] analysis cuts us, the middle class parents, down to size. Our verbosity and insincerity and fundamental uncertainty are revealed . . . The elaborated code is far from glorious when the hidden implications of the central system that generates it are laid bare.' In a generous letter to *The Atlantic* (vol. 230, no. 5, November 1972), Labov has expressed regret for any way in which his own writings have led to a misinterpretation of Bernstein's work.

only partial or conditional control over this code, that group would be at a disadvantage.

Harried by the linguists, Bernstein attempted to define the codes in linguistic terms, beginning with inventories of features and progressing towards a concept of 'syntactic prediction' according to which elaborated code was characterized by a wider range of syntactic choices, restricted code by a more limited range. Those like myself who categorically rejected this interpretation were partly confounded by some interesting early studies which showed that, in the performance of certain tasks, the amount of grammatical variation that was found in respect of (i) modification in the nominal group and (ii) the use of modalities, by children of various ages, was in fact linked to social class. It was clear, however, that any significant linguistic generalizations that could be made would be at the semantic level, since it was through meanings that the codes were manifested in language. Bernstein then went on to identify a small number of 'critical socializing contexts', generalized situation types from which the child, in the milieu of the primary socializing agencies of family, peer group and school, derives his essential information about the social system. The hypothesis was that, in a given context, say that of parental control of the child's behaviour, various different subsystems within the semantic system might typically be deployed; hence the 'codes' could be thought of as differential orientation to areas of meaning in given social situations.

It seemed that if in some sense access to the codes is controlled by social class, this control was achieved through the existence of different family types, defined in terms of role relationships within the family: the 'positional' and 'personal' family types (cf. 1.3 above). With important qualifications and subcategorizations, it appeared that strongly positional families would tend towards restricted-code forms of interaction – at least in their modes of parental control, in the regulative context. Family types do not coincide with classes; but it is likely that, in the British context, the more purely positional family is found most frequently among the lower working class – just that section of the population where the proportion of educational failure is the highest. The model then looks something like this:

> (different) social classes
> ↘
> (different) family role systems
> ↘
> (different) semiotic codes
> ↘
> (different) 'orders of meaning and relevance'

The later development of Bernstein's thought is set out in the final papers of *Class, Codes and Control*, vol. I, which are too rich to be summarized in a short space. Bernstein's theory is a theory of social learning and cultural transmission, and hence of social persistence and social change. As Mary Douglas puts it (1972, 312),

Whatever [Bernstein] does, . . . he looks at four elements in the social process. First the sytem of control, second the boundaries it sets up, third the justification or ideology which sanctifies the boundaries, and fourth he looks at the power which is hidden by the rest. . . .

I think Professor Bernstein's work is the first to argue that the distribution of speech forms is equally a realization of the distribution of power.

It is a theory of society in which language plays a central part, both as determiner and as determined: language is controlled by the social structure, and the social structure is maintained and transmitted through language. Hence it offers the foundation for interpreting processes of semantic change.

3.4 In terms of the framework we set up in the first section, there are two possible mechanisms of sociosemantic change: feedback and transmission – that is, feedback from the text to the system, and transmission of the system to the child. As far as feedback is concerned, there is the possibility of changes in the meanings that are typically associated with particular contexts or situation types, taking place in the course of time. These changes come about, for example, through changes in the family role systems, under conditions which Bernstein has suggested; or through other social factors – changes in educational ideologies, for example. Such changes could relate to rather specific situation types, such as those in the two illustrations given above.

We are familiar with instances of small subsystems realizing specific areas of symbolic behaviour. A good example is the 'pronouns of power and solidarity' (Brown and Gilman 1960). The semantic system of modern English is quite different at this point from that of Elizabethan English, so much so that we can no longer even follow, for example, the detailed subtleties and the shifts which take place in the personal relationship of Celia and Rosalind in *As You Like It*, which is revealed by their sensitive switching between *thou* and *you* (McIntosh 1963). This is simply not in our semantic system. But such instances are limited, not only in that they represent somewhat specific semantic options but also in that they reflect only those social relationships that are created by language (and that do not exist independently of language: the form *you* has meaning only as the encoding of a purely linguistic relationship) – or else, as in the case of changes in the use of kin terms, they affect only the direct expression of the social relationships themselves. Bernstein's work allows us to extend beyond these limited instances in two significant ways. First, it provides an insight into how the relations within the social system may come to shape and modify other meanings that language expresses, which may be meanings of any kind; sociosemantic variation and change is not confined to the semantics of interpersonal communication. Second, in the light of a functional account of the semantic system, Bernstein's work suggests how the changes in speech patterns that are brought about in this way become incorporated into the system, as a result of the innumerable minutiae of social interaction, and so have an effect on other options, not disturbing the whole system (whatever that would mean), but reacting specifically on those options that are functionally related to them.

Then there is transmission, and here we have considered the child's learning of the mother tongue from a sociolinguistic point of view: suggesting that the developmental origins of the semantic system are to be sought in the systems of meaning potential deriving from certain primary functions of language – instrumental, regulatory and so on. Let us postulate that a particular socializing agency, such as the family, tends to favour one set of functions over another: that is, to respond more positively to the child's meanings in that area, at least in certain significant socializing contexts. Then the semantic system associated with such contexts will show a relative orientation towards those areas of meaning potential. An indication of how this may come about at an early age is given in an interesting study by Katherine Nelson (1973), which suggests that the combination of educational level of parent with position of child in family may lead to differential semantic orientations and thus influence the child's functional strategy for language learning.

There is nothing surprising in this; it would be surprising if it was otherwise. The question that is of interest is to what extent such functional orientations become incorporated into the system. We noted earlier that the child, having begun by inventing his own language, in which the expression is unrelated to adult speech, at a certain point abandons the phylogenetic trail and takes over the adult system; there is a discontinuity in the realization. But there is (we suggested) no functional discontinuity; the child continues to build on the functional origins of the system, generalizing out of his original functional set of basic distinction of pragmatic versus mathetic – a pragmatic, or 'doing' function, which demands a response from the hearer, and a mathetic or 'learning' function, which is realized through observation, recall and prediction and which is self-sufficient: it demands no response from anyone. This, in turn, is a transitional pattern, which serves to transform the functional matrix so that it becomes the core of the adult language, taking the form of the ideational/interpersonal components in the semantic network; hence there is functional continuity in the system. At the same time the primary functions evolve into social contexts, the situation types encountered in the course of daily life. For example, the original interactional function of calls and responses to those on whom the child was emotionally dependent develops into the general interpersonal context within the family and peer group; the imaginative function of sound-play develops into that of songs and rhymes and stories; and so on. Thus there is functional continuity of use, that is, in the contexts in which selections are made from within the system. The meanings engendered by the social system, in other words, are such that the child is predisposed by his own language experience to adapt the linguistic mode of meaning to them.

Naturally, he 'makes semantic mistakes' in the process, mistakes which are often revealing. For example, towards the end of his second year Nigel learnt the grammatical distinction between declarative and interrogative. He located it, correctly, in the interpersonal component in the system, and related it to contexts of the exchange of information. But having at the time no concept of asking yes/no questions (i.e. isolating the polarity element in the demand for information), he used the system to realize a semantic distinction which he did make but which the adult language does not, namely that between imparting information to someone who knows it already, who has shared the relevant experience with him (declarative), and imparting information to someone who has not shared the experience and so does not know it (interrogative). Thus, for example, on one occasion while playing with his father he fell down; he got up and said to his father *you fell down* (*you* referred to himself at this stage). Then his mother, who had not been present, came into the room; he ran up to her and said *did you fall down*? The use of *you* for 'me' and the use of the interrogative for giving information are of course connected; they are both, in terms of cognitive development, features of the phase before role-playing in speech. But the modal pattern reveals a small semantic subsystem, not present in the adult language, which is both stable in terms of the child's meaning potential at the time, and transitional in the wider developmental context.

The functional continuity that we have postulated, according to which both the linguistic system itself and its environment evolve out of the initial set of functions which define the child's earliest acts of meaning, accounts for the fact that the child's meaning potential may develop different orientations under different environmental conditions – also, therefore, under the control of different symbolic codes. 'The social structure becomes the developing child's psychological reality by the shaping of his act of speech' (Bernstein 1971, 124). If there are changes in the social structure, especially changes affecting the family role systems, these may lead to changes in the child's orientation towards or away from certain ways of meaning in certain types of situation; and this, particularly in the environment of what Bernstein calls the 'critical socializing contexts', may lead to changes in learning strategies, and hence to changes in the meaning potential that is typically associated with various environments – i.e. in the semantic system. These changes in meaning potential would take place gradually and without essential discontinuity. A sociosemantic change of this kind does not necessarily imply, and probably usually does not imply, the complete disappearance of a semantic choice, or the appearance of a totally new one. It is likely to mean rather that certain choices become more, or less, differentiated; or that certain choices are more, or less, frequently taken up. These things too are features of the system. It seems possible, therefore, that semantic changes may be brought about by changes in the social structure, through the operation of the sort of processes described by Labov, in the course of the transmission of language to the child. Whether or not it is true that, as Weinreich, Labov and Herzog claim (1968, 145), 'the child normally acquires his particular dialect pattern, including recent changes, from children only slightly older than himself', it seems clear that only when we interpret language development in the context of the construction and transmission of social reality can we hope to find in it the sources and mechanisms of linguistic change.

We can call the field of study sociolinguistics; but if our goal is the pursuit of system-in-language (Fishman 1971, 8), this is surely linguistics, and linguistics always has, throughout all its shifts of emphasis, accepted what Hymes (1967) calls the 'sociocultural dimensions of its subject-matter', the link between language and the social factors that must be adduced to explain observed linguistic phenomena. By the same token, however, we do not need 'communicative competence', which has to be adduced only if the system has first been isolated from its social context. If we are concerned with 'what the speaker-hearer knows', as distinct from what he can do, and we call this his 'competence', then competence is communicative competence; there is no other kind. But this seems to be a needless complication. The system can be represented directly in 'inter-organism' terms, as 'what the speaker-hearer can do', and more specifically what he can mean. To shift to an 'intra-organism' perspective adds nothing by way of explanation.

The sociology of language is a different question, as Fishman says; here the aims are wider than the characterization of the linguistic system. Sociology of language implies the theoretical relation of the linguistic system to prior, independently established sociological concepts, as in Bernstein's work, where each theory is contingent on the other: the linguistic system is as essential to the explanation of social phenomena as is the social system to the explanation of linguistic phenomena.

In considering the social conditions of linguistic change, we are asking not only the 'sociolinguistic' question, to what extent are changes in the linguistic system relatable to social factors, but also, and perhaps more, the 'sociology of language' question, to what extent are changes in the linguistic system essential concomitants of features of (including changes in) the social system. Labov's work on phonetic change has not yet, so far as I know, been taken up by sociologists; but it reveals patterns and principles of intra- and inter-group communication which seem to me to have considerable significance for theories of social interaction and social hierarchy. And from another angle, Bernstein's research into language in the transmission of culture is equally central both to an understanding of language, including language development in children and linguistic change, and to an understanding of society, of persistence and change in the social structure. Here we are in a genuine interdiscipline of sociology and linguistics, an area of convergence of two different sets of theories, and ways of thinking about people.

Bernstein once reproached sociologists for not taking into account the fact that humans speak. If linguists seek to understand the phenomena of persistence and change in the linguistic system – how the innermost patterns both of language and of culture are transmitted through the countless microsemiotic processes of social interaction – we for our part must learn to take account of the fact that humans speak, not in solitude, but to each other.

4

Social dialects and socialization*

This book* is the record of a conference on social dialects organized by the Center for Applied Linguistics late in 1969. It is 'crossdisciplinary' in the sense that, of the ten participants, two were invited as specialists in speech and communication, two in psychology, two in sociolinguistics, two in education and two in linguistics/anthropology. Under each of these disciplinary headings, one of the two contributes a paper and the other a response.

The five papers are, in corresponding sequence, 'Social dialects and the field of speech', by Frederick Williams; 'Developmental studies of communicative competence', by Harry Osser; 'Social dialects in developmental sociolinguistics', by Susan M. Ervin-Tripp; 'Approaches to social dialects in early childhood education', by Courtney Cazden; and 'Sociolinguistics from a linguistic perspective', by Walt Wolfram. Finally, there is a contribution entitled 'The inadequacies of the linguistic approach in teaching situations', by Siegfried Engelmann, who was specially invited by the editor to comment on criticisms made of the 'Bereiter–Engelmann approach' in certain of the papers contained in the book.

Not surprisingly, the emphasis throughout is strongly pragmatic, with an orientation towards programme development. The context for such a conference is inevitably the critical situation in American education; the crisis is not limited to the United States, of course, but it is the American scene which is under focus here. The Center for Applied Linguistics' Urban Language Series reflects the same growing preoccupation. In the centre of attention is 'black English', and there is frequent reference, especially in the responses to the papers, to the negative aspects of study and intervention programmes: the lack of understanding of black culture, language use and language aspirations, the assumption that it is speech habits that must be changed instead of the attitudes towards them, the reluctance to look objectively into the school as a social institution, and so on. In Claudia Mitchell Kernan's words, 'Reaction in the black community to black English as it is portrayed in some grammars and readers has often been negative. . . . Many representations of black English differ to such a degree from the language as it is presently used that they ought to presage the reaction. The search for a new identity underway in black communities everywhere and the spirit of rebellion against an identity defined by outsiders should be

* Review of *Sociolinguistics: a crossdisciplinary perspective* (Washington, DC: Center for Applied Linguistics).

adequate forewarnings to non-blacks making efforts to define and institutionalize a black language' (p. 68).

Each of the papers consists of three parts, 'research assumptions', 'research review' and 'research suggestions'. These vary greatly in length and amount of detail; but all are thoughtful, informative and lively in presentation. Williams distinguishes the two main components of speech studies, 'speech and hearing' (communicative disorders) and 'general speech' (rhetoric and communication); neither is likely to be a major source of social dialect research, but Williams finds signs of increasing concern and a greater objectivity on the 'deficiency-difference issue'. The tendency of speech educators and speech clinicians to confuse dialect differences with language disorders, and to treat nonstandard forms as speech defects, is still, however, a major problem of socially conditioned attitudes. The need to 'accept a wide range of speech behaviour', rather than trying to change people's speech habits, is the keynote of the response by Orlando J. Taylor, who, urging the acceptance of a Black Standard English ('Why can't Black Standard English be included in the rubric of Standard English, described, and then left alone?' (p. 15)), makes the point that it is as a reading skill that Standard English is less likely to evoke resistance among nonstandard speakers, 'perhaps . . . because reading is a less intimate issue than speech and, therefore, less tender' (p. 19).

Stressing the factor of bias in typical experimental procedures, Osser underlines the necessity of discovering the 'sociolinguistic rules' that make up 'communicative competence', and in particular of expanding the sort of classroom interaction studies undertaken by Bellack *et al.* (1966) in order to find out 'how language functions for children of different ages and from different subcultural backgrounds in various educational contexts' (p. 29). Referring to the work of Flavell *et al.* (1968), Osser distinguishes two elements in the development of communicative competence: the ability to analyse the listener's role characteristics, and the ability to use one's linguistic resources in appropriate communication strategies. Studies such as that of Williams and Naremore (1969), taken together with those of Bernstein and his colleagues (e.g. Hawkins 1969), seem to suggest social class differences in the functions of speech; but 'we have to be very wary of developing a mythology about differences in communicative competence': children from different social classes may have quite different ideas of what the situation demands, but when they are told what is required of them the differences disappear (cf. Ervin-Tripp on p. 51). In a brief comment, Vera John subjects the role of the educational psychologist to a general critical appraisal.

Ervin-Tripp begins by distinguishing between 'comparative studies of language development', which may have little sociolinguistic content, and 'developmental sociolinguistics' which, based largely on the work of Hymes and Gumperz, seeks to explore language development in the context of the social milieu. She likewise refers to the bias that is inherent in many of the testing materials and procedures, citing Joan Baratz (1969) as an example of how this can be avoided; and suggests that perhaps 'until one is able to construct materials in which the minority group does better . . . one does not understand the unique features of the skills children acquire in those groups' (p. 37). By contrast, the 'ethnography of speaking' approach studies speech in its natural settings, on the assumption that 'social groups vary in the uses to which they most often put speech and in the value they attach to different uses' (p. 40); it provides a framework for investigating types and conditions of dialect switching (Blom and Gumperz, 1972) and for following up concepts such as Labov's 'monitoring' (attending to and modifying one's own speech) and 'marking' (conveying social information by the use of noncongruent forms). Pointing out that 'standard English' is in many instances a matter of the relative frequency and consistency of the use of certain forms, rather than of their presence or absence in absolute terms, Ervin-Tripp suggests contexts for the use of nonstandard in school, commenting that the main value of this lies in its helping to modify teachers' attitudes. She lists twelve research directions, among them the study of how the written language functions in children's lives, of how children learn different speech styles, and of how teachers can be trained 'to understand nonstandard speech' (in what sense is 'understand' being used here?). Kernan's response refers to the load of ills that the 'social dialect' concept has been made to bear ('Social dialect is probably not as directly a source of academic failure as we are prone to assume' (p. 67)), and looks towards a culturally unbiased account of communicative competence. Cazden's paper neatly summarizes the false assumptions, confusions and misconceptions that befog the issue, and identifies three research and development areas: the conceptions of language held by researchers and educators, and how to change them; the educational implications of dialect differences; and the nature of educational programmes and objectives. In his response, Robert D. Hess asks for clarification of 'the differences among: (1) the prestige value of a language, (2) linguistic competence, (3) the versatility of a language as a vehicle for communicating feelings and ideas', which seems an odd formulation but is perhaps interpretable as the 'deficit or difference' question in another form. He adds a reminder about linguistic variation within ethnic groups.

Wolfram's paper, the longest, is also an excellent summary of the field of social dialect studies in the United States. Its exclusively American orientation leads to some oversimplifying – it is implied, for example, that the only alternative interpretations of language development are those of Chomsky and Skinner; but the picture he gives is a representative one. Beginning with the dichotomy of the cognitive and behavioural functions of language (which he comes round to questioning in the end), he gives a clear summary of the deficit theory, remarking that 'such a position can only be taken when actual descriptive and sociolinguistic facts are ignored' (p. 93); he then treats of language as cultural behaviour and makes a firm commitment to the social explanation of linguistic differences. He offers a general definition of a standard language, referring to Garvin and Mathiot's (1956) characterization of its functions as unifying, separatist, prestige, and frame-of-reference, and noting that 'more specific definition is dependent on the particular language situation' (p. 98); after a brief history of dialect research in the United States, he then turns to the newer kind of dialectology, one that is urban, social and quantitative, inaugurated by Labov's (1966) New York City studies and continued by others such as Shuy *et al.* (1967) in Detroit and Fasold (1970) in Washington.

Wolfram then gives a critical summary of descriptive work on black English, and discusses the two opposed views regarding its origins: the earlier view that it is the form of English associated with speakers having certain socioregional profiles, whether black or white, and the views of Stewart, Bailey and others who see it as a language with its own 'deep structure' having evolved by a process of 'decreolization'. He introduces Labov's (1969) concept of 'inherent variability' as a systematic feature in language, and refers to the difference between 'sharp stratification' and 'gradient stratification' (discontinuity versus continuity in the frequency of variants in the speech of contiguous groups), noting that 'the phonological differences between social groups tend to be quantitative [gradient] whereas the grammatical differences are often qualitative [sharp]' (p. 112). He enumerates research tasks in the three areas of field techniques, descriptive studies and theoretical issues, singling out within the last problems of varia-tion, of 'pandialectal' description, and of 'modification' (the last related to what Ferguson (1971a) calls 'simplification'), as well as a number of more specific issues. Finally he makes a plea, which may readily be endorsed, for 'a general approach to sociolinguistics' (p. 128).

In a pleasantly refreshing response, William J. Samarin asks the sociolin-guists to tell us who the American people are and how they use language symbolically to build their backyard fences. He asks pointedly whether a society within a larger society can afford the luxury of its own language – to which we might offer the tentative observation that sociolinguistic history suggests that such 'microsocieties' come and go and their social dialects come and go with them: hence they create their 'languages' in the process of their own evolution and change.

The rather irritable polemic by Engelmann that concludes the volume does no service to his own cause. It contains a number of confusions about language, and some strange notions about linguists. Examples (my italics throughout): 'Let's say that we wanted to teach a child a *new concept*. This child does not have the concept red. He *speaks a foreign language*, which means that he has probably never *produced a statement* such as, "It's red. The truck is red" and so forth' (p. 142); 'Let's accept the linguist's orien-tation for the sake of argument. Let's say the problem with children *who lack language skills* is not a language problem, but rather *one of logical opera-tions*' (p. 145). But it is the general smugness that is most disturbing. We can perhaps understand the impatience of an educator who finds that linguistics is not a comfortable single-faceted theory with a box of remedies to hand, even if his expectations seem somewhat naïve: 'For every language program that [the linguist] proposes another linguist can propose a different program. Yet, all of the linguists work *from the same theory*, the same evidence' (p. 146); 'We are given statements about how language "develops", but we are not *told how* to *change language*' (p. 142). We can even sympathize with his exasperation at the superior attitude of linguists towards his views about language, an attitude of which this book is by no means free. Many linguists are equally critical of the limitations and one-sidedness which characterized the recent history of their own discipline. But it is dangerous to let the impatience and exasperation become the excuse for ignoring a whole realm of understanding about people that is centrally relevant to the educational process. A discussion of the nature of compensatory programmes and their highly complex implications for what we know about language and language development is outside our scope here; there is an extremely relevant discussion in Bernstein's (1971) two concluding chapters on the sociology of education, 'A critique of the concept of compensatory education' and 'On the classification and framing of educational knowledge'. But the linguists' plea for caution, which is essentially a plea for taking language seriously, and for approaching a child's linguistic development with imagination and some humility rather than with a sort of myopic violence, is not one just to be verbally bulldozed aside.

Let us now consider the book in its broader perspective. It is an admirable survey and reference handbook; but why the pretentious title? Out of a dozen and more current topics that could be cited as falling within the domain of sociolinguistics, the book deals with one or two at the most. It might better have been called 'Social dialect in America: an educational perspective' – although it is crossdisciplinary, there is also a great uniformity in the underlying preoccupations of the contributors.

It is not surprising that Labov's name occurs on practically every other page. His contribution is unique, in its originality and also in its range, which covers urban dialectology, the nature of the linguistic system, the language of the peer group, linguistic interaction and much else besides; he is now bringing radically new ideas into the history of language. It is all the more striking that, while the references to his work by scholars (including those in this book) relate mainly to these contributions, Labov's influence on the educational process in the United States – which some think is already considerable – has been achieved largely by the simple act of saying forcefully and colourfully what every linguist knows already: 'Look – *they* have language too!' It is a sad commentary on our time that we go on 'providing data to prove their humanity', as Taylor expresses it (p. 18). Useful as Labov's popular polemic undoubtedly has been, there are dangers in this kind of thing. However interesting the linguistic repartee of adolescent peer groups is to the sociolinguist (and we are still almost totally ignorant of young children's peer group speech and its role in cultural transmission), it is presumably a feature of all cultures in some form or other; in itself it is trivial, and it should not be necessary to focus attention on it in order to demonstrate that blacks have the same linguistic skills as whites. Much of what Cazden calls the 'crisis of confidence' of black people in research and educational programmes conducted by whites probably stems from the apparently constant need to harp on this elementary truth.

Hardly any reference is made in the book to social dialects which are not ethnic in origin. It might be argued that in the United States it is ethnic differences rather than social class differences that are more basic and more divisive; but this at least needs stating. In this respect social dialect questions are in some ways easier to discuss in the British context, where the work that has been done has no racial overtones; not that there are no comparable patterns affecting recent immigrants to Britain – though the issue is initially and still mainly one of social class – but because the relevant research, that of Bernstein and his colleagues, has been done among whites. (A black graduate student with whom I was working last year told me that when she first read Bernstein it was quite some time before she realized that his working-class subjects were not black.) Bernstein is the other truly original thinker in this field; his name too crops up at times in the book, and he receives an unusually sympathetic and enlightened reading. Like Labov, whose ideas get distorted into a sort of naïve romanticism, Bernstein is also widely misunderstood, being interpreted in terms of a crude class dialectology which is totally at variance with his actual views. It is unfortunate that Labov himself has contributed to this misunderstanding – the more so because Bernstein's theories form a necessary complement to Labov's own. Labov's work presupposes some general theory of cultural transmission and social change; and it is this that Bernstein has to offer. It is not too fanciful to speak of a 'Bernstein–Labov hypothesis' in this connection.

The point is that we need to look beyond questions of ethnicity and social class, at subcultural variety in the broader context of the social system. Neither so-called 'black/white speech differences' nor linguistic differences between social classes can be adequately accounted for in terms of phonological and lexicogrammatical features, whether qualitative or quantitative. Such differences exist; but they do not explain things. To cite one small piece of evidence, despite the linguistic distance separating black nonstandard from standard English in America, the surviving *rural* dialects in Britain are separated from standard British English by at least as great a distance, in lexicogrammar as well as in phonology; yet the problem of educational failure, in Britain as in America, is one not of the countryside but of the cities, involving children whose dialect is much closer to, and would be regarded by most linguists as a form of, the standard language (cf. Fishman and Lueders-Salmon 1972).

The sort of differences that are in question, insofar as they are linguistic, are probably to be interpreted along the lines of Bernstein's 'codes', as linguistic manifestations of differences in the social semiotic, different subcultural 'angles' on the social system. There are styles of meaning distinguishing one culture or one subculture from another: semiotic melodies and rhythms which may be actualized in various ways, for example as behavioural rhythms, various forms of body symbolism and the like. Language is just one of the forms through which these meanings are realized. Hence perhaps the observations by the McDavids (1951, where they credit it to William M. Austin) that 'many of the significant differences between the speech of Negroes and that of whites may not be linguistic at all.' The same kind of semiotic variety can be seen between male and female, between old and young, between rural and urban; and it would be surprising if it did not also manifest itself as a function of social class. We are merely adopting the Lévi-Straussian view of a culture as a system of meanings, and extending the principle to the subculture. The question then is not how social class differences in meaning arise so much as how they are maintained and transmitted from one generation to the next, and how they can change in the course of time. Bernstein relates this first to the family – to systems of family role relationships and the typical communication patterns that derive from them; then to the peer group and, later, to the educational process itself. These are the loci of the child's socialization, the contexts through which he becomes a person in the environment of other people.

In the socializing process, as in everyday social interaction (the two are the same thing looked at from different points of view), among the various semiotic modes language no doubt plays a uniquely prominent part. But there is a variable here too: as a number of contributors to the book point out, different cultures may vary in the roles that are assigned to language. The interpretation that is offered, however, stops short at the level of 'communicative competence'; it is confined to differences in the functions of language, with 'function' being equivalent to 'use'. Little mention is made of semantics, or of language in the social construction of reality. Perhaps we are still seeing here the after-effects of the series of false equations

language intra-organism = 'competence' = explanation = high value
language inter-organism = 'performance' = observation = low value

which relegated the social meaning of language to 'language behaviour' and denied it theoretical content. At all events, notions like 'communicative competence' and 'uses of language' are really temporary structures of a heuristic kind (they may also represent developmental strategies of a child, heuristic in another sense); they point the way to more general notions. The concept 'uses of language' can lead us to an interpretation of function in the sense of the underlying functional organization of the semantic system; that of 'communicative competence' to an appreciation of the meaning potential that is inherent in the social system as it is interpreted by the members of this or that subculture. The concept of social dialect becomes more revealing when it is related to more general concepts such as these (cf. Hasan 1973).

Many of us who have worked in research and development projects concerned with the teaching of English as a mother tongue are convinced, despite Engelmann's assertion that 'linguistic theory contains not a single principle that is needed in the teaching situation' (p. 143), that a combination of insights drawn from linguistics, psychology and sociology with each other and with the teacher's professional expertise can revitalize and in fact is revitalizing the educational process at the points where this is most needed. In the Schools Council Programme in Linguistics and English Teaching, we tried among other things to incorporate some sociolinguistic understanding into our initial literacy programme, which was a programme designed for general use, not as a compensatory exercise, though developed with a special view to the children who are most likely to fail and tested first in schools which faced major social problems (Mackay *et al.* 1970). The authors remark in the *Teacher's Manual*:

> Unlike psychology, the contributions of linguistics, sociology and the study of children's literature have not yet been accepted either in the education of teachers or in research work. The search for a theory of literacy is a search for a way to bring all these studies together and to balance their contributions so that no one of them is isolated, over-emphasized or omitted. (80)

These subjects are not branches of educational theory and it would be naïve to expect that everything a linguist or a psychologist or sociologist has to say holds some message for a teacher of language. Nevertheless the development of a general sociolinguistic theory, or sociology of language, is, indirectly but unmistakably, of fundamental significance for the teacher who is faced with the present critical situation in inner-city education.

A child is one who is learning how to mean. He is growing up in the context of a social semiotic, the network of meanings that constitute the culture; and he has the ability to master the system. As part of the process, he learns a linguistic system, a particular family and neighbourhood variant of a particular socioregional dialect of a particular language; it serves him well, expanding to meet each new demand. Later on he moves into another medium, that of written language – still as part of a continuous process, the extension of his functional meaning potential; and he may learn other variants, other dialects and even other languages. All this may take place without the crossing of any major boundaries, as it typically does for the middle-class child. But semiotic systems can clash; this is especially likely to happen in a pluralistic society marked, as Dumont (1970) expresses it, by 'the contradiction between the egalitarian ideal . . . and [the fact that] difference, differentiation, tends . . . to assume a hierarchical aspect, and to become permanent or hereditary inequality, or discrimination.' The child becomes aware that his own semiotic is in conflict with that of the school and the dominant culture it represents. It is this discontinuity and conflict that Bernstein sees as the heart of the problem. Differences of social dialect are then merely symptomatic; we do not even know whether they necessarily enter into the picture at all. But where they do, the dialect is the form of realization of patterns of social meaning. In this way a study of social dialects can be a source of insight into the deeper issues involved; and this book makes a solid contribution to the understanding of their role.

5

The significance of Bernstein's work for sociolinguistic theory*

The work of Basil Bernstein has sometimes been referred to as 'a theory of educational failure'. This seems to me misleading; the truth is both more, and less, than this implies. More, because Bernstein's theory is a theory about society, how a society persists and how it changes; it is a theory of the nature and processes of cultural transmission, and of the essential part that is played by language therein. Education is one of the forms taken by the transmission process, and must inevitably be a major channel for persistence and change; but there are other channels – and the education system itself is shaped by the social structure. Less, because Bernstein does not claim to be providing a total explanation of the causes of educational failure; he is offering an interpretation of one aspect of it, the fact that the distribution of failure is not random but follows certain known and sadly predictable patterns – by and large, it is a problem which faces children of the lower working class in large urban areas. Even here Bernstein is not trying to tell the whole story; what he is doing is to supply the essential link that was missing from the chain of relevant factors.

Nevertheless, it is perhaps inevitable that Bernstein's work should be best known through its application to educational problems, since these are the most striking and the most public of the issues with which he is concerned. After the relative confidence of fifteen postwar years, the 1960s were marked by growing awareness of a crisis in education, a realization that it was not enough to ensure that all children were adequately nourished and spent a certain number of years receiving formal education in school. The 'crisis' consists in the discovery that large numbers of children of normal intelligence, who have always had enough to eat, pass through the school system and come out as failures. We say, 'society has given them the opportunity, and they have failed to respond to it'; we feel hurt, and we want to know the reason why. (The formulation is not intended to imply a lack of genuine concern.)

Many people are aware of the existence of a hypothesis that educational failure is in some sense to be explained as linguistic failure. Something has gone wrong, it is suggested, with the language. This notion is in the air, so to speak; and the source of it is to be found in Bernstein's work – even though the various forms in which it is mooted often bear little relation to Bern-

* Foreword to Basil Bernstein (ed.), *Class, codes and control 2: applied studies towards a sociology of language* (London: Routledge & Kegan Paul, 1973).

stein's ideas. The terms that have become most widely current are Bernstein's 'elaborated code' and 'restricted code'; and in spite of the care which Bernstein has taken to emphasize that neither is more highly valued than the other, and that the hypothesis is that both are necessary for successful living – though the processes of formal education may demand the elaborated code – there is a widespread impression that Bernstein is saying (1) that some children speak elaborated code and some children speak restricted code, and (2) that the latter is an inferior form of speech, and therefore children who speak it are likely to fail. With these is sometimes compounded a further distortion according to which elaborated code is somehow equated with standard language and restricted code with nonstandard. And the confusion is complete.

But if there is confusion, it is because there is something to be confused about. The difficulty is a very real one, and it is this. If language is the key factor, the primary channel, in socialization, and if the form taken by the socialization process is (in part) responsible for educational failure, then language is to blame; there must be something wrong about the language of the children who fail in school. So the reasoning goes. Either their language is deficient in some way, or, if not, then it is so different from the 'received' language of the school (and, by implication, of the community) that it is *as if* it was deficient – it acts as a barrier to successful learning and teaching. So we find two main versions of the 'language failure' theory, a 'deficit' version and a 'difference' version; and these have been discussed at length in the context of 'black English' in the United States, where the problem of educational failure tends to be posed in ethnic rather than in social class terms. The language failure theory is sometimes referred to Bernstein's work, and he has even been held responsible for the deficit version of the theory, although nothing could be further removed from his own thinking. The fact that language failure is offered both as an interpretation of Bernstein's theories and as an alternative to them shows how complex the issues are and how easily they become clouded.

Let us consider the notion of language failure. According to the deficit version of the theory, the child who fails in school fails because he has not got enough language. It then becomes necessary to say where, in his language, the deficiency lies; and according to linguistic theory there are four possibilities, although these are combinable – the deficiency might lie in more than one: sounds, words, constructions and meanings.

Probably few people nowadays would diagnose the trouble as deficiency in sounds, although the 'our job is to teach them to talk properly' view of education is still with us, and might be taken to imply some such judgement of the case. If we leave this aside, there are two variants of the theory, and possibly a third: not enough vocabulary, not enough grammar (or 'structures', in contemporary jargon), and a rarer and rather sophisticated alternative, not enough meanings. (Perhaps we should recognize another variant, according to which the child has no language at all. This cannot seriously be called a theory; but some people who would vigorously deny it if it was put to them in that form behave as if they held this view – 'they have been exposed to good English, so obviously they have not the resources with which to absorb it.') We have to take these views seriously; they are held by serious-minded people of good faith who have thought about the problem and are anxious to find a solution. At the same time it needs to be said quite firmly that they are wrong.

There is no convincing evidence that children who fail in school have a smaller available vocabulary, or a less rich grammatical system, than those who succeed. Studies measuring the extent of the vocabulary used by children in the performance of specific tasks, though very valuable, do not tell us much about their total resources; and formulations of the overall size of a child's vocabulary tend to conceal some doubtful assumptions about the nature of language. In the first place, one cannot really separate vocabulary from grammar; the two form a single component in the linguistic system, and measuring one without the other is misleading. It may well be that one individual extends his potential more by enlarging his grammatical resources, while another, or the same individual at a different time, does so by building up a larger vocabulary; and different varieties of a language, for example its spoken and written forms, tend to exploit these resources differentially. Second, there are so many problems in counting – how do we decide what a person *could* have said, or whether two things he *did* say were the same or different? – that it is hardly possible to assess an individual's linguistic resources accurately in quantitative terms. Finally, even if we could do so, it would tell us very little about his linguistic potential, which depends only in the last resort on the size of inventory. One does not count the gestures in order to evaluate the qualities of an actor, or judge a composer by the number of different chords and phrases he uses; it is only necessary to think of the immense variation, among writers, in the extent of the linguistic resources they typically deploy. In other words, there is no reliable way of saying 'this child has a smaller linguistic inventory (than that one, or than some presumed standard)'; and it would not help us much if we could.

But there are more serious weaknesses in the deficit theory. If there is a deficit, we have to ask: is it that the child has not got enough language, or that he does not know how to use what he has? But this question is meaningless. There is no sense in which we can maintain that he knows a linguistic form but cannot use it. (Of course one may get the meaning of a word or a construction wrong, but that is not what the question is about; in that case one does not know it.) The fact that we are led to pose the question in this way is an indication of the basic fallacy in the theory, a fallacy the nature of which we can see even more clearly when we pose another awkward question: is the presumed deficit an individual matter, or is it subcultural? Here we must assume the second, since the former would not offer any explanation of the pattern of educational failure. In other words the supposition is that there are groups of people – social class groups, ethnic groups, family types or some other – whose language is deficient; in linguistic terms, that there are deficient social dialects. As soon as we put it like that, the fallacy becomes obvious. Unfortunately, as Joan Baratz pointed out in a similar context (1970), the idea of a deficient dialect is so patently self-contradictory and absurd that no linguist has ever taken the trouble to deny it. Perhaps the time has come to make an explicit denial.

We are left with the 'difference' version of the theory. This holds that some children's language is different from others'; this is undeniable, so the question is whether it is relevant. If one child's language differs from another's, but neither is deficient relative to the other, why is one of the children at a disadvantage?

The answer comes in two forms, one being a stronger variant of the other. We assume that the difference is that between a dialect and the standard language (in linguistic terms, between nonstandard and standard dialects). Then, in the weaker variant, the child who speaks the nonstandard dialect is at a disadvantage because certain contexts demand the use of the standard. Many such factors could be cited, but they tend to fall under three headings: the teacher, the subject-matter, and the system. The child who speaks nonstandard may be penalized by the teacher for doing so; he has to handle material presented in the standard language, for example in textbooks; and he has to adjust to an educational process and a way of life that is largely or entirely conducted in the standard language. This already raises the odds against him; and they are raised still higher if we now take the stronger variant of the difference theory, which adds the further explanation that nonstandard dialects are discriminated against by society. In other words, the standard language is required not only by specific factors in the child's education but also by social pressures and prejudices, which have the effect that the child's own mother tongue is downgraded and he is stereotyped as likely to fail.

Now all this is certainly true. Moreover, as Frederick Williams found in testing the 'stereotype hypothesis' in the United States, the teacher's expectations of a pupil's performance tend to correspond rather closely to the extent to which that pupil's dialect diverges from the standard – and children, like adults, tend to act out their stereotypes: if you have decided in advance that a child will fail, he probably will (Williams 1970b). Many of the assumptions of the difference theory are justified, and these undoubtedly play some part in educational failure.

But there is still one question unanswered. If children are suffering because of their dialect, why do they not learn another one? Children have no difficulty in doing this; in many parts of the world it is quite common for a child to learn three or even four varieties of his mother tongue. Rural dialects in Britain differ from the standard much more widely than the urban dialects do, either in Britain or in America; yet rural children do not have the problem, which is well known to be an urban one. Moreover there is considerable evidence that these children who, it is claimed, are failing because they cannot handle the standard language can imitate it perfectly well outside the classroom, and often do. Perhaps then the problem lies in the written language: has the dialect-speaking child a special difficulty in learning to read in the standard? But here we are on even weaker ground, because the English writing system is splendidly neutral with regard to dialect. It is as well adapted to Glaswegian or Harlem speech as it is to standard British or American; that is its great strength. There are no special *linguistic* problems involved in learning to read just because one happens to speak a nonstandard variety of English.

In other words, the 'difference' version of the language failure theory does not explain why dialect-speaking children come off badly – for the very good reason that the child who speaks a nonstandard dialect is not under any linguistic disadvantage at all. His disadvantage is a social one. This does not mean that it is not real; but it means that it is misleading to treat if as if it was linguistic and to seek to apply linguistic remedies. Part of the social disadvantage lies in society's attitudes to language and to dialect – including those of the teacher, who may interpose false notions about language which *create* problems of a linguistic nature. But these are only manifestations of patterns in the social structure; they do not add up to a linguistic explanation of the facts.

So the language failure theory, in both its versions, stands rejected. We have removed all linguistic content from the hypothesis about educational failure. The fault rests neither with language as a system (the deficit version) nor with language as an institution (the difference version); the explanation is a social one (and, in Bernstein's words, 'education cannot compensate for society'). And here, in my own thinking, the matter rested, for a considerable time; I did not accept that there was any essentially linguistic element in the situation.

But, reconsidering in the light of Bernstein's work, especially his more recent thinking, we can see that the question 'deficit or difference?' is the wrong question. It is not what the issue is about. If we look at the results of investigations carried out by Bernstein and his colleagues, as reported in the present volume, and in other monographs in the series, we find that these studies reveal certain differences which correlate significantly with social class; these differences are there, and they are in some sense linguistic – they have to do with language. But the differences do not usually appear undisguised in the linguistic forms, the grammar and vocabulary, of the children's speech. They are, rather, differences of interpretation, evaluation, orientation, on the part of the children and of their mothers. Even where the primary data are drawn from samples of children's spontaneous speech, and this is analysed in linguistic terms, the focus of attention is always on the principles of the social functioning of language. Two features of the research stand out in this connection. One is the emphasis on 'critical socializing contexts', as Bernstein has defined and identified them: generalized situation types which have greatest significance for the child's socialization and for his interpretation of experience. The other is the focus on the variable *function* of language within these contexts, and on the functional meaning potential that is available to, and typically exploited by, the child who is participating.

What Bernstein's work suggests is that there may be differences in the relative orientation of different social groups towards the various functions of language in given contexts, and towards the different areas of meaning that may be explored within a given function. Now if this is so, then when these differences manifest themselves in the contexts that are critical for the socialization process they may have a profound effect on the child's social learning; and therefore on his response to education, because built into the educational process are a number of assumptions and practices that reflect differentially not only the values but also the communication patterns and learning styles of different subcultures. As Bernstein has pointed out, not only does this tend to favour certain modes of learning over others, but it also creates for some children a continuity of culture between home and school which it largely denies to others.

This puts the question of the role of language in a different light. We can interpret the codes, from a linguistic point of view, as differences of orientation within the total semiotic potential. There is evidence in Bernstein's work that different social groups or subcultures place a high value on different orders of meaning. Hence differences arise in the prominence accorded to one or another sociosemantic 'set', or meaning potential within a given context. For any particular subculture, certain functions of language, or areas of meaning within a given function, may receive relatively greater emphasis; these will often reflect values which are implicit and submerged, but in other instances the values might be explicitly recognized – such different concepts as 'fellowship', 'soul', 'blarney', 'brow' (highbrow, lowbrow), suggest certain functional orientations which might well be examined from this standpoint. And there will be other orders of meaning, and other functions of language, that are relatively less highly valued and receive less emphasis. In general this does not matter. But let us now suppose that the semiotic modes that are relatively stressed by one group are *positive* with respect to the school – they are favoured and extended in the educational process, either inherently or because this is how education has come to be actualized – while those that are relatively stressed by another group are largely irrelevant, or even *negative*, in the educational context. We then have a plausible interpretation of the role of language in educational failure. It is, certainly, much oversimplified, as we have stated it here. But it places language in a perspective that is relevant to education – namely as the key factor in cultural transmission – instead of isolating it as if it were something on its own.

This is somewhat removed from the notion of 'language failure', in either the deficit or the difference versions. We have had to direct attention beyond the forms of language, beyond accent and dialect and the morphological and syntactic particulars of this or that variety of English, on to meaning and social function. Of course, there are myths and misconceptions about, and attitudes towards, the forms of language, and these enter into and complicate the picture. It is important to make it clear that speakers of English who have no initial *h* or no postvocalic *r*, no verbal substitute or no definite article or no -*s* on the third person singular present tense, are not verbal defectives (if they are, then we all are, since any such list could always be made up – as this one was – of standard as well as nonstandard features); nor is the underlying logic of one group any different from that of another. But just as the language element in educational failure cannot be reduced to a question of linguistic forms, so also it cannot be wholly reduced to one of attitudes to those forms and the stereotypes that result from them. It cannot be reduced to a concept of linguistic failure at all.

However, if we reject the equation 'educational failure = linguistic failure', this does not mean that we reject any interpretation of the problem in linguistic terms. Language is central to Bernstein's theory; but in order to understand the place that it occupies, it is necessary to think of language as meaning rather than of language as structure. The problem can then be seen to be one of linguistic success rather than linguistic failure. Every normal child has a fully functional linguistic system; the difficulty is that of reconciling one functional orientation with another. The remedy will not lie in the administration of concentrated doses of linguistic structure. It *may* lie, in part, in the broadening of the functional perspective – that of the school, as much as that of the individual pupil. This, in turn, demands a broadening of our own conceptions, especially our conceptions of meaning and of language. Not the least of Bernstein's contributions is the part that his work, and that of his colleagues, has played in bringing this about.

6

Language as social semiotic

1 Introductory

Sociolinguistics sometimes appears to be a search for answers which have no questions. Let us therefore enumerate at this point some of the questions that do seem to need answering.

1 How do people decode the highly condensed utterances of everyday speech, and how do they use the social system for doing so?

2 How do people reveal the ideational and interpersonal environment within which what they are saying is to be interpreted? In other words, how do they construct the social contexts in which meaning takes place?

3 How do people relate the social context to the linguistic system? In other words, how do they deploy their meaning potential in actual semantic exchanges?

4 How and why do people of different social class or other subcultural groups develop different dialectal varieties and different orientations towards meaning?

5 How far are children of different social groups exposed to different verbal patterns of primary socialization, and how does this determine their reactions to secondary socialization especially in school?

6 How and why do children learn the functional–semantic system of the adult language?

7 How do children, through the ordinary everyday linguistic interaction of family and peer group, come to learn the basic patterns of the culture: the social structure, the systems of knowledge and of values, and the diverse elements of the social semiotic?

2 Elements of a sociosemiotic theory of language

There are certain general concepts which seem to be essential ingredients in a sociosemiotic theory of language. These are the text, the situation, the text variety or register, the code (in Bernstein's sense), the linguistic system (including the semantic system), and the social structure.

2.1 Text

Let us begin with the concept of *text*, the instances of linguistic interaction in which people actually engage: whatever is said, or written, in an operational context, as distinct from a citational context like that of words listed in a dictionary.

For some purposes it may suffice to conceive of a text as a kind of 'supersentence', a linguistic unit that is in principle greater in size than a sentence but of the same kind. It has long been clear, however, that discourse has its own structure that is not constituted out of sentences in combination; and in a sociolinguistic perspective it is more useful to think of text as *encoded* in sentences, not as composed of them. (Hence what Cicourel (1969) refers to as omissions by the speaker are not so much omissions as encodings, which the hearer can decode because he shares the principles of realization that provide the key to the code.) In other words, a text is a semantic unit; it is the basic unit of the semantic process.

At the same time, text represents choice. A text is 'what is meant', selected from the total set of options that constitute what can be meant. In other words, text can be defined as actualized meaning potential.

The meaning potential, which is the paradigmatic range of semantic choice that is present in the system, and to which the members of a culture have access in their language, can be characterized in two ways, corresponding to Malinowski's distinction between the 'context of situation' and the 'context of culture' (1923, 1935). Interpreted in the context of culture, it is the entire semantic system of the language. This is a fiction, something we cannot hope to describe. Interpreted in the context of situation, it is the particular semantic system, or set of subsystems, which is associated with a particular type of situation or social context. This too is a fiction; but it is something that may be more easily describable (cf. 2.5 below). In sociolinguistic terms the meaning potential can be represented as the range of options that is characteristic of a specific situation type.

2.2 Situation

The situation is the environment in which the text comes to life. This is a well-established concept in linguistics, going back at least to Wegener (1885). It played a key part in Malinowski's ethnography of language, under the name of 'context of situation'; Malinowski's notions were further developed and made explicit by Firth (1957, 182), who maintained that the context of situation was not to be interpreted in concrete terms as a sort of audiovisual record of the surrounding 'props' but was, rather, an abstract representation of the environment in terms of certain general categories having relevance to the text. The context of situation may be totally remote from what is going on round about during the act of speaking or of writing.

It will be necessary to represent the situation in still more abstract terms if it is to have a place in a general sociolinguistic theory; and to conceive of it not as situation but as situation *type*, in the sense of what Bernstein refers to as a 'social context'. This is, essentially, a semiotic structure. It is a constellation of meanings deriving from the semiotic system that constitutes the culture.

If it is true that a hearer, given the right information, can make sensible guesses about what the speaker is going to mean – and this seems a necessary assumption, seeing that communication does take place – then this 'right information' is what we mean by the social context. It consists of those general properties of the situation which collectively function as the determinants of text, in that they specify the semantic configurations that the speaker will typically fashion in contexts of the given type.

However, such information relates not only 'downward' to the text but also 'upward', to the linguistic system and to the social system. The 'situation' is a theoretical sociolinguistic construct; it is for this reason that we interpret a particular situation type, or social context, as a semiotic structure. The semiotic structure of a situation type can be represented as a complex of three dimensions: the ongoing social activity, the role relationships involved, and the symbolic or rhetorical channel. We refer to these respectively as 'field', 'tenor' and 'mode' (following Halliday *et al.* 1964, as modified by Spencer and Gregory 1964; and cf. Gregory 1967). The field is the social action in which the text is embedded; it includes the subject-matter, as one special manifestation. The tenor is the set of role relationships among the relevant participants; it includes levels of formality as one particular instance. The mode is the channel or wavelength selected, which is essentially the function that is assigned to language in the total structure of the situation; it includes the medium (spoken or written), which is explained as a functional variable. (Cf. above, chapter 1, p. 33, and chapter 3, pp. 62–4.)

Field, tenor and mode are not kinds of language use, nor are they simply components of the speech setting. They are a conceptual framework for representing the social context as the semiotic environment in which people exchange meanings. Given an adequate specification of the semiotic properties of the context in terms of field, tenor and mode we should be able to make sensible predictions about the semantic properties of texts associated with it. To do this, however, requires an intermediary level – some concept of text variety, or register.

2.3 Register

The term 'register' was first used in this sense, that of text variety, by Reid (1956); the concept was taken up and developed by Jean Ure (Ure and Ellis 1972), and interpreted within Hill's (1958) 'institutional linguistic' framework by Halliday *et al.* (1964). The register is the semantic variety of which a text may be regarded as an instance.

Like other related concepts, such as 'speech variant' and '(sociolinguistic) code' (Ferguson 1971, chs. 1 and 2; Gumperz 1971, part I), register was originally conceived of in lexicogrammatical terms. Halliday *et al.* (1964) drew a primary distinction between two types of language variety: dialect, which they defined as variety according to the user, and register, which they defined as variety according to the use. The dialect is what a person speaks, determined by who he is; the register is what a person is speaking, determined by what he is doing at the time. This general distinction can be accepted, but, instead of characterizing a register largely by its lexicogrammatical properties, we shall suggest, as with text, a more abstract definition in semantic terms. (See table 1, p. 35.)

A register can be defined as the configuration of semantic resources that the member of a culture typically associates with a situation type. It is the meaning potential that is accessible in a given social context. Both the situation and the register associated with it can be described to varying degress of specificity; but the existence of registers is a fact of everyday experience – speakers have no difficulty in recognizing the semantic options and combinations of options that are 'at risk' under particular environmental conditions. Since these options are realized in the form of grammar and vocabulary, the register is recognizable as a particular selection of words and structures. But it is defined in terms of meanings; it is not an aggregate of conventional forms of expression superposed on some underlying content by 'social factors' of one kind or another. It is the selection of meanings that constitutes the variety to which a text belongs.

2.4 Code

'Code' is used here in Bernstein's sense; it is the principle of semiotic organization governing the choice of meanings by a speaker and their interpretation by a hearer. The code controls the semantic styles of the culture.

Codes are not varieties of language, as dialects and registers are. The codes are, so to speak, 'above' the linguistic system; they are types of social semiotic, or symbolic orders of meaning generated by the social system (cf. Hasan 1973). The code is actualized in language through the register, since it determines the semantic orientation of speakers in particular social contexts; Bernstein's own use of 'variant' (as in 'elaborated variant') refers to those characteristics of a register which derive from the form of the code. When the semantic systems of the language are activated by the situational determinants of text – the field, tenor and mode – this process is regulated by the codes.

Hence the codes transmit, or control the transmission of, the underlying patterns of a culture or subculture, acting through the socializing agencies of family, peer group and school. As a child comes to attend to and interpret meanings, in the context of situation and in the context of culture, at the same time he takes over the code. The culture is transmitted to him with the code acting as a filter, defining and making accessible the semiotic principles of his own subculture, so that as he learns the culture he also learns the grid, or subcultural angle on the social system. The child's linguistic experience reveals the culture to him through the code, and so transmits the code as part of the culture.

2.5 The linguistic system

Within the linguistic system, it is the *semantic system* that is of primary concern in a sociolinguistic context. Let us assume a model of language with a semantic, a lexicogrammatical and a phonological stratum; this is the basic pattern underlying the (often superficially more complex) interpretations of language in the work of Trubetzkoy, Hjelmslev, Firth, Jakobson, Martinet, Pottier, Pike, Lamb, Lakoff and McCawley (among many others). We can then adopt the general conception of the organization of each stratum, and of the realization between strata, that is embodied in Lamb's stratification theory (Lamb 1971; 1974).

The semantic system is Lamb's 'semological stratum'; it is conceived of here, however, in functional rather than in cognitive terms. The conceptual framework was already referred to in chapter 3, with the terms 'ideational', 'interpersonal', and 'textual'. These are to be interpreted not as functions in the sense of 'uses of language', but as functional components of the semantic system – 'metafunctions' as we have called them. (Since in respect both of the stratal and of the functional organization of the linguistic system we are adopting a ternary interpretation rather than a binary one, we should perhaps explicitly disavow any particular adherence to the magic number three. In fact the functional interpretation could just as readily be stated in terms of four components, since the ideational comprises two distinct sub-parts, the experiential and the logical; see Halliday 1973; 1976; also chapter 7 below.)

What are these functional components of the semantic system? They are the modes of meaning that are present in every use of language in every social context. A text is a product of all three; it is a polyphonic composition in which different semantic melodies are interwoven, to be realized as integrated lexicogrammatical structures. Each functional component contributes a band of structure to the whole.

The ideational function represents the speaker's meaning potential as an observer. It is the content function of language, language as 'about something'. This is the component through which the language encodes the cultural experience, and the speaker encodes his own individual experience as a member of the culture. It expresses the phenomena of the environment: the things – creatures, objects, actions, events, qualities, states and relations – of the world and of our own consciousness, including the phenomenon of language itself; and also the 'metaphenomena', the things that are already encoded as facts and as reports. All these are part of the ideational meaning of language.

The interpersonal component represents the speaker's meaning potential as an intruder. It is the participatory function of language, language as doing something. This is the component through which the speaker intrudes himself into the context of situation, both expressing his own attitudes and judgements and seeking to influence the attitudes and behaviour of others. It expresses the role relationships associated with the situation, including those that are defined by language itself, relationships of questioner-respondent, informer-doubter and the like. These constitute the interpersonal meaning of language.

The textual component represents the speaker's text-forming potential; it is that which makes language relevant. This is the component which provides the texture; that which makes the difference between language that is suspended *in vacuo* and language that is operational in a context of situation. It expresses the relation of the language to its environment, including both the verbal environment – what has been said or written before – and the nonverbal, situational environment. Hence the textual component has an enabling function with respect to the other two; it is only in combination with textual meanings that ideational and interpersonal meanings are actualized.

These components are reflected in the lexicogrammatical system in the form of discrete networks of options. In the clause, for example, the ideational function is represented by transitivity, the interpersonal by mood and modality, and the textual by a set of systems that have been referred to collectively as 'theme'. Each of these three sets of options is characterized by strong internal but weak external constraints: for example, any choice made in transitivity has a significant effect on other choices within the transitivity systems, but has very little effect on choices within the mood or theme systems. Hence the functional organization of meaning in language is built in to the core of the linguistic system, as the most general organizing principle of the lexicogrammatical stratum.

2.6 *Social structure*
Of the numerous ways in which the social structure is implicated in a sociolinguistic theory, there are three which stand out. In the first place, it defines and gives significance to the various types of social context in which meanings are exchanged. The different social groups and communication networks that determine what we have called the 'tenor' – the status and role relationships in the situation – are obviously products of the social structure; but so also in a more general sense are the types of social activity that constitute the 'field'. Even the 'mode', the rhetorical channel with its associated strategies, though more immediately reflected in linguistic patterns, has its origin in the social structure; it is the social structure that generates the semiotic tensions and the rhetorical styles and genres that express them (Barthes 1970).

Secondly, through its embodiment in the types of role relationship within the family, the social structure determines the various familial patterns of communication; it regulates the meanings and meaning styles that are associated with given social contexts, including those contexts that are critical in the processes of cultural transmission. In this way the social structure determines, through the intermediary of language, the forms taken by the socialization of the child. (See Bernstein 1971; 1975.)

Thirdly, and most problematically, the social structure enters in through the effects of social hierarchy, in the form of caste or class. This is obviously the background to social dialects, which are both a direct manifestation of social hierarchy and also a symbolic expression of it, maintaining and reinforcing it in a variety of ways: for example, the association of dialect with register – the fact that certain registers conventionally call for certain dialectal modes – expresses the relation between social classes and the division of labour. In a more pervasive fashion, the social structure is present in the forms of semiotic interaction, and becomes apparent through incongruities and disturbances in the semantic system. Linguistics seems now to have largely abandoned its fear of impurity and come to grips with what is called 'fuzziness' in language; but this has been a logical rather than a sociological concept, a departure from an ideal regularity rather than an organic property of sociosemiotic systems. The 'fuzziness' of language is in part an expression of the dynamics and the tensions of the social system. It is not only the text (what people mean) but also the semantic system (what they can mean) that embodies the ambiguity, antagonism, imperfection, inequality and change that characterize the social system and social structure. This is not often systematically explored in linguistics, though it is familiar enough to students of communication and of general semantics, and to the public at large. It could probably be fruitfully approached through an extension of Bernstein's theory of codes (cf. Douglas 1972). The social structure is not just an ornamental background to linguistic interaction, as it has tended to become in sociolinguistic discussions. It is an essential element in the evolution of semantic systems and semantic processes.

3 A sociolinguistic view of semantics

In this section we shall consider three aspects of a sociological semantics: the semantics of situation types, the relation of the situation to the semantic system, and the sociosemantics of language development. The discussion will be illustrated from a sociolinguistic study of early language development.

3.1 The semantics of situation types

A sociological semantics implies not so much a general description of the semantic system of a language but rather a set of context-specific semantic descriptions, each one characterizing the meaning potential that is typically associated with a given situation type. In other words, a semantic description is the description of a register.

This approach has been used to great effect by Turner in a number of studies carried out under Bernstein's direction in London (Turner 1973). Turner's contexts in themselves are highly specific; he constructs semantic networks representing, for example, the options taken up by mothers in response to particular questions about their child control strategies. At the same time they are highly general in their application, both because of the size of the sample investigated and, more especially, because of the sociological interpretation that is put upon the data, in terms of Bernstein's theories of cultural transmission and social change. (See figure 7, pp. 82–3.)

The sociolinguistic notion of a situation type, or social context, is variable in generality, and may be conceived of as covering a greater or smaller number of possible instances. So the sets of semantic options that constitute the meaning potential associated with a situation type may also be more or less general. What characterizes this potential is its truly 'sociolinguistic' nature. A semantics of this kind forms the interface between the social system and the linguistic system; its elements realize social meanings and are realized in linguistic forms. Each option in the semantic network, in other words, in interpreted in the semiotics of the situation and is also represented in the lexicogrammar of the text. (Note that this is not equivalent to saying that the entire semiotic structure of the situation is represented in the semantic options, and hence also in the text, which is certainly not true.)

Figure 9 (pp. 118–20) shows an outline semantic network for a particular situation type, one that falls within the general context of child play; more specifically, it is that of a small child manipulating vehicular toys in interaction with an adult. The network specifies some of the principal options, together with their possible realizations. The options derive from the general functional components of the semantic system (2.5 above) and are readily interpretable in terms of the grammar of English; we have not attempted to represent the meaning potential of the adult in the situation, but only that of the child. The networks relate, in turn, to a general description of English, modified to take account of the child's stage of development.

3.2 Structure of the situation, and its relation to the semantic system
The semiotic structure of a situation type can be represented in terms of the three general concepts of field, tenor and mode (cf. 2.2 above). The 'child play' situation type that was specified by the semantic networks in figure 9 might be characterized, by reference to these concepts, in something like the following manner:

Field Child at play: manipulating movable objects (wheeled vehicles) with related fixtures, assisted by adult; concurrently associating (i) similar past events, (ii) similar absent objects; also evaluating objects in terms of each other and of processes.
Tenor Small child and parent interacting: child determining course of action, (i) announcing own intentions, (ii) controlling actions of parent; concurrently sharing and seeking corroboration of own experience with parent.
Mode Spoken, alternately monologue and dialogue, task-oriented; pragmatic, (i) referring to processes and objects of situation, (ii) relating to and furthering child's own actions, (iii) demanding other objects; interposed with narrative and exploratory elements.

Below is a specimen of a text having these semiotic properties. It is taken from a study of the language development of one subject, Nigel, from nine months to three and a half years; the passage selected is from age 1;11. [Note: ` = falling tone; ´ = rising tone; ˇ = fall-rise tone; tonic nucleus falls on syllables having tone marks; tone group boundaries within an utterance shown by . . . . For analysis of intonation, cf. Halliday 1967a.]

Nigel [small wooden train in hand, approaching track laid along a plank sloping

from chair to floor]: Here the ràilway line . . . but it not for the trǎin to go on that.
Father: Isn't it?
Nigel: Yès tís. . . . I wonder the train will carry the lòrry [*puts train on lorry* (sic)].
Father: I wonder.
Nigel: Oh yes it wíll. . . . I don't wànt to send the train on this flóor . . . you want to send the train on the ràilway line [*runs it up plank onto chair*] . . . but it doesn't go very well on the chǎir. . . . [*makes train go round in circles*] The train all round and ròund . . . it going all round and ròund . . . [*tries to reach other train*] have that tráin . . . have the blue tráin ('give it to me') [*Father does so*] . . . send the blue train down the ráilway line . . . [*plank falls off chair*] lèt me put the railway line on the cháir ('you put the railway line on the chair!') [*Father does so*] . . . [*looking at blue train*] Daddy put sèllotape on it ('previously') . . . there a very fierce lìon in the train . . . Daddy go and see if the lion still thére. . . . Have your éngine ('give me my engine').
Father: Which engine? The little black engine?
Nigel: Yés . . . Daddy go and find it fór you . . . Daddy go and find the black éngine for you.

Nigel's linguistic system at this stage is in a state of transition, as he approximates more and more closely to the adult language, and it is unstable at various points. He is well on the way to the adult system of mood, but has not quite got there – he has not quite grasped the principle that language can be used as a *substitute* for shared experience, to impart information not previously known to the hearer; and therefore he has not yet learnt the general meaning of the yes/no question. He has a system of person, but alternates between *I/me* and *you* as the expression of the first person 'I'. He has a transitivity system, but confuses the roles of agent (actor) and medium (goal) in a non-middle (two-participant) process. It is worth pointing out perhaps that adult linguistic systems are themselves unstable at many points – a good example being transitivity in English, which is in a state of considerable flux; what the child is approximating to, therefore, is not something fixed and harmonious but something shifting, fluid and full of indeterminacies.

What does emerge from a consideration of Nigel's discourse is how, through the internal organization of the linguistic system, situational features determine text. If we describe the semiotic structure of the situation in terms of features of field, tenor and mode, and consider how these various features relate to the systems making up the semantic networks shown in figure 9, we arrive at something like the picture presented in table 2.

There is thus a systematic correspondence between the semiotic structure of the situation type and the functional organization of the semantic system. Each of the main areas of meaning potential tends to be determined or activated by one particular aspect of the situation:

Semantic components		*Situational elements*
ideational	systems activated by features of	field
interpersonal	"	tenor
textual	"	mode

In other words, the type of symbolic activity (field) tends to determine the range of meaning as content, language in the observer function (ideational); the role relationships (tenor) tend to determine the range of meaning as participation, language in the intruder function (interpersonal); and the rhetorical channel (mode) tends to determine the range of meaning as texture, language in its relevance to the environment (textual). There are of course many indeterminate areas – though there is often some system even in the indeterminacy: for example, the child's evaluation of objects lies on the borderline of 'field' and 'tenor', and the system of 'modulation' likewise lies on the borderline of the ideational and interpersonal components of language (Halliday 1969). But there is an overall pattern. This is not just a coincidence: presumably the semantic system evolved as symbolic interaction among people in social contexts, so we should expect the semiotic structure of these contexts to be embodied in its internal organization. By taking account of this we get an insight into the form of relationship among the three concepts of situation, text and semantic system. The semiotic features of the situation activate corresponding portions of the semantic system, in this way determining the register, the configuration of potential meanings that is typically associated with this situation type, and becomes actualized in the text that is engendered by it.

Table 2 Determination of semantic features by elements of semiotic structures of situation (text in 3.2)

	Situational	Semantic	
Field	manipulation of objects assistance of adult movable objects and fixtures movability of objects & their relation to fixtures recall of similar events evaluation	process type and participant structure benefactive type of relevant object type of location and movement past time modulation	**Ideational**
Tenor	interaction with parent determination of course of action enunciation of intention control of action sharing of experience seeking corroboration of experience	person mood and polarity demand, 'I want to' demand, 'I want you to' statement/question, monologue statement/question, dialogue	**Interpersonal**
Mode	dialogue reference to situation textual cohesion: objects textual cohesion: processes furthering child's actions orientation to task spoken mode	ellipsis (question-answer) exophoric reference anaphoric reference conjunction theme (in conjunction with transitivity and mood; typically, parent or child in demands, child in two-participant statements, object in one-participant statements) lexical collocation and repetition information structure	**Textual**

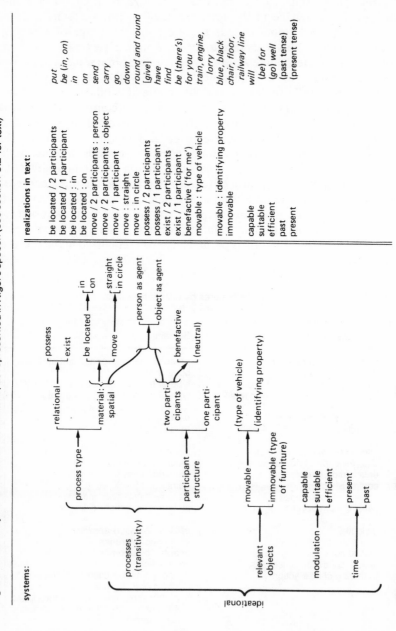

Fig. 9 Semantic systems and their realizations, as represented in Nigel's speech (see section 3.2 for text)

Fig. 9(a) Ideational systems and their realizations

systems:

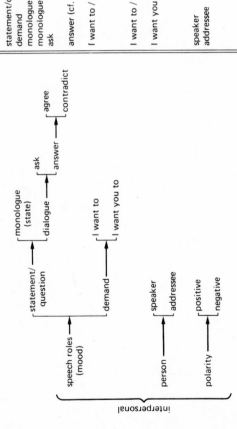

realizations in text:

statement/question	(falling tone)
demand	(rising tone)
monologue / positive	(indicative)
monologue / negative	(indicative +) *not*
ask	*I wonder* (+ indicative)
answer (cf. textual component)	*yes*[/*no*] (+ indicative)
I want to / positive	(*I*/*you*) *want*; (subjectless non-finite, e.g. *have that*)
I want to / negative	(*I*/*you*) *don't want*
I want you to	*let me* [sic] ; (proper name) ; (*I*/*you*) *want* (proper name) *to*
speaker	*I*; *you* [sic]
addressee	*you*; (proper name, e.g. *Daddy*)

Fig. 9(b) Interpersonal systems and their realizations

systems:

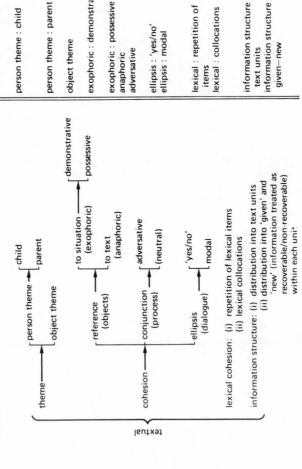

textual

theme → person theme → child / parent
      → object theme

cohesion → reference (objects) → to situation (exophoric) → demonstrative / possessive
                               → to text (anaphoric)
         → conjunction (process) → adversative / (neutral)
         → ellipsis (dialogue) → 'yes/no' / modal

lexical cohesion: (i) repetition of lexical items
                  (ii) lexical collocations

information structure: (i) distribution into text units
                       (ii) distribution into 'given' and 'new' (information treated as recoverable/non-recoverable) within each unit

realizations in text:

person theme : child	I/you (initial); (subjectless non-finite)
person theme : parent	(proper name initial)
object theme	(object name initial)
exophoric : demonstrative	this, that, the, here
exophoric : possessive	your ('my')
anaphoric	it, that, the
adversative	but; (fall-rise tone)
ellipsis : 'yes/no'	yes [no]
ellipsis : modal	(modal element, e.g. it is, it will)
lexical : repetition of items	(e.g. train . . . train)
lexical : collocations	(e.g. chair . . . floor; train . . . railway line)
information structure : text units	(organization in tone groups)
information structure : given—new	(location of tonic nucleus)

Fig. 9(c) Textual systems and their realizations

3.3 Sociosemantics of language development

A child learning his mother tongue is learning how to mean; he is building up a meaning potential in respect of a limited number of social functions. These functions constitute the semiotic environment of a very small child, and may be thought of as universals of human culture.

The meanings the child can express at this stage derive very directly from the social functions. For example, one of the functions served by the child's 'proto-language' is the regulatory function, that of controlling the behaviour of other people; and in this function he is likely to develop meanings such as 'do that some more' (continue or repeat what you've just been doing), and 'don't do that'. How does he get from these to the complex and functionally remote meanings of the adult semantic system?

These language-engendering functions, or 'proto-contexts', are simultaneously the origin both of the social context and of the semantic system. The child develops his ability to mean by a gradual process of generalization and abstraction, which in the case of Nigel appeared to go somewhat along the following lines. Out of the six functions of his proto-language (instrumental, regulatory, interactional, personal, heuristic and imaginative), he derived a simple but highly general distinction between language as a means of doing and language as a means of knowing – with the latter, at this stage, interpretable functionally as 'learning'. As he moved into the phase of transition into the adult system, at around 18 months, he assigned every utterance to one or other of these generalized functional categories, encoding the distinction by means of intonation: all 'learning' utterances were on a falling tone, and all 'doing' utterances on a rising tone. As forms of interaction, the latter required a response (increasingly, as time went on, a *verbal* response) while the former did not.

From the moment when this semantic principle was adopted, however, it ceased to satisfy, since Nigel already needed a semiotic system which would enable him to do both these things at once – to use language in both the learning mode and the doing mode within a single utterance. Without this ability he could not engage in true dialogue; the system could not develop a dynamic for the adoption and assignment of semiotic roles in verbal interaction. At this point, two steps were required, or really one complex step, for effectively completing the transition to the adult system. One was a further abstraction of the basic functional opposition, such that it came to be incorporated into his semantic system, as the two components of 'ideational' and 'interpersonal'; in the most general terms, the former developed from the 'learning' function, the latter from the 'doing' function. The other step was the introduction of a lexicogrammar, or syntax, making it possible for these two modes of meaning to be expressed simultaneously in the form of integrated lexicogrammatical structures.

The term 'sociosemantics of language development' refers to this process, whereby the original social functions of the infant's proto-language are reinterpreted, first as 'macro-functions', and then as 'meta-functions', functional components in the organization of the semantic system. These components, as remarked earlier (2.5), are clearly seen in the adult language; the options show a high degree of mutual constraint within one component but a very low degree of constraint between components. At the same time, looked at from another point of view, what the child has done is finally to dissociate the concept of 'function' from that of 'use'; the functions evolve into components of the semantic system, and the uses into what we are calling social contexts or situation types. For a detailed treatment of this topic see Halliday (1975a).

4 Towards a general sociolinguistic theory

In this final section we shall try to suggest how the main components of the sociolinguistic universe relate to one another, the assumption being that this network of relations is the cornerstone of a general sociolinguistic theory.

4.1 Meaning and text
The *text* is the linguistic form of social interaction. It is a continuous progression of meanings, combining both simultaneously and in succession. The meanings are the selections made by the speaker from the options that constitute the *meaning potential*; text is the actualization of this meaning potential, the process of semantic choice (cf. chapter 7).

The selections in meaning derive from different functional origins, and are mapped onto one another in the course of their realization as lexico-grammatical structure. In our folk linguistic terminology, the 'meaning' is represented as 'wording' – which in turn is expressed as 'sound' ('pronouncing') or as 'spelling'. The folk linguistic, incidentally, shows our awareness of the tri-stratal nature of language.

4.2 Text and situation
A text is embedded in a context of *situation*. The context of situation of any text is an instance of a generalized social context or situation type. The situation type is not an inventory of ongoing sights and sounds but a semiotic structure; it is the ecological matrix that is constitutive of the text.

Certain types of situation have in their semiotic structure some element which makes them central to the processes of cultural transmission; these are Bernstein's 'critical socializing contexts'. Examples are those having a regulative component (where a parent is regulating the child's behaviour), or an instructional component (where the child is being explicitly taught).

4.3 Situation as semiotic structure
The semiotic structure of the situation is formed out of the three sociosemiotic variables of field, tenor and mode. These represent in systematic form the type of activity in which the text has significant function (field), the status and role relationships involved (tenor) and the symbolic mode and rhetorical channels that are adopted (mode). The field, tenor and mode act collectively as determinants of the text through their specification of the

register (4.5 below); at the same time they are systematically associated with the linguistic system through the functional components of the semantics (4.4).

4.4 Situation and semantic system

The semiotic components of the situation (field, tenor and mode) are systematically related to the functional components of the semantics (ideational, interpersonal and textual): *field* to the *ideational* component, representing the 'content' function of language, the speaker as observer; *tenor* to the *interpersonal* component, representing the 'participation' function of language, the speaker as intruder; and *mode* to the *textual* component, representing the 'relevance' function of language, without which the other two do not become actualized. There is a tendency, in other words, for the field of social action to be encoded linguistically in the form of ideational meanings, the role relationships in the form of interpersonal meanings, and the symbolic mode in the form of textual meanings.

4.5 Situation, semantic system and register

The semiotic structure of a given situation type, its particular pattern of field, tenor and mode, can be thought of as resonating in the semantic system and so activating particular networks of semantic options, typically options from within the corresponding semantic components (4.4). This process specifies a range of meaning potential, or *register*: the semantic configuration that is typically associated with the situation type in question.

4.6 Register and code

The specification of the register by the social context is in turn controlled and modified by the *code*: the semiotic style, or 'sociolinguistic coding orientation' in Bernstein's term, that represents the particular subcultural angle on the social system. This angle of vision is a function of the social structure. It reflects, in our society, the pattern of social hierarchy, and the resulting tensions between an egalitarian ideology and a hierarchical reality. The code is transmitted initially through the agency of family types and family role systems, and subsequently reinforced in the various peer groups of children, adolescents and adults.

4.7 Language and the social system

The foregoing synthesis presupposes an interpretation of the social system as a *social semiotic*: a system of meanings that constitutes the 'reality' of the culture. This is the higher-level system to which language is related: the semantic system of language is a realization of the social semiotic. There are many other forms of its symbolic realization besides language; but language is unique in having its own semantic stratum.

This takes us back to the 'meaning potential' of 4.1. The meaning potential of language, which is realized in the lexicogrammatical system, itself realizes meanings of a higher order; not only the semiotic of the particular social context, its organization as field, tenor and mode, but also that of the total set of social contexts that constitutes the social system. In this respect language is unique among the modes of expression of social meanings: it operates on both levels, having meaning both in general and in particular at the same time. This property arises out of the functional organization of the semantic system, whereby the meaning potential associated with a particular social context is derived from corresponding sets of generalized options in the semantic system.

4.8 Language and the child

A child begins by creating a proto-language of his own, a meaning potential in respect of each of the social functions that constitute his developmental semiotic. In the course of maturation and socialization he comes to take over the adult language. The text-in-situation by which he is surrounded is filtered through his own functional-semantic grid, so that he processes just as much of it as can be interpreted in terms of his own meaning potential at the time.

As a strategy for entering the adult system he generalizes from his initial set of functions an opposition between language as doing and language as learning. This is the developmental origin of the interpersonal and ideational components in the semantic system of the adult language. The concept of function is now abstracted from that of use, and has become the basic principle of the linguistic organization of meaning.

4.9 The child and the culture

As a child learns language, he also learns *through* language. He interprets text not only as being specifically relevant to the context of situation but also as being generally relevant to the context of culture. It is the linguistic system that enables him to do this; since the sets of semantic options which are characteristic of the situation (the register) derive from generalized functional components of the semantic system, they also at the same time realize the higher order meanings that constitute the culture, and so the child's focus moves easily between microsemiotic and macrosemiotic environment.

So when Nigel's mother said to him 'Leave that stick outside; stop teasing the cat; and go and wash your hands. It's time for tea', he could not only understand the instructions but could also derive from them information about the social system: about the boundaries dividing social space, and 'what goes where'; about the continuity between the human and the animal world; about the regularity of cultural events; and more besides. He does not, of course, learn all this from single instances, but from the countless sociosemiotic events of this kind that make up the life of social man. And as a corollary to this, he comes to rely heavily on social system for the decoding of the meanings that are embodied in such day-to-day encounters.

In one sense a child's learning of this mother tongue is a process of progressively freeing himself from the constraints of the immediate context – or, better, of progressively redefining the context and the place of language within it – so that he is able to learn through language, and interpret an exchange of meanings in relation to the culture as a whole. Language is not the only form of the realization of social meanings, but it is the only form of it that has this complex property: to mean, linguistically, is at once both to reflect and to act – and to do both these things both in particular and in general at the same time. So it is first and foremost through language that the culture is transmitted to the child, in the course of everyday interaction in the key socializing agencies of family, peer group and school. This process, like other semiotic processes, is controlled and regulated by the code; and so, in the course of it, the child himself also takes over the coding orientation, the subcultural semiotic bias that is a feature of all social structures except those of a (possibly nonexistent) homogeneous type, and certainly of all complex societies of a pluralistic and hierarchical kind.

4.10 Summary

Figure 4 (chapter 3) was an attempt to summarize the discussion in dia-grammatic form; the arrow is to be read as 'determines'. What follows is a rendering of it in prose.

Social interaction typically takes a linguistic form, which we call *text*. A text is the product of infinitely many simultaneous and successive choices in meaning, and is realized as lexicogrammatical structure, or 'wording'. The environment of the text is the context of situation, which is an instance of a social context, or *situation type*. The situation type is a semiotic construct which is structured in terms of *field, tenor* and *mode*: the text-generating activity, the role relationships of the participants, and the rhetorical modes they are adopting. These situational variables are related respectively to the *ideational, interpersonal* and *textual* components of the *semantic system*: meaning as content (the observer function of language), meaning as par-ticipation (the intruder function) and meaning as texture (the relevance function). They are related in the sense that each of the situational features typically calls forth a network of options from the corresponding semantic component; in this way the semiotic properties of a particular situation type, its structure in terms of field, tenor and mode, determine the semantic configuration or *register* – the meaning potential that is characteristic of the situation type in question, and is realized as what is known as a 'speech variant'. This process is regulated by the *code*, the semiotic grid or principles of the organization of social meaning that represent the particular sub-cultural angle on the social system. The subcultural variation is in its turn a product of the *social structure*, typically the social hierarchy acting through the distribution of family types having different familial role systems. A child, coming into the picture, interprets text-in-situation in terms of his generalized functional categories of *learning (mathetic)* and *doing (prag-matic)*; from here by a further process of abstraction he constructs the functionally organized semantic system of the adult language. He has now gained access to the social semiotic; this is the context in which he himself will learn to mean, and in which all his subsequent meaning will take place.

I have been attempting here to interrelate the various components of the sociolinguistic universe, with special reference to the place of language within it. It is for this reason that I have adopted the mode of interpretation of the social system as a semiotic, and stressed the systematic aspects of it: the concept of system itself, and the concept of function within a system. It is all the more important, in this context, to avoid any suggestion of an idealized social functionalism, and to insist that the social system is not something static, regular and harmonious, nor are its elements held poised in some perfect pattern of functional relationships.

A 'sociosemiotic' perspective implies an interpretation of the shifts, the irregularities, the disharmonies and the tensions that characterize human interaction and social processes. It attempts to explain the semiotic of the social structure, in its aspects both of persistence and of change, including the semantics of social class, of the power system, of hierarchy and of social conflict. It attempts also to explain the linguistic processes whereby the members construct the social semiotic, whereby social reality is shaped, constrained and modified – processes which, far from tending towards an ideal construction, admit and even institutionalize myopia, prejudice and misunderstanding (Berger and Luckmann 1966, ch. 3).

The components of the sociolinguistic universe themselves provide the sources and conditions of disorder and of change. These may be seen in the text, in the situation, and in the semantic system, as well as in the dynamics of cultural transmission and social learning. All the lines of determination are *ipso facto* also lines of tension, not only through indeterminacy in the transmission but also through feedback. The meaning of the text, for example, is fed back into the situation, and becomes part of it, changing it in the process; it is also fed back, through the register, into the semantic system, which it likewise affects and modifies. The code, the form in which we conceptualize the injection of the social structure into the semantic process, is itself a two-way relation, embodying feedback from the semantic configurations of social interaction into the role relationships of the family and other social groups. The social learning processes of a child, whether those of learning the language or of learning the culture, are among the most permeable surfaces of the whole system, as one soon becomes aware in listening to the language of young children's peer groups – a type of semiotic context which has hardly begun to be seriously studied. In the light of the role of language in social processes, a sociolinguistic perspective does not readily accommodate strong boundaries. The 'sociolinguistic order' is neither an ideal order nor a reality that has no order at all; it is a human artefact having some of the properties of both.

III
The social semantics of text

7

The sociosemantic nature of discourse*

1 The semantic system

We shall start with the assumption that the semantic system is one of three strata, that constitute the linguistic system:

Semantic (the meaning)
Lexicogrammatical (the wording, i.e. syntax, morphology and lexis)
Phonological (the sound)

Second, we shall assume that the semantic system consists of four functional components: experiential, logical, interpersonal and textual. The first two of these are closely related, more so than other pairs, and can be combined under the heading of 'ideational' (but see p. 131 below):

Third, we shall assume that each stratum, and each component, is described as a network of options, sets of interrelated choices having the form 'if a, then either b or c.' Variants of this general form include: 'if a, then either x or y or z and either m or n; if x, or if m, then either p or q; if both y and n, then either r or s or t.' The description is, therefore, a paradigmatic one, in which environments are also defined paradigmatically: the environment of any option is the set of options that are related to it, including those that define its condition of entry. The description is also open-ended: there is no point at which no further subcategorization of the options is possible.

Fourth, we shall assume that each component of the semantic system specifies its own structures, as the 'output' of the options in the network (so each act of choice contributes to the formation of the structure). It is the function of the lexicogrammatical stratum to map the structures one onto another so as to form a single integrated structure that represents all components simultaneously. With negligible exceptions, every operational instance of a lexicogrammatical construct in the adult language – anything that realizes text – is structured as the expression of all four components. In

---

* The text provided for this interpretative exercise was 'The lover and his lass', from *Further fables for our time*, by James Thurber. It is reproduced at the end of this chapter (p. 151).

other words, any instance of language in use 'means' in these various ways, and shows that it does so in its grammar.

Fifth, we shall assume that the lexicogrammatical system is organized by rank (as opposed to by immediate constituent structure); each rank is the locus of structural configurations, the place where structures from the different components are mapped on to each other. The 'rank scale' for the lexicogrammar of English is:

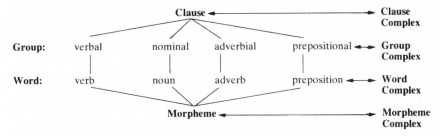

Complexes are univariate (recursive) structures formed by paratactic or hypotactic combinations – coordination, apposition, modification and the like – at the rank in question; a clause complex may be formed for example by two clauses in coordination. All other structures are multivariate (non-recursive). A 'sentence' is defined as a clause complex. See Huddleston 1965, Hudson 1967, Hudson 1971, and Sinclair 1972.

It follows from the above that each type of unit – clause, verbal group, nominal group etc. – is in itself a structural composite, a combination of structures each of which derives from one or other component of the semantics.

A clause, for example, has a structure formed out of elements such as agent, process, extent; this structure derives from the system of transitivity, which is part of the experiential component. Simultaneously it has a structure formed out of the elements modal and propositional: this derives from the system of mood, which is part of the interpersonal component. It also has a third structure composed of the elements theme and rheme, deriving from the theme system, which is part of the textual component.

For example (see text at end of chapter, p. 151):

	The Grays	retired	to their beds
experiential: (transitivity)	Medium	Process	Location: Locative
interpersonal: (mood)	Modal	Propositional	
textual: (theme)	Theme	Rheme	

It is not the case that the same constituent structure (same bracketing) holds throughout, with only the labels differing. This is already clear from this example: the thematic and modal structures are simple binary ones, whereas the transitivity structure is not. In any case, the representation just given is oversimplified; the modal constituent includes the finite element in the verb, and consists of subject plus finiteness, yielding an analysis as follows:

clause:		The Grays	'did	retire'	to their beds
	1	Medium	Process		Location: Locative
	2	Modal		Propositional	
		Subject	Finite		
	3	Theme	Rheme		

There may be differences at other points too; in general it is characteristic of lexicogrammatical structures that the configurations deriving from the various functional components of the semantic system will differ not only in their labelling but in their bracketing also.

The logical component is distinct from the other three in that all logical meanings, and only logical meanings, are expressed through the structure of 'unit complexes': clause complex, group complex and so on. For example:

clause complex:	The Grays stopped maligning the hippopotamuses	and retired to their beds
logical: (coordination)	(clause) A ——————► (clause) B	

2 Functional components of the system

The grouping of semantic components differs according to the perspective from which we look at them.

From the standpoint of their realization in the lexicogrammatical system (i.e. 'from below'), the logical component is the one that stands out as distinct from all the others, since it alone is, and always is, realized through recursive structures.

From the standpoint of the functions of the linguistic system in relation to some higher-level semiotic that is realized through the *linguistic* semiotic (i.e. 'from above'), it is the textual component that appears as distinct, since the textual component has an enabling function in respect of the other components: language can effectively express ideational and interpersonal meanings only because it can create text. Text is language in operation; and the textual component embodies the semantic systems by means of which text is created.

From the point of view of the organization within the semantic system itself (i.e. 'from the same level'), the experiential and the logical go together because there is greater systemic interdependence between these two than between other pairs. This shows up in various places throughout the English semantic system (the general pattern may well be the same in all languages, though the specifics are different): for example, the semantics of time reference, of speaking ('X said —'), and of identifying ('A = B') all involve some interplay of experiential and logical systems. To illustrate this from the semantics of speaking, the *process* 'say' is an option in the transitivity system, which is experiential; whereas the *relation* between the process of saying and what is said – the 'reporting' relation – is an option in the logical system of inter-clause relations.

The picture is therefore something like the following:

Functional components of semantic system, seen from different vantage points:

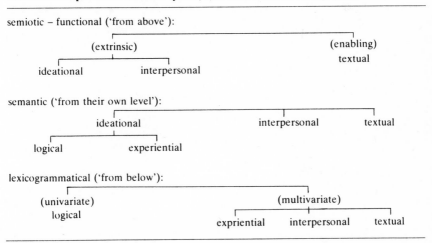

Table 3 (p. 132) sets out the principal semantic systems arranged by function and rank, showing their functional location in the semantic system and their point of origin in the lexicogrammar.

In considering the nature of text, we have to take note of the fact that certain semantic systems are realized through the medium of phonological systems which have no counterpart in the written language. One of these is the information system.

The information system, which derives from the textual component, determines how the text is organized as a flow of messages. It does not operate through a unit on the lexicogrammatical rank scale but specifies a distinct constituent structure of its own, which we refer to as 'information structure'. The information structure is realized through the intonation

Table 3 Functional components of the semantic system

IDEATIONAL		INTERPERSONAL	TEXTUAL	
LOGICAL	EXPERIENTIAL			(COHESION)
	STRUCTURAL			NONSTRUCTURAL
	(1) Clause structure			
expansion	clause: transitivity, modulation; polarity	clause: mood, modality	clause: theme	reference
identity				substitution/ellipsis
projection	verbal group: types of process; tense	verbal group: person; polarity	verbal group: voice; contrast	conjunction
& (paratactic & hypotactic)	nominal group: types of participant; class, quality, quantity etc.	nominal group: person ('role')	nominal group: deixis	lexical cohesion: reiteration collocation
	adverbial group: prepositional group: types of circumstance	adverbial group: prepositional group: comment	adverbial group: prepositional group: conjunction	
		connotations of attitude etc.		
		(2) Information structure		
Complexes at all ranks (clause complex etc.)		information unit: key	information unit: Information distribution and focus	

system of the phonology; and the structural unit, the 'information unit', is realized as a phonological constituent (i.e. a unit on the phonological rank scale), the one which is generally known as the tone group, or tone unit. This is the carrier of one complete tone contour. See Halliday 1967b, Elmenoufy 1969, Halliday 1970.

Since it is realized through intonation, which is not shown in the writing system, the information structure is a feature of the spoken language only; and any interpretation of the information structure of a written text depends on the 'implication of utterance' which is a feature of written language. There are two aspects to this: (i) the interpretation of the paragraphological signals that the written language employs, such as punctuation, underlining and other forms of emphasis; (ii) the assumption of the 'good reason' principle, namely that the mapping of the information structure onto other structures will take the unmarked form except where there is good reason for it to do otherwise (or, to put the same thing in another way, the assumption that it will take the form that is *locally* unmarked).

This does not mean that we are left with only one possible reading of a text, because in any real text there will be both ambiguities and conflicts in the 'co-text', the relevant textual environment at any point. Different features may be counted as relevant; some features will allow more than one interpretation; and some features will run counter to others in the pressures they exert. But there will always be a vast number of theoretically possible readings that are ruled out by the co-text, so that the number of sensible interpretations is reasonably small.

3 The nature of text

Within this functional framework, there is one semantic component that we have labelled 'textual'; this component embodies the specifically text-forming resources of the linguistic system. One part of these resources consists of the theme and information systems (Halliday 1968; 1976, ch. 12); these are structural, in the sense that options in these systems contribute to the derivation of structure: thematic options contribute to the lexico-grammatical structure, being realized through the clause, and information systems contribute to what we have called the information structure, a distinct though related hierarchy that is realized directly in the phonological system, through the tone group. The cohesive relations are nonstructural, not being realized through any form of structural configuration (Halliday and Hasan 1976).

All these are aspects of the semantic system. They are options in meaning, which like other options in meaning are realized through the organization at other strata.

In order to give a complete characterization of texture, we should have to make reference also to 'generic' structure, the form that a text has as a property of its genre. The fact that the text under discussion is a narrative, and of a particular kind, as made explicit in the general title *Fables for our time* – that is, it is a complex of a traditional narrative form, the fable, and a later form, the humorous essay, to which this has been adapted – defines for it a certain generic structure, which determines such things as its length, the types of participant (typically animals given human attributes, or at least human roles, and engaging in dialogue), and the culmination in a moral.

The generic structure is outside the linguistic system; it is language as the projection of a higher-level semiotic structure. It is not simply a feature of literary genres; there is a generic structure in all discourse, including the most informal spontaneous conversation (Sacks *et al*. 1974). The concept of generic structure can be brought within the general framework of the concept of register, the semantic patterning that is characteristically associated with the 'context of situation' of a text; see the sections on text and situation (pp. 141–50) below, and also Gregory 1967, Hasan 1973. The structure of narrative genre, especially traditional forms of narrative, has been extensively studied across a wide range of different languages, and we shall not attempt to discuss it here; see for example Taber 1966, Chabrol and Marin 1971.

These three factors – generic structure, textual structure (thematic and informational), and cohesion – are what distinguish text from 'non-text'. One does not normally meet 'non-text' in real life, though one can construct it for illustrative purposes. Here is a passage in which only the thematic structure has been scrambled; everything else, including all other aspects of the texture, is well-formed:

> Now comes the President here. It's the window he's stepping through to wave to the crowd. On his victory his opponent congratulates him. What they are shaking now is hands. A speech is going to be made by him. 'Gentlemen and ladies. That you are confident in me honours me. I shall, hereby pledge I, turn this country into a place, in which what people do safely will be live, and the ones who grow up happily will be able to be their children.'

Thematic patterns are not optional stylistic variants; they are an integral part of the meaning of language. Texture is not something that is achieved by superimposing an appropriate text form on a preexisting ideational content. The textual component is a component of meaning along with the ideational and interpersonal components. Hence a linguistic description is not a progressive specification of a set of structures one after the other, ideational, then interpersonal, then textual. The system does not first generate a representation of reality, then encode it as a speech act, and finally recode it as a text, as some writing in philosophical linguistics seems to imply. It embodies all these types of meaning in simultaneous networks of options, from each of which derive structures that are mapped onto one another in the course of their lexicogrammatical realization. The lexicogrammar acts as the integrative system, taking configurations from all the components of the semantics and combining them to form multilayered, 'polyphonic' structural compositions.

4 The text as a semantic unit

The quality of texture is not defined by size. There is a concept of a text as a kind of super-sentence, something that is larger than a sentence but of the same nature. But this is to misrepresent the essential quality of a text. Obviously one cannot quarrel with the use of the term 'text' to refer to a string of sentences that realize a text; but it is important to stress that the sentences are, in fact, the *realization* of text rather than constituting the text itself. Text is a semantic concept.

The same problem has arisen in linguistics with the conception of the sentence as a super-phoneme. A sentence is not an outsize phonological unit; it is a lexicogrammatical unit that is realized in the phonological system, which has its own hierarchy of units. It may be that the sentence in some language or other is marked off by the phonological system, so that it can be identified at the phonological level; but that does not make the sentence a phonological concept. There is developmental evidence that a child builds up his phonology from both ends, as it were, constructing a phonological system on the one hand and individual phonological representations of lexicogrammatical elements on the other – both particular word-phonologies and generalized syllable-phonologies at the same time (Ferguson and Farwell 1973). In other words a system is built up both as a tactic system in its own right and as the piecemeal realization of elements of a higher-level system. We find an analogous process taking place at the next level up. The child both constructs a lexicogrammatical system and, simultaneously, lexicogrammatical representations of semantic elements. Just as he develops a word phonology side by side with a syllable phonology, he also develops a text grammar side by side with a clause grammar. The 'text grammar' in this sense is the realization, in the lexicogrammar, of particular elements on the semantic stratum; and it explains the important part played in language development by the learning of large stretches of 'wording' as uninterrupted wholes.

A text, as we are interpreting it, is a semantic unit, which is not composed of sentences but is realized in sentences. A text is to the semantic system what a clause is to the lexicogrammatical system and a syllable to the phonological system. It may be characterized by certain lexicogrammatical features, just as a clause may be characterized by certain phonological features; but this does not make it a lexicogrammatical unit (given that such a unit is to be defined, as we have defined it, by its being the locus of lexicogrammatical structures).

Whether or not, and in what sense, there is a rank scale, or hierarchy, of semantic units, as some linguists have suggested, must be left undecided. A clause is only one of a number of structure-carrying units in the grammar, and it is not entirely clear why it should be singled out as *the* primary grammatical constituent; the same applies to the syllable, or any unit that is selected as *the* basic unit for phonology. The concept of semantic units is much less clearcut, since the concept of semantic structure is less clearcut.

In any case the linguistic system as a whole is not symmetrical, as Lamb pointed out in his review of Hjelmslev 1961 (Lamb 1966). Moreover the distinguishing feature of the semantic system is its organization into functional components. These determine, not units of different sizes, but simultaneous configurations of meanings of different kinds. The semantic analogue of the rank scale would appear to be not some kind of a hierarchy of structural units but the multiple determination of the text as a unit in respect of more than one property, or 'dimension', of meaning.

Let me express this more concretely in relation to the text that is under consideration. This constitutes 'a text' as defined by the textual component: not only has it a generic structure, but it is also internally cohesive, and it functions as a whole as the relevant environment for the operation of the theme and information systems. In other words it has a unity of what we have called 'texture', deriving from the specifically text-forming component within the semantic system, and this is sufficient to define it as a text. But we are likely to find this unity reflected also in its ideational and interpersonal meanings, so that its quality as a text is reinforced by a continuity of context and of speaker-audience relationship. In fact this 'artistic unity' is already contained in the concept of generic structure, and reflected in the specific forms taken by the cohesive relations. So there is a continuity in the time reference (every finite verb in the narrative is in simple past tense, every one in the dialogue is in simple present); in the transitivity patterns (the process types are those of perception, cognition, verbalization, and attribution, except for the very last sentence; and there is a rather even distribution among them); in the attitudinal modes, the form of the dialogue, and so on.

In other words, a text is a semantic unit defined by the textual component. This is not a tautology; rather it is the reason for calling the textual component by that name. A text has a generic structure, is internally cohesive, and constitutes the relevant environment for selection in the 'textual' systems of the grammar. But its unity as a text is likely to be displayed in patterns of ideational and interpersonal meaning as well. A text is the product of its environment, and it functions in that environment. In the next section I shall explore briefly the way in which we can conceptualize the relation of text to its environment, and the processes whereby specific aspects of a speaker's or writer's semantic system tend to be activated by – and hence, in turn, to shape and modify – specific aspects of the environment in which meanings are exchanged.

Meanwhile, we should stress the essential indeterminacy of the concept of 'a text'. Clauses, or syllables, are relatively well-defined entities: we usually know how many of them there are, in any instance, and we can even specify, in terms of some theory, where they begin and end. A text, in the normal course of events, is not something that has a beginning and an ending. The exchange of meanings is a continuous process that is involved in all human interaction; it is not unstructured, but it is seamless, and all that one can observe is a kind of periodicity in which peaks of texture alternate with

troughs – highly cohesive moments with moments of relatively little continuity. The discreteness of a literary text is untypical of texts as a whole.

By 'text', then, we understand a continuous process of semantic choice.
Text is meaning and meaning is choice, an ongoing current of selections each
in its paradigmatic environment of what *might have* been meant (but was
not). It is the paradigmatic environment – the innumerable subsystems that
make up the semantic system – that must provide the basis of the description,
if the text is to be related to higher orders of meaning, whether social,
literary or of some other semiotic universe. The reason why descriptions
based on structure are of limited value in text studies is that in such theories
the paradigmatic environment is subordinated to a syntagmatic frame of
reference; when paradigmatic concepts are introduced, such as transformation, they are embedded in what remains essentially a syntagmatic
theory. By what at first sight appears as a paradox, since text is a syntagmatic
process (but see Hjelmslev 1961, section 11), it is the paradigmatic basis of a
description that makes it significant for text studies. Hence in glossematics,
and similarly in the 'systemic' version of system-structure theory, the syntagmatic concept of structure is embedded in a theory that is essentially
paradigmatic. Here the description is based on system; and text is interpreted as the process of continuous movement through the system, a process
which both expresses the higher orders of meaning that constitute the 'social
semiotic', the meaning systems of the culture, and at the same time changes
and modifies the system itself.

5 The text as projection of meanings at a higher level

What is 'above' the text? If text is semantic process, encoded in the lexicogrammatical system, what does it encode in its turn?

What is 'above' depends on one's perspective, on the nature of the inquiry
and the ideology of the inquirer. There are different higher-level semiotics,
and often different levels of meaning within each.

This point emerges very clearly if one considers literary texts. To say that a
text has meaning as literature is to relate it specifically to a literary universe
of discourse as distinct from others, and thus to interpret it in terms of
literary norms and assumptions about the nature of meaning. The linguistic
description of a text which is contextualized in this way attempts to explain
its meaning as literature – why the reader interprets it as he does, and why he
evaluates it as he does. This involves relating the text to a higher-level
semiotic system which is faceted and layered in much the same way as the
linguistic system itself. An example of this 'layering' from the present text is
the use of the generic form of the fable as the vehicle of a humorous essay,
already referred to above. The 'level of literary execution' is part of the total
realizational chain (Hasan 1971).

When there is foregrounding of lexicogrammatical or phonological features in a literary text, particular forms of linguistic prominence that relate
directly to some facet of its literary interpretation, this is closely analogous to

the 'bypassing' phenomenon that is found within the linguistic system when some element in the semantics is realized directly in phonological terms (cf. p. 133 above). At this point there is isomorphism between two adjacent strata, and the phenomenon can be represented as a straight pass through one of the stratal systems. An example from the semantics of English is the bandwidth of a falling tone expressing the degree of 'newness' or semantic contrast involved in a statement. It is possible in such a case to set up a grammatical system as an interface between the semantics and the phonology; and there are strong reasons for doing so, since there is a systematic interrelationship between this and other grammatical systems, although strictly in its own terms the grammatical representation is redundant because there is neither neutralization nor diversification at this point.

The point is a significant one because a great deal of stylistic foregrounding depends on an analogous process, by which some aspect of the underlying meaning is represented linguistically at more than one level: not only through the semantics of the text – the ideational and interpersonal meanings, as embodied in the content and in the writer's choice of his role – but also by direct reflection in the lexicogrammar or the phonology. For an example of this from a study of William Golding's novel *The Inheritors* see Halliday 1971, where it is suggested that the particular impact of this novel on reader and critic may be explained by the fact that the underlying semiotic is projected simultaneously both onto the semantics, in the content of narrative and dialogue, and onto the grammar, in the highly untypical transitivity patterns that characterize, not so much individual clauses (none of which is in itself deviant), but the distribution of clause types in the writing as a whole.

The text under discussion does not display this feature of multilevel foregrounding to any great extent because it is both short and prose. A verse text, however short, provides scope by virtue of its generic form for the sort of patterned variability of patterns which is involved in this kind of multiple projection; whereas in a prose text it is likely to appear only in rather long-range effects, as deflections in the typical patterns of cooccurrence and relative frequency. But there are minor instances: for example the phonaesthetic motif of the final syllable in *snaffle, bumble, wuffle* and *gurble*, and incongruity involved in the use of synonyms of different 'tenor' (see p. 144 below) such as *mate, lover, inamoratus*.

To summarize this point: a text, as well as being realized in the lower levels of the linguistic system, lexicogrammatical and phonological, is also itself the realization of higher-level semiotic structures with their own modes of interpretation, literary, sociological, psychoanalytic and so on. These higher-level structures may be expressed not only by the semantics of the text but also by patterning at these lower levels; when such lower-level patterning is significant at some higher level it becomes what is known as 'foregrounded'. Such foregrounded patterns in lexicogrammar or phonology may be characteristic of a part or the whole of a text, or even of a whole class or genre of texts, a classic example being the rhyme schemes of the

Petrarchan and Shakespearean sonnets as expression of two very different modes of artistic semiotic (patterns of meaning used as art forms).

6 The text as a sociosemiotic process

In its most general significance a text is a sociological event, a semiotic encounter through which the meanings that constitute the social system are *exchanged*. The individual member is, by virtue of his membership, a 'meaner', one who means. By his acts of meaning, and those of other individual meaners, the social reality is created, maintained in good order, and continuously shaped and modified.

It is perhaps not too farfetched to put it in these terms: reality consists of meanings, and the fact that meanings are essentially indeterminate and unbounded is what gives rise to that strand in human thought – philosophical, religious, scientific – in which the emphasis is on the dynamic, wavelike aspect of reality, its constant restructuring, its periodicity without recurrence, its continuity in time and space. Here there is no distinction between relations among symbols and relations among the 'things' that they symbolize – because both are of the same order; both the things and the symbols are meanings. The fact that aspects of reality can be digitalized and reduced to ordered operations on symbols is still consistent with the view of reality as meaning: certain aspects of meaning are also captured in this way. Pike (1959) expressed this property of the linguistic system (though one may question the details of his application of these concepts) by viewing language as particle, wave and field; each of these perspectives reveals a different kind of truth about it.

Linguistic theory has remained at a stage at which particulateness is treated as the norm, and a number of different and not very clearly related concepts are invoked to handle its non-particulate aspects. As far as text studies, and text meaning, is concerned, however, we cannot relegate the indeterminacy to an appendix. The text is a continuous process. There is a constantly shifting relation between a text and its environment, both paradigmatic and syntagmatic: the syntagmatic environment, the 'context of situation' (which includes the semantic context – and which for this reason we interpret as a semiotic construct), can be treated as a constant for the text as a whole, but is in fact constantly changing, each part serving in turn as environment for the next. And the ongoing text-creating process continually modifies the system that engenders it, which is the paradigmatic environment of the text. Hence the dynamic, indeterminate nature of meaning, which can be idealized out to the margins if one is considering only the system, or only the text, emerges as the dominant mode of thought as soon as one comes to consider the two together, and to focus on text as actualized meaning potential.

The essential feature of text, therefore, is that it is interaction. The exchange of meanings is an interactive process, and text is the means of exchange: in order for the meanings which constitute the social system to be exchanged between members they must first be represented in some exchangeable symbolic form, and the most accessible of the available forms is language. So the meanings are encoded in (and through) the semantic system, and given the form of text. And so text functions as it were as potlatch: it is perhaps the most highly coded form of the gift. The contests in meaning that are a feature of so many human groups – cultures and sub-cultures – are from this point of view contests in giving, in a re-encoded form in which the gift, itself an element in the social semiotic (a 'meaning') but one that in the typical or at least the classic instance is realized as a thing, is realized instead as a special kind of abstract symbol, as meanings in the specifically linguistic sense. Such a gift has the property that, however great its symbolic value (and however much it may enrich the recipient), it does not in the slightest degree impoverish the giver.

We can see this aspect of text, its role as a gift, most clearly in the phenomenon of semantic contest: in competitive story-telling, exchange of insults, 'capping' another's jokes and other forms of verbal exploit. Oral verse forms such as ballads, lyrics, and epigrammatic and allusive couplets figure in many cultures as modes of competing, and even written composition may be predominantly a competitive act: late Elizabethan sonnets provide an outstanding example. In all such instances the aim is to excel in meaning, in the act of giving and the value of the gift. But it is not too fanciful to see the element of the gift as one component in all literature, and in this way to show how the act of meaning, and the product of this act, namely text, comes to have value in the culture.

The reason for making this point here needs to be clarified. It is natural to conceive of text first and foremost as conversation: as the spontaneous interchange of meanings in ordinary, everyday interaction. It is in such contexts that reality is constructed, in the microsemiotic encounters of daily life. The reason why this is so, why the culture is transmitted to, or recreated by, the individual in the first instance through conversation rather than through other acts of meaning, is that conversation typically relates to the environment in a way that is perceptible and concrete, whereas other genres tend to depend on intermediate levels of symbolic interpretation. A literary text such as the one under discussion creates its own immediate context of situation, and the relating of it to its environment in the social system is a complex and technical operation. Conversation, while it is no less highly structured, is structured in such a way as to make explicit its relationship to its setting; though it is no less complex in its layers of meaning, the various semiotic strategies and motifs that make it up are (by no means always, but in significantly many instances, and typically in the case of contexts that are critical in the socialization of a child: see Bernstein 1971) derivable from features of the social environment. Hence to understand the nature of text as social action we are led naturally to consider spontaneous conversation, as being the most accessible to interpretation; and to draw a rather clear line between this and other, less immediately contextualizable acts of meaning such as a poem or prose narrative. It is perhaps useful in text studies, therefore, to bring out those aspects of the semiotic act that are common to all, and that encompass what is traditional as well as what is spontaneous, and relate to literary as well as to conversational texts. The very general concept of a text as an exchange of meanings covers both its status as gift and its role in the realization and construction of the social semiotic.

7 The situation as a determinant of text

We have taken as our starting point the observation that meanings are created by the social system and are exchanged by the members in the form of text. The meanings so created are not, of course, isolates; they are integrated systems of meaning potential. It is in this sense that we can say that the meanings *are* the social system: the social system is itself interpretable as a semiotic system.

Persistence and change in the social system are both reflected in text and brought about by means of text. Text is the primary channel of the transmission of culture; and it is this aspect – text as the semantic process of social dynamics – that more than anything else has shaped the semantic system. Language has evolved as the primary mode of meaning in a social environment. It provides the means of acting on and reflecting on the environment, to be sure – but in a broader context, in which acting and reflecting on the environment are in turn the means of *creating* the environment and transmitting it from one generation to the next. That this is so is because the environment is a social construct. If things enter into it, they do so as bearers of social values.

Let us follow this line of reasoning through. The linguistic system has evolved in social contexts, as (one form of) the expression of the social semiotic. We see this clearly in the organization of the semantic system, where the ideational component has evolved as the mode of reflection on the environment and the interpersonal component as the mode of action on the environment. The system is a meaning potential, which is actualized in the form of text; a text is an instance of social meaning in a particular context of situation. We shall therefore expect to find the situation embodied or enshrined in the text, not piecemeal, but in a way which reflects the systematic relation between the semantic structure and the social environment. In other words, the 'situation' will appear, as envisaged by Hymes (1971a), as constitutive of the text; provided, that is, we can characterize it so as to take account of the ecological properties of language, the features which relate it to its environment in the social system.

A text is, as I have stressed, an indeterminate concept. It may be very long, or very short; and it may have no very clear boundaries. Many things about language can be learnt only from the study of very long texts. But there is much to be found out also from little texts; not only texts in the conventional forms of lyric poetry, proverbs and the like, but also brief transactions, casual encounters, and all kinds of verbal micro-operations. And among these there is a special value to the linguist in children's texts, since these tend to display their environmental links more directly and with less metaphorical mediation. A description of a short piece of child language, showing its relationship to the context of situation which engendered it, was given in chapter 6. We find all the time in the speech of young children examples of the way in which they themselves expect text to be related to its environment: their own step-by-step building up of layers of metaphorical meaning affords a clear and impressive illustration of this point.

The question to be resolved is, how do we get from the situation to the text? What features of the environment, in any specific instance, called for these particular options in the linguistics system? It may be objected that this is asking the old question, why did he say (or write) what he did? and that is something we can never know. Let me make it clear, therefore, that I am not asking any questions that require to be answered in terms of individual psychology. I am asking: what is the potential of the system that is likely to be at risk, the semantic configurations that are typically associated with a specific situation type? This can always be expressed in personal terms, if it seems preferable to do so; but in that case the question will be: what meanings will the hearer, or reader, expect to be offered in this particular class of social contexts? The meanings that constitute any given text do not present themselves to the hearer out of the blue; he has a very good idea of what is coming. The final topic that will be discussed here is that of text and situation. In what sense can the concept of 'situation' be interpreted in a significant way as the environment of the text?

8 Semiotic structure of the situation: field, tenor and mode

It was suggested in the first section that the options that make up the semantic system are essentially of three or four kinds – four if we separate the experiential from the logical, as the grammar very clearly does.

We shall be able to show something of how the text is related to the situation if we can specify what aspects of the context of situation 'rule' each of these kinds of semantic option. In other words, for each component of meaning, what are the situational factors by which it is activated?

The question then becomes one of characterizing the context of situation in appropriate terms, in terms which will reveal the systematic relationship between language and the environment. This involves some form of theoretical construction that relates the situation simultaneously to the text, to the linguistic system, and to the social system. For this purpose we interpret the situation as a semiotic structure; it is an instance of the meanings that make up the social system. Actually it is a class of instances, since what we characterize will be a situation *type* rather than a particular situation considered as unique.

The situation consists of:

(i) *the social action*: that which is 'going on', and has recognizable meaning in the social system; typically a complex of acts in some ordered configuration, and in which the text is playing some part, and including 'subject-matter' as one special aspect;

(ii) *the role structure*: the cluster of socially meaningful participant relationships, both permanent attributes of the participants and role relationships that are specific to the situation, including the speech roles, those that come into being through the exchange of verbal meanings;

(iii) *the symbolic organization*: the particular status that is assigned to the text within the situation; its function in relation to the social action and the role structure, including the channel or medium, and the rhetorical mode.

We refer to these by the terms 'field', 'tenor' and 'mode'. The environment, or social context, of language is structured as a *field* of significant social action, a *tenor* of role relationships, and a *mode* of symbolic organization. Taken together these constitute the situation, or 'context of situation', of a text.

We can then go on to establish a general principle governing the way in which these environmental features are projected onto the text.

Each of the components of the situation tends to determine the selection of options in a corresponding component of the semantics. In the typical instance, the field determines the selection of experiential meanings, the tenor determines the selection of interpersonal meanings, and the mode determines the selection of textual meanings.

semiotic structures of situation	associated with	functional component of semantics
field (type of social action)	,,	experiential
tenor (role relationships)	,,	interpersonal
mode (symbolic organization)	,,	textual

8.1 Field

The selection of options in experiential systems – that is, in transitivity, in the classes of things (objects, persons, events etc.), in quality, quantity, time, place and so on – tends to be determined by the nature of the activity: what socially recognized action the participants are engaged in, in which the exchange of verbal meanings has a part. This includes everything from, at one end, types of action defined without reference to language, in which language has an entirely subordinate role, various forms of collaborative work and play such as unskilled manipulation of objects or simple physical games; through intermediate types in which language has some necessary but still ancillary function, operations requiring some verbal instruction and report, games with components of scoring, bidding, planning, and the like; to types of interaction defined solely in linguistic terms, like gossip, seminars, religious discourse and most of what is recognized under the heading of literature. At the latter end of the continuum the concept of 'subject-matter' intervenes; what we understand as subject-matter can be interpreted as one element in the structure of the 'field' in those contexts where the social action is inherently of a symbolic, verbal nature. In a game of football, the social action is the game itself, and any instructions or other verbal interaction among the players are *part of* this social action. In a discussion about a game of football, the social action is the discussion and the verbal interaction among the participants is *the whole of* this social action. Here the game constitutes a second order of 'field', one that is brought into being by that of the first order, the discussion, owing to its special nature as a type of social action that is itself defined by language. *It is to this second-order field of discourse that we give the name of 'subject-matter'.*

8.2 Tenor

The selection of interpersonal options, those in the systems of mood, modality, person, key, intensity, evaluation and comment and the like, tends to be determined by the role relationships in the situation. Again there is a distinction to be drawn between a first and a second order of such role relationships. Social roles of the first order are defined without reference to language, though they may be (and typically are) realized through language as one form of role-projecting behaviour; all social roles in the usual sense of the term are of this order. Second-order social roles are those which are defined by the linguistic system: these are the roles that come into being only in and through language, the discourse roles of questioner, informer, responder, doubter, contradicter and the like. (Other types of symbolic action, warning, threatening, greeting and so on, which may be realized either verbally or nonverbally, or both, define roles which are some way intermediate between the two.) These discourse roles determine the selection of options in the mood system. There are systematic patterns of relationship between the first-order and the second-order roles. An interesting example of this emerged from recent studies of classroom discourse, which showed that in the teacher-pupil relationship the role of teacher is typically combined with that of questioner and the role of pupil with that of respondent, and not the other way round (cf. *Five to Nine* (1972); Sinclair *et al.* 1972) – despite our concept of education, it is not the learner who asks the questions.

8.3 Mode

The selection of options in the textual systems, such as those of theme, information and voice, and also the selection of cohesive patterns, those of reference, substitution and ellipsis, and conjunction, tend to be determined by the symbolic forms taken by the interaction, in particular the place that is assigned to the text in the total situation. This includes the distinction of medium, written or spoken, and the complex subvarieties derived from these (written to be read aloud, and so on); we have already noted ways in which the organization of text-forming resources is dependent on the medium of the text. But it extends to much more than this, to the particular semiotic function or range of functions that the text is serving in the environment in question. The rhetorical concepts of expository, didactic, persuasive, descriptive and the like are examples of such semiotic functions. All the categories under this third heading are second-order categories, in that they are defined by reference to language and depend for their existence on the prior phenomenon of text. It is in this sense that the textual component in the semantic system was said to have an 'enabling' function vis-à-vis the other two: it is only through the encoding of semiotic interaction *as text* that the ideational and interpersonal components of meaning can become operational in an environment.

The concept of genre discussed above is an aspect of what we are calling the 'mode'. The various genres of discourse, including literary genres, are the specific semiotic functions of text that have social value in the culture. A genre may have implications for other components of meaning: there are often associations between a particular genre and particular semantic features of an ideational or interpersonal kind, for example between the genre of prayer and certain selections in the mood system. Hence labels for generic categories are often functionally complex: a concept such as 'ballad' implies not only a certain text structure with typical patterns of cohesion but also a certain range of content expressed through highly favoured options in transitivity and other experiential systems – the types of process and classes of person and subject that are expected to figure in association with the situational role of a ballad text. The 'fable' is a category of a similar kind.

The patterns of determination that we find between the context of situation and the text are a general characteristic of the whole complex that is formed by a text and its environment. We shall not expect to be able to show that the options embodied in one or another particular sentence are determined by the field, tenor or mode of the situation. The principle is that each of these elements in the semiotic structure of the situation activates the corresponding component in the semantic system, creating in the process a semantic configuration, a grouping of favoured and foregrounded options from the total meaning potential, that is typically associated with the situation type in question. This semantic configuration is what we understand by the 'register': it defines the variety ('diatypic variety' in the sense of Gregory 1967) of which the particular text is an instance. The concept of register is the necessary mediating concept that enables us to establish the continuity between a text and its sociosemiotic environment.

9 The situation of the Thurber text

The 'situation' of a written text tends to be complex; and that of a fictional narrative is about as complex as it is possible for it to be. The complexity is not an automatic feature of language in the written medium: some written texts have relatively simple environments, which do not involve layers of interpretation. An example is a warning notice such as *Beware of the dog*.

The complexity of the environment of a written text arises rather from the semiotic functions with which writing is typically associated. In the case of fictional narrative, this is not even necessarily associated with writing: it is a feature just as much of oral narrative, traditional or spontaneous (in their different ways).

In a fictional text, the field of discourse is on two levels: the social act of narration, and the social acts that form the content of the narration. For our present text the description of the field would be in something like these terms:

1 (a) Verbal art: entertainment through story-telling
   (b) (i) Theme: human prejudice ('they're different, so hate them!'). Projected through:
       (ii) Thesis ('plot'): fictitious interaction of animals: male/female pairs of hippopotamuses, parrots.

The tenor is also on two levels, since two distinct sets of role relationships are embodied in the text: one between the narrator and his readership, which is embodied in the narrative, and one among the participants in the narrative, which is embodied in the dialogue:

2 (a) Writer and readers; writer adopting role as recounter: specifically as humorist (partly projected through subsidiary role as moralist), and assigning complementary role to audience.
   (b) Mate and mate: animal pair as projection of husband and wife; each adopting own (complementary) role as reinforcer of shared attitudes.

Since under each of the headings of 'field' and 'tenor' the text has appeared as a complex of two distinct levels, we might be tempted to conclude that a fictional narrative of this kind was really two separate 'texts' woven together. As a purely abstract model this could be made to stand; but it is really misleading, not only because it fails to account for the integration of the text – and in any sensible interpretation this is one text and not two – but also because the relation between the two levels is quite different in respect of the tenor from what it is in respect of the field. As regards the tenor, the text does fall into two distinct segments, the narrative and the dialogue; each is characterized by its own set of role relationships, and the two combine to form a whole. As regards the field, however, there is no division in the text corresponding to the two levels of social action: the whole text is at one and the same time an act of malicious gossip *and* an act of verbal art, the one being the realization of the other. We could not, in other words, begin by separating out the two levels and then go on to describe the field and the tenor of each; we have to describe the field of the text, and then the tenor of the text, and both in different ways then reveal its two-level semiotic organization.

The oneness of the text also appears in the characterization of the mode, the symbolic structure of the situation and the specific role assigned to the text within it:

3 Text as 'self-sufficient', as *only* form of social action by which 'situation' is defined.

Written medium: to be read silently as private act.

Light essay; original (newly-created) text projected onto traditional fable genre, structured as narrative-with-dialogue, with 'moral' as culminative element.

Even a general sketch such as this suggests something of the complexity of the concept of 'situation' applied to a written narrative. The complexity increases if we seek to make explicit the semiotic overtones that are typically associated with the interpretation of a literary text; in particular, as in this instance, the manysided relationship between the plot and the theme or themes underlying it. If the 'context of situation' is seen as the essential link between the social system (the 'context of culture', to use another of Malinowski's terms) and the text, then it is more than an abstract representation of the relevant material environment; it is a constellation of social meanings, and in the case of a literary text these are likely to involve many orders of cultural values, both the value systems themselves and the many specific subsystems that exist as metaphors for them. At the same time, one of the effects of a sociosemiotic approach is to suggest that *all* language is literature, in this sense; it is only when we realize that the same things are true of the spontaneous verbal interaction of ordinary everyday life (and nothing demonstrates this more clearly than the late Harvey Sacks' brilliant exegesis of conversational texts, which was in the best traditions of literary interpretation) that we begin to understand how language functions in society – and how this, in turn, has moulded and determined the linguistic system.

If therefore there are limits on the extent to which we can demonstrate, in the present instance, that the text has its effective origin in the context of situation, this is only partly because of its peculiarly difficult standing as a complex genre of literary fiction; many other types of linguistic interaction are not essentially different in this respect. There *are* more favourable instances; we have already referred in this connection to children's language, where there is not so much shifting of focus between different orders of meaning. Not that the speech of children is free of semiotic strategies – far from it; but the resources through which their strategies are effected tend to be less complex, less varied and less ambiguous – children cannot yet mean so many things at once. The present text, which is a good example of adult multivalence, is for that very reason less easy to derive from the context of situation, without a much more detailed interpretative apparatus. But certain features do emerge which illustrate the link between the semantic configurations of the text and the situational description that we have given of the field, tenor and mode. These are set out in the following section.

10 Situational interpretation of the text

1 Story-telling – tense: every finite verb in narrative portions is in simple past tense.

Theme/thesis – (i) transitivity: predominantly (a) mental process: perception, e.g. *listen*; cognition, e.g. *believe*; reaction, e.g. *surprise, shock*; (b) verbal process, introducing quoted speech. Animal participant as medium of process (cognizant, speaker); note that there is a grammatical rule in English that the cognizant in a mental-process clause is always 'human', i.e. a thing endowed with the attribute of humanity.

Theme/thesis – (ii) vocabulary as content (denotative meanings), e.g. *inamoratus* as expression of 'mate'.

2 Writer as recounter – mood: every clause in narrative portions is declarative (narrative statement).

Writer as humorist – vocabulary as attitude (connotative meanings), e.g. *inamoratus* as expression of mock stylishness.

Writer as moralist – mood: special mood structure for proverbial wisdom, *laugh and the world laughs* . . .

'Husband and wife' as players in game of prejudice-reinforcement – mood and modulation: clauses in dialogue portions switch rapidly among different moods and modulations, e.g. the sequence declarative, modulated interrogative, negative declarative, moodless, declarative (statement, exclamatory question, negative response, exclamation, statement).

3 Self-sufficiency of text – cohesion: reference entirely endophoric (within text itself). Note reference of *her* to *Lass* in title, suggesting highly organized text.

Written medium – information: no information structure, except as implied by punctuation, but 'alternative' devices characteristic of written language, viz. (i) higher lexical density per unit grammar, (ii) less complexity, and more parallelism, of grammatical structure, (iii) thematic variation (marked and nominalized themes), which suggests particular information structure because of association between the two systems, typically of the form ([theme] [given rheme) (new)]. i.e. theme within given, new within rheme.

Genre: narrative with dialogue – Quoting structures: thematic form of quoted followed by quoting, with the latter (*said* + Subject) comprising informational 'tail', e.g. '*He calls her snooky-ookums,*' *said Mrs Gray*, expresses 'dialogue in context of original fictional narrative'.

When the text is located in its environment, in such a way as to show what aspects of the environment are projected onto what features of the text, a pattern emerges of systematic relationship between the two. The linguistic features that were derived from the 'field' were all features assigned to the ideational component in the semantic system. Those deriving from the 'tenor' are all assigned to the interpersonal component; and those deriving from the 'mode', to the textual component.

The logical component enters into the picture in a dual perspective which I shall not attempt to discuss in detail here. The meanings that make up this component are generalized ideational relations such as coordination, apposition, reported speech, modification and submodification; as such they form a part of the ideational component. But once in being, as it were, they may also serve to relate elements of the other components, interpersonal and textual. To take a simplest example, the meaning 'and' is itself an ideational one, but the 'and' relation can as well serve to link interpersonal as ideational meanings: *hell and damnation!* as well *snakes and ladders*. Compare, in the present text, the 'and-ing' of alliterative (textual) features in *disdain and derision, mocking and monstrous*.

It should perhaps be stressed in this connection that the interpretation of the semantic system in terms of these components of ideational (experiential, logical), interpersonal and textual is prior to and independent of any consideration of field, tenor and mode. Such an interpretation is imposed by the form of internal organization of the linguistic system. Hence we can reasonably speak of the determination of the text by the situation, in the sense that the various semantic systems are seen to be activated by particular environmental factors that stand in a generalized functional relationship to them.

This picture emerges from a description of the properties of the text, especially one in terms of the relative frequency of options in the different systems. Much of the meaning of a text resides in the sort of foregrounding that is achieved by this kind of environmentally motivated prominence, in which certain sets of options are favoured (selected with greater frequency than expected on the assumption of unconditioned probability), as a realization of particular elements in the social context. The inspection of these sets of options one by one, each in its situational environment, is of course an analytical procedure; their selection by the speaker, and apprehension by the hearer, is a process of dynamic simultaneity, in which at any moment that we stop the tape, as it were, a whole lot of meaning selections are going on at once, all of which then become part of the environment in which further choices are made. If we lift out any one piece of the text, such as a single sentence, we will find the environment reflected not in the individual options (since these become significant only through their relative frequency of occurrence in the text), but in the particular combination of options that characterizes this sentence taken as a whole. As an example, consider the sentence:

'I would as soon live with a pair of unoiled garden shears,' said her inamoratus.

This sentence combines the relational process of accompaniment, in *live with*; the class of object, *unoiled garden shears*, as circumstantial element; and the comparative modulation *would as soon* (all of which are ideational meanings) as realization of the motif of human prejudice (field, as in 1 (b) (i) above). It combines declarative mood, first person (speaker) as subject, and the attitudinal meaning of *would as soon*, expressing personal preference (these being interpersonal meanings) as realization of the married couple's sharing of attitudes (tenor). Not very much can be said, naturally, about the specific text-forming elements within a single sentence; but it happens that in its thematic structure, which is the clause-internal aspect of texture, this sentence does combine a number of features that relate it to the 'mode': it has the particular quoting pattern referred to above as characteristic of dialogue in narrative, together with, in the quoted clause, the first person theme in active voice that is one of the marks of informal conversation. In fact it displays in a paradigm form the crescendo of 'communicative dynamism' described by Firbas (1964; 1968) as typical of spoken English.

We shall not find the entire context of situation of a text neatly laid out before us by a single sentence. It is only by considering the text as a whole that we can see how it springs from its environment and is determined by the specific features of that environment. And until we have some theoretical model of this relationship we shall not really understand the processes by which meanings are exchanged. This is the significance of attempts towards a 'situational' interpretation of text. Verbal interaction is a highly coded form of social act, in which the interactants are continuously supplying the information that is 'missing' from the text; see on this point Cicourel 1969. They are all the time unravelling the code – and it is the situation that serves them as a 'key'. The predictions that the hearer or reader makes from his knowledge of the environment allow him to retrieve information that would otherwise be inaccessible to him. To explain these predictions requires some general account of the systematic relations among the situation, the linguistic system and the text.

The text is the unit of the semantic process. It is the text, and not the sentence, which displays patterns of relationship with the situation. These patterns, the characteristic semantic trends and configurations that place the text in its environment, constitute the 'register'; each text can thus be treated as an instance of a class of texts that is defined by the register in question. The field, tenor and mode of the situation collectively determine the register and in this way function as constitutive of the text.

What is revealed in a single sentence, or other unit of lexicogrammatical structure, is its origin in the functional organization of the semantic system. Each of the semantic components, ideational (experiential and logical), interpersonal and textual, has contributed to its makeup. A piece of wording – sentence, clause, phrase or group – is the product of numerous micro-acts of semantic choice. The semantic system has its own further context in the total sociosemiotic cycle, the series of networks that extend from the social system (the culture as a semiotic construct), through the linguistic system on the one hand and the social context on the other, down to the wording and the sounds and written symbols, which are the ultimate linguistic manifestations of the text.

The lover and his lass

An arrogant gray parrot and his arrogant mate listened, one African afternoon, in disdain and derision, to the lovemaking of a lover and his lass, who happened to be hippopotamuses.

'He calls her snooky-ookums,' said Mrs Gray. 'Can you believe that?'

'No,' said Gray. 'I don't see how any male in his right mind could entertain affection for a female that has no more charm than a capsized bathtub.'

'Capsized bathtub, indeed!' exclaimed Mrs Gray. 'Both of them have the appeal of a coastwise fruit steamer with a cargo of waterlogged basketballs.'

But it was spring, and the lover and his lass were young, and they were oblivious of the scornful comments of their sharp-tongued neighbors, and they continued to bump each other around in the water, happily pushing and pulling, backing and filling, and snorting and snaffling. The tender things they said to each other during the monolithic give-and-take of their courtship sounded as lyric to them as flowers in bud or green things opening. To the Grays, however, the bumbling romp of the lover and his lass was hard to comprehend and even harder to tolerate, and for a time they thought of calling the A.B.I., or African Bureau of Investigation, on the ground that monolithic lovemaking by enormous creatures who should have become decent fossils long ago was probably a threat to the security of the jungle. But they decided instead to phone their friends and neighbors and gossip about the shameless pair, and describe them in mocking and monstrous metaphors involving skidding buses on icy streets and overturned moving vans.

Late the evening, the hippopotamus and the hippopotama were surprised and shocked to hear the Grays exchanging terms of endearment.

'Listen to those squawks,' wuffled the male hippopotamus.

'What in the world can they see in each other?' gurbled the female hippopotamus.

'I would as soon live with a pair of unoiled garden shears,' said her inamoratus.

They called up their friends and neighbors and discussed the incredible fact that a male gray parrot and a female gray parrot could possibly have any sex appeal. It was long after midnight before the hippopotamuses stopped criticizing the Grays and fell asleep, and the Grays stopped maligning the hippopotamuses and retired to their beds.

MORAL: *Laugh and the world laughs with you, love and you love alone.*

(James Thurber, *Further fables for our time* (London 1956), 36–9)

IV

Language and social structure

8

Language in urban society

A city is a place of talk. It is built and held together by language. Not only do its inhabitants spend much of their energies communicating with one another; in their conversation they are all the time reasserting and reshaping the basic concepts by which urban society is defined. If one listens to city talk, one hears constant reference to the institutions, the times and places, the patterns of movement and the types of social relationship that are characteristic of city life.

We might describe this by using the familiar term 'speech community' (Gumperz 1968). A city is a speech community. But this is a very general label that might be applied to almost any aggregate of people. We would have to say what it means, and what particular meaning is being ascribed to it as a description of urban society.

The 'speech community' is an idealized construct, and it is one which combines three distinct concepts: those of social group, communication network, and linguistically homogeneous population. Each of these three embodies some idea of a norm. A speech community, in this idealized sense, is a group of people who (1) are linked by some form of social organization, (2) talk to each other, and (3) all speak alike.

Dialectologists have always recognized that this is an idealized construction, to which actual human groups only approximate. If we think of the inhabitants of an old-established European village, they probably did form some sort of a communication network: in Littleby, or Kleinstadt or Malgorod, strangers were rare. But they hardly formed a single social unit, other than as defined by the fact of their living in the village; and they certainly did not all speak alike, particularly if one took the landlord and the priest into account.

Nevertheless, as a model for linguistics in a rural context the 'speech community' notion works reasonably well. 'The dialect of Littleby' can be taken, and by consent is taken, to refer to the most highly differentiated form of Littleby speech, that which is most clearly set apart from the speech of the neighbouring villages. Nowadays this variety is usually to be found spoken only by the oldest inhabitant. Rural dialectology leans rather heavily on the oldest inhabitant, and always has done; partly no doubt because there was some hope that he might turn out to be the linguist's ideal of a naïve informant, but also because he was more likely to speak 'pure Littleby'. There is an apparent contradiction here. In the history of languages, as we are accustomed to conceptualize it, the normal picture is one of divergence:

dialects grow further apart as time goes by. But by the time dialects began to be systematically studied, this trend towards linguistic divergence had been replaced in these rural communities by a trend towards convergence. The younger speakers no longer focused on the village, and so in their speech they were already moving away from the more highly differentiated forms of the village dialect.

It was not until the 1960s that serious interest came to be directed towards the speech of the cities. The modern development of urban dialectology is due largely to the innovations of one linguist, William Labov, who first took linguistics into the streets of New York (actually, in the first instance, into the department stores (Labov 1966)). In an urban context, the classical speech community model soon begins to break down; it no longer serves as a useful form of idealization to which to relate the facts. Labov very soon found that the inhabitants of a metropolis are united much more by their linguistic attitudes and prejudices, which are remarkably consistent, than by their own speech habits, which are extremely variable. The average New Yorker (or Chicagoan, or Londoner, or Frankfurter) not only does not speak like all other New Yorkers (or Chicagoans etc.); he does not even speak like himself. He may be consistent in his judgement on others – Labov's subjects showed striking agreement in their ratings of recorded utterances when asked to assign the speaker to her appropriate place on an occupational scale – but he is far from being consistent in his own practice. What is more, he is often aware of not being consistent, and is worried by the fact. He has a conception of certain norms, from which he regards himself as deviating, so that there is a difference among (1) what he says, (2) what he thinks he says, and (3) what he thinks he ought to say. Labov went so far as to devise an 'index of linguistic insecurity' as a measure of the extent of a speaker's deviation, as he himself imagines it, from his own assumed norms.

The urban 'speech community' is a heterogeneous unit, showing diversity not only between one individual and another but also within one individual. And this leads us to recognize a basic fact about urban speech: that the language itself is variable. The linguistic system, in other words, is a system of variation. We cannot describe urban speech in terms of some invariant norm and of deviation from it; the variation is intrinsic in the system. To put this another way, the norms for urban speech are made up of spaces, not of points. Many linguists, in fact, would claim that this is a general truth about language. They would see language not as a system of invariants, the way the layman (or the philosopher of language) tends to see it, but as a system with a great deal of flexibility in it.

There is no evidence that the man in the city street has some overall integrated speech system lurking somewhere at the back of his mind. Rather, he has internalized a pattern that is extraordinarily heterogeneous; and he reacts to this by picking out a few variables and assigning normative value to them. The uniformity, such as it is, takes the form of a consensus about these values. In a hierarchical social structure such as is characteristic of our culture, the values that are assigned to linguistic variants are social values, and variation serves as a symbolic expression of the social structure. To say that there is a consensus does not mean that every social group within the city interprets the social value of a linguistic variant in precisely the same way. What for one group is a prestige form, to be aimed at at least in specifiable social contexts, for another group may be a source of ridicule and social aversion. But this is essentially no different; it is the same phenomenon seen from another point of view. The variable in question is highlighted as a carrier of social meaning.

So the immediate picture of language in an urban context is one of variation in which some variables have social value; they are certified, so to speak, as social indices, and are attended to in careful speech. If we take the simplest case, that of a variable having just two forms, or 'variants', then the variants form a contrasting pair of one 'high' and one 'low'. In the following pair of sentences, either of which might be heard in London, there are five such pairs of variants:

I saw the man who did it, but I never told anybody
I seen the bloke what done it, but I never told nobody

The variants are: I saw / I seen, man / bloke, who / what, (he) did / (he) done, never . . . anybody / never . . . nobody. There are also a number of phonetic features, which are continuous rather than paired, and which are not shown in the spelling; the vowel sounds, principally those in *I* and *told*, and also the final consonant in *but*. Any speaker knows which are the high and which are the low variants (whereas there is no way for an outsider to guess). If he controls both, his choice between them is in some way related to the situation of use: the high form is likely to be used in contexts of careful speech but not in those of casual speech. So it seems as if variation in the system is in some way regulated by the social context.

And so it is, in a way, though not in any simple deterministic fashion. A speaker may use high variants in formal contexts and low variants in informal contexts: let us call this the congruent pattern. But he may also use the forms incongruently: that is, outside the contexts which define them as the norm. In so doing, he achieves a foregrounding effect, an effect that may be humorous, or startling, or derisory or many other things according to the environment. The significant fact is that such variation is meaningful. The meaning of a particular choice in a particular instance is a function of the whole complex of environmental factors, factors which when taken together define any exchange of meanings as being at some level a realization of the social system.

I shall suggest below that this is only the tip of the iceberg. It is not only isolated features of grammar and pronunciation that are the bearers of social value. There is a sense in which the whole linguistic system is value-charged, though it is a sense that is rather different from and also deeper than that which we have been considering. First however let me return briefly to the concept of variation in the linguistic system. The linguistic system is, as I expressed it, a system of variation – but the variation is within limits. In general, urban speech variants are variants of one particular dialect; and they are not, in objective terms, very far apart. In this they are rather different from the surviving rural dialects as found, for example, in Britain. The British rural dialects, those few that remain, almost certainly differ from each other more widely than do any urban speech forms, British or American, in their pronunciation, grammar and vocabulary. This last point – in pronunciation, grammar and vocabulary – constitutes a very important proviso, to which I shall return. But with this proviso, we can say that even the most highly differentiated forms of speech in American, British, Australian or other English-speaking cities – for example, Midwestern upper-middle-class speech on the one hand and so-called Black English Vernacular on the other – are not so far apart as rural Yorkshire and rural Somerset, or even as rural Yorkshire and urban London. Let us admit straight away that this is an impressionistic judgement; we cannot measure these differences. We can point to the fact that the pair of rural dialects just cited would largely be mutually unintelligible; unfortunately this does not help us very much, because speech varieties that in objective terms are not very far apart are sometimes believed by their speakers to be vastly different, and this creates a gulf which is interpreted as (and so turned into) a condition of mutual unintelligibility. Speakers' judgements of these matters tend to be social rather than linguistic: 'we don't understand them' is an observation about the social structure rather than about the linguistic system. So linguistic distance, if we treat it as a purely linguistic concept, is not very helpful or reliable. Nevertheless it is true that, in terms of variation in language as a whole, city dialects are varieties that are confined within relatively narrow limits.

In talking about 'dialect' and 'standard', we need to refer once again to the distinction between dialect and register. A dialect is any variety of a language that is defined by reference to the speaker: the dialect you speak is a function of who you are. In this respect, a dialect differs from the other dimension of variety in language, that of register: a register is a variety defined by reference to the social context – it is a function of what you are doing at the time. The dialect is what you speak; the register is what you are speaking. It seems to be typical of human cultures for a speaker to have more than one dialect, and for his dialect shifts, where they occur, to symbolize shifts in register. A 'standard' dialect is one that has achieved a distinctive status, in the form of a consensus which recognizes it as serving social functions which in some sense transcend the boundaries of dialect-speaking groups. This is often associated with writing – in many cultures the standard dialect is referred to as the 'literary [i.e. written] language' – and with formal education. Because of its special status, speakers generally find it hard to recognize that the standard dialect is at heart 'just a dialect' like any other. In English-speaking countries, received terminology makes a contrast between 'standard' (or 'standard language') and 'dialect', in this way embodying the distinctive social status of the standard dialect by refusing to classify it as a dialect at all. (For 'dialect' and 'register', see table 1, p. 35.)

To return to the facts of variation in the context of the city. Typically the various subcultures – social class, generational and others – mark themselves off by their patterns of selection within the range of linguistic variety. Certain fairly general features of pronunciation or of grammar come to be associated with a particular group within the society – by others, at first, but subsequently perhaps by themselves also – and hence to serve as a symbol of that group. For example, one group may be known for putting in the *r* sound after a vowel; or for leaving it out; or for affricating initial voiceless plosives, as in *a cup of t^{s}ea, in the p^{f}ark*; or for not affricating them; or for having no definite article; or for the particular type of negation it uses; or for the type of sentence structure it favours, e.g. *he's not here isn't Tom* versus *Tom isn't here*. Particular words may also function in this way, provided they are words of reasonably high frequency. (This is not a reference to slang. Slang is more subject to conscious choice, and so is often used by people who are deliberately adopting a certain speech variant for social purposes.) If you come from outside, you are not sensitized to these variants and may find it hard to believe in their symbolic load; but to the insider they are ludicrously obvious.

A dialect, in principle, is simply the sum of any set of variants that always go together, or at least that typically go together. In city speech, such configurations are by no means fixed; we cannot set up a neat classification of dialects with dialect A having just such and such features, always co-occurring, dialect B having a different set of features, and so on. The actual pattern is more continuous and more indeterminate. At the same time, not everything goes with everything else. For any one variable, we can usually recognize a scale from high to low; and it is more likely for high variants to cooccur with each other, and for low variants to cooccur with each other, than for the two to be randomly mixed. Hence there are regular groupings of features that are recognizable as typical configurations, and these tend to correspond with the main socioeconomic groupings in the community. An insider soon knows, when he starts talking to the man next to him in the train, where he comes from, what education he has had, and what kind of a job he does.

We still understand very little of the processes by which this rather systematic pattern of social dialect variation arises. No detailed account can yet be given of patterns of interpersonal communication in urban contexts; but obviously people of different social classes do talk to each other – there is no mountain or river separating them (only the tracks). Yet the urban speech varieties, as they evolve in the course of time, do not show (as it was once expected they would) any noticeable tendency to converge. Changes take place, but not such as to eliminate the differences. If anything, Labov finds the diversity increasing. There is a tendency to convergence, but it is not in the language itself – it is in the attitudes towards language: people come more and more to share the same evaluations of each own and others' speech. My interpretation of the social functions of language will suggest that this apparent paradox, of increasingly uniform attitudes going together

with increasingly diversified performance, is not really a paradox at all;
it is not so much the total diversity that is increasing, but rather, the extent of the correlation between this diversity and the social class structure. Language comes more and more to function as a measure of social
distance.

Some of the actual forces and mechanisms of change are probably to be
found in the young child's peer group. Of the three primary socializing
agencies, the family, the peer group and the school, the peer group is the one
we know least about – for obvious reasons, since it has no adults in it. It is a
neighbourhood organization which in some subcultures may be very close-
knit – a centre of linguistic solidarity, clearly identifying who's in and who's
out and at the same time allowing for movement in and out, including the
very important function of getting back in again. It is also a centre of
linguistic innovation. The vowel-breaking game, for example, seems to have
been going on in English-speaking city children's peer groups since the
middle ages, and it still is. (Vowel breaking is what makes the girl's name
Ann sound like the boy's name Ian. Related to it is a general tendency for the
English vowels to chase themselves up and over inside the mouth like milk
boiling in a saucepan, to use Angus McIntosh's lively simile.) This seems to
be one possible source of changes of the kind that take place within just one
social group.

But whatever their origin, social dialects are clearly recognized and identified in the community. A social dialect is a dialect – a configuration of
phonetic, phonological, grammatical and lexical features – that is associated
with, and stands as a symbol for, some more or less objectively definable
social group. Such groups typically carry popular labels of a socioregional
kind: 'lower middle class south side', and so on. These labels are popular in
the sense that there is a conception in people's minds that corresponds to
them, and corresponds rather specifically and consistently, on the whole. In
another sense, they are not popular: people are often embarrassed about
using them.

Most individuals probably have one social dialect that is their normal
usage, a form of speech that is in some sense natural to them, always with the
proviso that considerable variation is possible within it. At the same time
they can and often do move outside this. An individual in an urban speech
community is not, typically, imprisoned within one set of speech habits. He
tends to have one linguistic identity which is unmarked, a speech range
within which his speech typically falls. But he also has, very frequently, a
range of variation above and beyond this, within which he moves about
freely, in part at random and in part systematically. The variation is partly
under conscious control; and so a pattern of variants can be used by a
speaker either where the situation demands it, or where the situation does
not demand it and hence its use as it were creates the situation. If you
typically speak in a certain way among your work group, then this form of
speech will evoke that environment when it is not present. (This is the most
significant evidence for saying that speech variety is linked to that envi-

ronment in the first place.) In this way dialect variation comes to play a part in the linguistic contests and verbal humour in which urban speakers typically excel.

Language lends itself to play, and urban speech is no exception; it is characteristically associated with verbal games and contests of all kinds. Story telling is a common mode, and like many others it is often competitive: a clever storyteller can not only tell rich stories himself but can also contrive to impoverish everyone else's. The swapping of insults in young children's and adolescents' peer groups is at once both an instance of language play and an apprenticeship in it, resembling many other forms of play in having this dual character. But verbal play also extends to highly elaborate forms, ranging from competitive versifying to highly ritualized and often very cruel games such as 'the law' in southern Italy, as described by Vailland (1958). The types of verbal play that have received most attention seem to have been predominantly male activities; it would be interesting to know to what extent they have their counterparts among women.

Verbal play involves all elements in the linguistic system, from rhyme and rhythm to vocabulary and structure. But the essence of verbal play is playing with meaning; including, as in the examples cited earlier, playing with the meaning that is inherent in the social structure. Variation in language is one of the principal sources of material for the sociolinguistic game. To imitate the pronunciation or grammar of another group at the same time as taking on particular roles and attitudes that are thought to be associated with that group is a powerful means of creating stereotypes, and of upholding those that already exist. At the same time, there is an important defensive aspect to developing the sociolinguistic play potential of one's own variety of the language. A social group under pressure, aware that its own linguistic norms are disvalued by other groups, will often elaborate complex forms of verbal play in which its own speech is uniquely highly valued.

This brings me back to the point made earlier, that 'there is a sense in which the whole linguistic system is value-charged.' This is something we have to understand if we are trying to interpret the significance of linguistic diversity in urban societies. Let me pose the question in this way: if we all live in the same city, do we all mean the same things?

The immediate answer is obviously no. We all recognize our friends by their individual habits of meaning, as much as by their faces or voices or their dress and way of moving. A person is what he means. But individuals do not exist out of context; they exist in interaction with others, and meaning is the principal form that this interaction takes. Meaning is a social act, and it is constrained by the social structure. Our habits of meaning are those of the people we identify ourselves with, the primary reference groups that define our semiotic environment. Anyone who in the course of his own life has shifted from one social group to another in the same city, for example middle-class family and working-class peer group, or vice versa, knows that he has had to learn to mean different things in the process. Moving from one ethnic neighbourhood to another involves considerable semantic readjustment. So does going into the army, going to a different kind of job, or going to jail.

Why is this? We are accustomed to thinking of dialect differences in terms of pronunciation, morphology or vocabulary – the more obvious sets of variables, which are also the things that change most quickly in language over the course of time. But what are the first things to appear when an infant is learning to talk? They are the features at the 'outer limits' of the linguistic system, the two planes where language impinges on other aspects of reality: at one end, the fundamental rhythms and intonation patterns of speech, the springs of sound in chest and throat; and, at the other end, the meanings, or rather the essential ways of meaning, the semantic habits that are associated with the various contexts of language use. These are very deeply sunk into our consciousness. They persist through time, and through all kinds of changes in the formal elements of the system. This is the proviso that was made earlier, in reference to the kind of distance separating urban speech varieties one from another. If there is an African substrate in Black English – and there are good reasons for thinking that there is – it is likely to be located in the underlying rhythms and intonation patterns, and airstream mechanisms, on the one hand, and in the deepest tendencies of meaning, the semantic patterns, on the other, rather than in the more obvious phonological and morphological features that are most frequently cited in this connection.

Within any pluralistic community, the different social groups have different habits of meaning: different 'sociolinguistic coding orientations', as Bernstein (1975) calls them. Different social groups tend to associate different kinds of meaning with a given social context; they have different concepts of the semiotic structure of the situation. What one group interprets as an occasion for a public declaration of private faith may be seen by the second group as an exchange of observations about the objective world, and by a third group as something else again – as a game, for example. Interaction between the generations, and between the sexes, is full of semiotic mismatches of this kind. It is not just the individual as an individual that we identify by his semantic profile; it is the individual as a member of his social group. The city-dweller is remarkable only in the number of different social groups in which he typically holds a membership at any one time.

Since social groups differ in what they adopt as their mode of meaning in any given context, the meaning styles come to be charged with the social value that attaches to these groups themselves. This is why people in cities tend to have very strongly felt attitudes towards the linguistic varieties in their own ambience. They distinguish with some force between an approved variety, the 'standard', and other varieties ('nonstandard', or 'dialect'), of which they disapprove. But since they cannot describe these varieties in any systematic way, they pick out from the wealth of phonological and grammatical features that are 'nonstandard' certain ones that serve as the focus of explicit social attitude and comment. In Britain, and also in ancient Rome, the 'dropping of aitches' (leaving out *h* in initial position) became foregrounded as a symbol of socially unacceptable speech. In New York it is the absence of postvocalic and final *r* (which in Britain is a feature of the 'standard' dialect; it is 'nonstandard' to put the *r* in). And there are certain phonological and morphological features of Black English Vernacular that are singled out and used to characterize this variety of English.

Linguists have been insisting for many decades, and no doubt will be insisting for many decades to come, on the fact that no one form of speech, no single dialect of a language, is intrinsically more worthy of respect than any other. The differences between dialects have to do not with language as a system, but with language as an institution – as a vehicle and a symbol for the social structure. The concept of a 'standard language' is an institutional concept; it refers to the status of a particular dialect, and to the spread of functions that it serves, not to any intrinsic elements in the dialect itself. What then is the source of the very deeply held attitudes? Why are many city people so violent in condemning what they consider 'substandard' forms of speech.

The answer seems to be that, although the attitudes are explicitly formulated in connection with immediately accessible matters of pronunciation and word formation, what is actually being reacted to is something much deeper. People are reacting to the fact that others mean differently from themselves; and they feel threatened by it. It is not just a simple question of disliking certain sounds, though that is the form it takes on the surface; but of being anxious about certain ways of meaning. The trouble lies not in a different vowel system but in a different value system. If I object to somebody's vowels sounds, or to the structure of their sentences, I am likely to express my objection either as aesthetic ('they are ugly') or as pragmatic ('they are a barrier to communication'), or both. This is how I feel it to be. But I am really objecting to these things as symbols. And being linguistic symbols, they are doubly charged: they function on the one hand directly, as indices of the social structure, like beards and styles of dress, and on the other hand indirectly, as part of the realization of the meanings through which the speaker is acting out his subcultural identity.

Language is only one of the ways in which people represent the meanings that are inherent in the social system. In one sense, they are represented (that is, expressed) also by the way people move, the clothes they wear, their eating habits and their other patterns of behaviour. In the other sense, they are represented (that is, metaphorized) by the way people classify things, the rules they set up, and other modes of thought. Language 'represents' in both these senses. It is able to do this because it encodes, at one and the same time, both our experience of reality and our relationships with each other. Language mediates between ourselves and the two components of our environment, the natural environment and the social environment; and it does so in such a way that each becomes a metaphor of the other. Every social group develops its own particular view of the world and of society. And the existence of these different and competing models, where they jostle each other in crowded cities, is very easily felt as a threat to the social order.

So it comes about that large numbers of city children learn to speak – that is, as I would interpret it, they learn to mean – in ways which are incompatible with established social norms. This would not matter, if it was not for the fact that these norms are embodied in the principles and practices of education. The result is a massive problem of educational failure, or educational resistance. The problem of educational failure is not a linguistic problem, if by linguistic we mean a problem of different urban dialects, though it is complicated by dialect factors, especially dialect attitudes; but it is at bottom a semiotic problem, concerned with the different ways in which we have constructed our social reality, and the styles of meaning that we have learnt to associate with the various aspects of it. My meanings, the semantic resources I deploy in a particular social context, may not be the same as your meanings, or as your expectation of what my meanings should be; and that can lead to a bewildering lack of communication between us.

A city is not a speech community, in the classical sense. Its inhabitants obviously do not all talk to each other. They do not all speak alike; and furthermore they do not mean alike. But a city is an environment in which meanings are exchanged. In this process, conflicts arise, symbolic conflicts which are no less real than conflicts over economic interest; and these conflicts contain the mechanism of change. It is fascinating to linguists to find that they contain some of the mechanisms of *linguistic* change, so that by studying these processes we gain new insights into the history of language. But they are also a source of new insights into the nature of cultural change, changes in the reality that each one of us constructs for himself in the course of interaction with others. The city-dweller's picture of the universe is not, in the typical instance, one of order and constancy. But at least it has – or could have, if allowed to – a compensating quality that is of some significance: the fact that many very different groups of people have contributed to the making of it.

9
Antilanguages

Of the various kinds of 'anti'-word, such as antibiotic, antibody, antinovel, antimatter and so on, the kind that is to be understood here is that represented by antisociety. An antisociety is a society that is set up within another society as a conscious alternative to it. It is a mode of resistance, resistance which may take the form either of passive symbiosis or of active hostility and even destruction.

An antilanguage is not only parallel to an antisociety; it is in fact generated by it. We do not know much about either the process or its outcome, because most of the evidence we have is on the level of travellers' tales; but it is reasonable to suppose that, in the most general terms, an antilanguage stands to an antisociety in much the same relation as does a language to a society. Either pair, a society and its language or an antisociety and its (anti) language, is, equally, an instance of the prevailing sociolinguistic order. It has commonly been found with other aspects of the human condition – the social structure, or the individual psyche – that there is much to be learnt from pathological manifestations, which are seldom as clearly set off from the 'normal' as they at first appear. In the same way a study of sociolinguistic pathology may lead to additional insight into the social semiotic.

In Elizabethan England, the counterculture of vagabonds, or 'cursitors' in Thomas Harman's (1567) mock-stylish designation, a vast population of criminals who lived off the wealth of the established society, had their own tongue, or 'pelting (= paltry) speech'; this is frequently referred to in contemporary accounts, though rarely described or even illustrated with any detailed accuracy. The antisociety of modern Calcutta has a highly developed language of its own, substantially documented by Bhaktiprasad Mallik in his book *Language of the underworld of West Bengal* (1972). The 'second life', the term used by Adam Podgórecki (1973) to describe the subculture of Polish prisons and reform schools, is accompanied by an elaborated antilanguage called 'grypserka'. We shall take these as our three cases for discussion.

What can be said about the characteristics of antilanguages? Like the early records of the languages of exotic cultures, the information usually comes to us in the form of word lists. These afford only very limited possibilities of interpretation, although they are perhaps slightly more revealing here than in other contexts because of the special relation that obtains between an antilanguage and the language to which it is counterposed.

The simplest form taken by an antilanguage is that of new words for old; it is a language relexicalized. It should not be assumed that it always arises by a process of fission, splitting off from an established language; but this is one possibility, and it is easier to talk about it in these terms. Typically this relexicalization is partial, not total: not all words in the language have their equivalents in the antilanguage. (For an interesting case of total relexicalization compare the Dyirbal mother-in-law language as described by Dixon (1970) – perhaps a related phenomenon, since this is the language used by the adult male to his affinal kin, who constitute a kind of institutionalized antisociety within society.) The principle is that of same grammar, different vocabulary; but different vocabulary only in certain areas, typically those that are central to the activities of the subculture and that set it off most sharply from the established society. So we expect to find new words for types of criminal act, and classes of criminal and of victim; for tools of the trade; for police and other representatives of the law enforcement structure of the society; for penalties, penal institutions, and the like. The Elizabethan chroniclers of the pelting speech list upwards of twenty terms for the main classes of members of the fraternity of vagabonds, such as *upright man, rogue, wild rogue, prigger of prancers* (= horse thief), *counterfeit crank, jarkman, bawdy basket, walking mort, kinchin mort, doxy* and *dell*; numerous terms for specific roles in their often highly elaborate villainies, and names for the strategies themselves, which are known collectively as *laws* – for example *lifting law* (stealing packages) which involves a *lift*, a *marker* and a *santer* (the one who steals the package, the one to whom it is handed, and the one who waits outside to carry it off); names for the tools, e.g. *wresters* (for picking locks), and for the spoils, e.g. *snappings*, or *garbage*; and names for various penalties that may be suffered, such as *clying the jerk* (being whipped) or *trining on the chats* (getting hanged).

Such features belong to our commonsense picture of an argot, or cant (to give it its Elizabethan name). By themselves, they are no more than the technical and semitechnical features of a special register; they amount to an antilanguage only if we admit into this category something that is simply the professional jargon associated with the activities of a criminal counterculture.

It is noticeable, however, that even these purely technical elements seem to be somewhat larger than life. The language is not merely *re*lexicalized in these areas; it is *over*lexicalized. So in Mallik's account of the Calcutta underworld language we find not just one word for 'bomb' but twenty-one; forty-one words for 'police', and so on (1972, 22–3). A few of these are also technical expressions for specific subcategories; but most of them are not – they are by ordinary standards synonymous, and their proliferation would be explained by students of slang as the result of a never-ending search for originality, either for the sake of liveliness and humour or, in some cases, for the sake of secrecy.

But there is more to it than that. If we consider underworld languages in terms of a general comparison with the languages of the overworld, we find in them a characteristic functional orientation, away from the experiential mode of meaning towards the interpersonal and the textual modes. Both the textual orientation (the 'set' towards the message, in Jakobson's terms) and the interpersonal (the 'set' towards addresser/addressee, although as we shall suggest this is to be interpreted rather as a set towards the social structure) tend to produce this overlexicalization: the former because it takes the form of verbal competition and display, in which kennings of all kinds are at a premium; the latter because sets of words which are denotatively synonymous are clearly distinguished by their attitudinal components. Mallik's twenty-four synonyms for 'girl' include the whole range of predictable connotations – given that, as he remarks, 'the language of the criminal world [with some exceptions] is essentially a males' language' (27).

Both of these are normal features of everyday language, in which textual and interpersonal meanings are interwoven with experiential meanings into a single fabric of discourse. What characterizes what we are calling antilanguages is their *relatively greater* orientation in this direction. In all languages, words, sounds and structures tend to become charged with social value; it is to be expected that, in the antilanguage, the social values will be more clearly foregrounded. This is an instance of what Bernstein refers to as the 'sociolinguistic coding orientation', the tendency to associate certain ways of meaning with certain social contexts. Any interpretation of the phenomenon of antilanguages involves some theory about what kinds of meaning are exchanged in different environments within a culture.

Let us try and answer more specifically the question why antilanguages are used. Mallik in fact put this question to 'a large number of criminals and antisocial elements' – 400 in all; he got 385 replies (including only 26 'don't know'), of which 158 explained it as the need for secrecy, and 132 as communicative force or verbal art. In Podgórecki's account of the 'second life', both these motifs figure prominently: one of the ways in which an inmate can be downgraded to the level of a 'sucker' in the social hierarchy is by breaking the rules of verbal contest, and another is by 'selling the secret language to the police' (1973, 9). But the fact that an antilanguage is *used for* closed communication and for verbal art does not mean that these are what gave rise to it in the first place. It would be possible to create a language just for purposes of contest and display; but this hardly seems sufficient to account for the origin of the entire phenomenon. The theme of secrecy is a familiar one in what we might call 'folk antilinguistics' – in members' and outsiders' explanations of the use of an antilanguage. No doubt it is a part of the truth: effective teamwork does depend, at times, on exchanging meanings that are inaccessible to the victim, and communication among prisoners must take place without the participation of the gaoler. But while secrecy is a necessary strategic property of antilanguages, it is unlikely to be the major cause of their existence. Secrecy is a feature of the jargon rather than a determinant of the language.

What then lies behind the emergence of the antilanguage? Yet another way of being 'suckered down' is by 'maliciously refusing to learn the *grypserka*'; and it is clear from Podgórecki's discussion that there is an inseparable connection between the 'second life' and the antilanguage that is associated with it. The 'grypserka' is not just an optional extra, serving to adorn the second life with contest and display while keeping it successfully hidden from the prison authorities. It is a fundamental element in the existence of the 'second life' phenomenon.

Here is Podgórecki's initial summing up:

> The essence of the second life consists in a secular stratification which can be reduced to the division of the inmates into 'people' and 'suckers'. . . . The people are independent and they have power over the suckers. Everyday second life is strongly ritualized. The body of these rituals are called *grypserka* (from *grypa* – a slang word designating a letter smuggled secretly to or from a prison); S. Malkowski defined this as 'the inmates' language and its grammar', In this language, certain . . . words . . . are insulting and noxious either to the speaker or to one to whom they are addressed. (7)

The language comes to the investigator's attention in the context of the familiar twin themes of ritual insult and secrecy. But Podgórecki's discussion of the 'second life' shows that it is much more than a way of passing the time. It is the acting out of a distinct social structure; and this social structure is, in turn, the bearer of an alternative social reality.

On closer scrutiny, the Polish investigators found that the division into people and suckers was only the principal division in a more elaborate social hierarchy. There were two classes of 'people' and three of 'suckers'; with some degree of mobility among them, though anyone who had once reached the highest or lowest category stayed there. There were a number of other variables, based on age, provenance (urban/rural), type of offence, and prison standing (first offender/old lag); and the place of an individual in the social structure was a function of his status in respect of each of these hierarchies. Account was also taken of his status in the free underworld, which, along with other factors, suggested that 'second life' was not a product of the prison, or of prison conditions, but was imported from the criminal subculture outside. Nevertheless

> . . . the incarcerated create in their own social system a unique stratification which is based on the caste principle. The caste adherence in the case of 'second life' is based not on a given social background or physical features, but is predominantly determined by a unique link with magical rules which are not functional for the social system in which they operate. The only function which these rules have is to sustain the caste system. (14)

Comparative data from American sources quoted by Podgórecki show the existence of a similar form of social organization in correctional institutions in the United States, differing mainly in that each of the two antisocieties appears as a distorted reflection of the structure of the particular society from which it derives.

Podgórecki cites explanations of the 'second life' as resulting from conditions of isolation, or from the need to regulate sexual behaviour, and rejects them as inadequate. He suggests instead that it arises from the need to maintain inner solidarity under pressure, and that this is achieved through an accumulation of punishments and rewards:

> Second life is a system which transforms the universal reciprocity of punishments into a pattern of punishments and rewards, arranged by the principles of stratification. Some members of the community are in a position to transform the punishments into rewards.
>
> It might be said that this type of artificial social stratification possesses features of collective representation which transform the structure of existing needs into an operating fabric of social life which tries to satisfy these needs in a way which is viable in the given conditions. (20)

The formula is therefore:

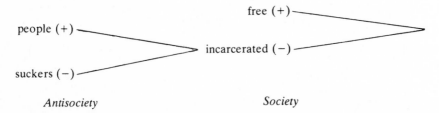

Antisociety   *Society*

which is the Lévi-Straussian proportion $b_1 : b_2 :: a : b$ (cf. Bourdieu 1971). At the individual level, the second life provides the means of maintaining identity in the face of its threatened destruction:

> In a world in which there are no real things, a man is reduced to the status of a thing. . . . The establishment of a reverse world (in which reducing others to things becomes a source of gratification by transforming a punitive situation into a rewarding one) can also be seen as a desperate attempt to rescue and reintegrate the self in the face of the cumulative oppression which threatens to disintegrate it. Thus 'second life' . . . can be interpreted as a defence and a means of reconstruction, to which the self resorts just before total disruption by means of mutually enhancing oppressive forces. (Podgórecki 1973, 24)

The second life is a reconstruction of the individual and society. It provides an alternative social structure, with its systems of values, of sanctions, of rewards and punishments; and this becomes the source of an alternative identity for its members, through the patterns of acceptance and gratification. In other words, the second life is an alternative reality.

It is in this light that we can best appreciate the function of the second life antilanguage, the grypserka. The grypserka serves to create and maintain this alternative reality. An antilanguage is, in this respect, no different from a language 'proper': both are reality-generating systems. But because of the special character of the second life reality – its status as an alternative, under constant pressure from the reality that is 'out there' (which is still a subjective reality, but nevertheless stands always ready to be reaffirmed as a norm) – the reality-generating force of the antilanguage, and especially its power to create and maintain social hierarchy, is strongly foregrounded.

At this point we should quote at some length a critically relevant passage from Berger and Luckmann's *The social construction of reality* (1966, 172–3):

> The most important vehicle of reality-maintenance is conversation. One may view the individual's everyday life in terms of the working away of a conversational apparatus that ongoingly maintains, modifies and reconstructs his subjective reality. Conversation means mainly, of course, that people speak with one another. This does not deny the rich aura of nonverbal communication that surrounds speech. Nevertheless speech retains a privileged position in the total conversational apparatus. It is important to stress, however, that the greater part of reality-maintenance in conversation is implicit, not explicit. Most conversation does not in so many words define the nature of the world. Rather, it takes place against the background of a world that is silently taken for granted. Thus an exchange such as, 'Well, it's time for me to get to the station', and 'Fine, darling, have a good day at the office', implies an entire world *within which* these apparently simple propositions make sense. By virtue of this implication the exchange confirms the subjective reality of this world.
>
> If this is understood, one will readily see that the great part, if not all, of everyday conversation maintains subjective reality. Indeed, its massivity is achieved by the accumulation and consistency of casual conversation – conversation that can *afford to be* casual precisely because it refers to the routine of a taken-for-granted world. The loss of casualness signals a break in the routines and, at least potentially, a threat to the taken-for-granted reality. Thus one may imagine the effect on casualness of an exchange like this: 'Well, it's time for me to get to the station', 'Fine, darling, don't forget to take along your gun.'
>
> At the same time that the conversational apparatus ongoingly maintains reality, it ongoingly modifies it. Items are dropped and added, weakening some sectors of what is still being taken for granted and reinforcing others. Thus the subjective reality of something that is never talked about comes to be shaky. It is one thing to engage in an embarrassing sexual act. It is quite another to talk about it beforehand or afterwards. Conversely, conversation gives firm contours to items previously apprehended in a fleeting and unclear manner. One may have doubts about one's religion: these doubts become real in a quite different way as one discusses them. One then 'talks oneself into' these doubts: they are objectified as reality within one's own consciousness. Generally speaking, the conversational apparatus maintains reality by 'talking through' various elements of experience and allocating them a definite place in the real world.
>
> This reality-generating potency of conversation is already given in the fact of linguistic objectification. We have seen how language objectifies the world, transforming the *panta rhei* of experience into a cohesive order. In the establishment of this order language *realizes* a world, in the double sense of apprehending and producing it. Conversation is the actualizing of this realizing efficacy of language in the face-to-face situation of individual existence. In conversation the objectifications of language become objects of individual

consciousness. Thus the fundamental reality-maintaining fact is the continuing use of the same language to objectify unfolding biographical experience. In the widest sense, all who employ this same language are reality-maintaining others. The significance of this can be further differentiated in terms of what is meant by a 'common language' – from the group-idiosyncratic language of primary groups to regional or class dialects to the national community that defines itself in terms of language.

An individual's subjective reality is created and maintained through interaction with others, who are 'significant others' precisely because they fill this role: and such interaction is, critically, verbal – it takes the form of conversation. Conversation is not, in general, didactic; the 'others' are not teachers, nor do they consciously 'know' the reality they are helping to construct. Conversation is, in Berger and Luckmann's term, casual. Berger and Luckmann do not ask the question, what must language be like for casual conversation to have this magic power? They are not concerned with the nature of the linguistic system. For linguistics, however, this is a central problem; and for linguistics in the perspective of a general social semiotic, it might be said to be *the* central problem: how can we interpret the linguistic system in such a way as to explain the magical powers of conversation?

Let us consider the antilanguage in this light. As Berger and Luckmann point out, subjective reality can be transformed:

> To be in society already entails an ongoing process of modification of sub-jective reality. To talk about transformation, then, involves a discussion of different degrees of modification. We will concentrate here on the extreme case, in which there is a near-total transformation; that is, in which the individual 'switches worlds'. . . . Typically, the transformation is subjectively apprehended as total. This, of course, is something of a misapprehension. Since subjective reality is never totally socialized, it cannot be totally transformed by social processes. At the very least the transformed individual will have the same body and live in the same physical universe. Nevertheless there are instances of transformation that appear total if compared with lesser modifications. Such transformations we will call alternations.
>
> Alternation requires processes of re-socialization.   (176)

The antilanguage is the vehicle of such *re*socialization. It creates an alter-native reality: the process is one not of construction but of reconstruction. The success condition for such a reconstruction is, in Berger and Luck-mann's words, 'the availability of an effective plausibility structure, that is, a social base serving as the 'laboratory' of transformation. This plausibility structure will be mediated to the individual by means of significant others, with whom he must establish strongly affective identification' (177).

The processes of resocialization, in other words, make special kinds of demand on language. In particular, these processes must enable the indi-vidual to 'establish strongly affective identification' with the significant others. Conversation in this context is likely to rely heavily on the fore-grounding of interpersonal meanings, especially where, as in the case of the second life, the cornerstone of the new reality is a new social structure – although, by the same token, the interpersonal elements in the exchange of meanings are likely to be fairly highly ritualized.

But it is a characteristic of an antilanguage that it is not just an ordinary language which happens to be, for certain individuals, a language of resocializing. Its conditions of use are different from the types of alternation considered by Berger and Luckmann, such as forms of religious conversion. In such instances an individual takes over what for others is *the* reality; for him it involves a transformation, but the reality itself is not inherently of this order. It is *somebody's* ordinary, everyday, unmarked reality, and its language is *somebody's* 'mother tongue'. An antilanguage, however, is nobody's mother tongue'; it exists solely in the context of *re*socialization, and the reality it creates is inherently an alternative reality, one that is constructed precisely in order to function in alternation. It is the language of an antisociety.

Of course, the boundary between the two is not hard and fast. The early Christian community was an antisociety, and its language was in this sense an antilanguage. But nevertheless there are significant differences. Alternation does not of itself involve any kind of antilanguage: merely the switch from one language to another. (It could be said that, in the perspective of the individual, the second is in fact functioning as an antilanguage. Thus for example in Agnes's reconstruction of an identity, as described by Garfinkel (1967) in his famous case-history, the language of femininity, or rather of femaleness, was for her an antilanguage, since it was required to construct what was in the context a counter-identity. But a language is a social construct; Agnes did not, and could not by herself, create a linguistic system to serve as the medium for the reconstruction. Indeed, to do so would have sabotaged the whole effort, since its success depended on the new identity appearing, and being accepted, as if it had been there from the start.) The antilanguage arises when the alternative reality is a *counter*-reality, set up *in opposition to* some established norm.

It is thus not the *distance* between the two realities but the *tension* between them that is significant. The distance need not be very great; the one is, in fact, a metaphorical variant of the other (just as grypserka is clearly a variant of Polish and not some totally alien language). Moreover unlike what happens in a transformation of the religious conversion kind, the individual may in fact switch back and forth between society and anti-society, with varying degrees of intermediate standing: the criminal subculture outside the prison is in that sense intermediate between the second life and the established society.

Mallik likewise identifies three distinct groups of people using the underworld language of Bengal: criminals, near-criminals, and students; and he notes significant differences among them, both in content and in expression: 'while the criminals speak with a peculiar intonation, the students or other cultured people speak normally' (1972, 26). There is continuity between language and antilanguage, just as there is continuity between society and antisociety. But there is also tension between them, reflecting the fact that they are variants of one and the same underlying semiotic. They may express different social structures: but they are part and parcel of the same social system.

An antilanguage is the means of realization of a subjective reality: not merely expressing it, but actively creating and maintaining it. In this respect, it is just another language. But the reality is a counter-reality, and this has certain special implications. It implies the foregrounding of the social structure and social hierarchy. It implies a preoccupation with the definition and defence of identity through the ritual functioning of the social hierarchy. It implies a special conception of information and of knowledge. (This is where the secrecy comes in: the language is secret because the reality is secret. Again there is a counterpart in individual verbal behaviour, in the techniques of information control practised by individuals having something to hide, which they do not want divulged; cf. Goffman's (1963) study of stigma.) And it implies that social meanings will be seen as oppositions: values will be defined by what they are *not*, like time and space in the Looking-Glass world (where one lives backwards, and things get further away the more one walks towards them).

Let me enumerate here some of the features of the Calcutta underworld language described by Mallik. Mallik states that it is 'a full and complete language, though mixed and artificial to some extent' (73); it is 'primarily Bengali, in which strains of Hindi infiltration are discernable' (62). He considers that the language has its own phonology and morphology, which could and should be described in their own terms. But these can also be interpreted in terms of variation within Bengali, and Mallik relates the underworld forms to standard Bengali wherever he can.

In phonology, Mallik distinguishes some thirty different processes: for example metathesis (e.g. *kodān* 'shop', from *dokān*; *karcā* 'servant', from *cākar*), back formation (e.g. *khum* 'mouth', from *mukh*), consonantal change (e.g. *konā* 'gold', from *sonā*), syllabic insertion (e.g. *biṭuṛi* 'old woman', from *buṛi*); and variation involving single features, such as nasality, cerebral articulation or aspiration. Many words, naturally, have more than one such process in their derivation (e.g. *chappi* 'buttock', from *pāch*; *ãske* 'eyes', from *akṣi*; *mākrā* 'joke', from *maskarā*).

In morphology also, Mallik identifies a number of derivational processes: for example suffixing (e.g. *koṭni* 'cotton bag', from English *cotton*; *dharān* 'kidnapper', from *dharā* 'hold'); compounding (e.g. *bilākhānā* 'brothel', from *bilā*, general derogatory term, + *khānā* '−orium, place for'); simplifying; shift of word class; lexical borrowing (e.g. *khālās* 'murder', from Arabic *xalās* 'end', replacing *khun*). Again, we find various combinations of these processes; and very many instances that are capable of more than one explanation.

All these examples are variants, in the sense in which the term is used in variation theory (Cedergren and D. Sankoff 1974; G. Sankoff 1974). Labov (1969) defines a set of variants as 'alternative ways of "saying the same thing" ' (his quotation marks); and while the principle behind variation is much more complex than this innocent-sounding definition implies, it is true that, in the most general terms, we can interpret a variant as an alternative realization of an element on the next, or on some, higher stratum. So, for example, *kodān* and *dokān* are variants (alternative phonological realizations) of the same *word* 'shop'. Similarly *koṭni* and its standard Bengali equivalent are variants (alternative lexicogrammatical realizations) of the same *meaning* 'cotton bag'. Assuming the semantic stratum to be the highest within the linguistic system, *all* sets of variants have the property of being identical semantically; *some* have the property of being identical lexicogrammatically as well:

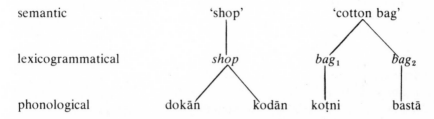

Now the significant thing about the items that are phonologically or morphologically distinctive in the underworld language is that many of them are not, in fact, variants at all; they have no semantic equivalent in standard Bengali. This does not mean they cannot be *translated* into standard Bengali (or standard English, or standard anything else): they can. But they do not function as *coded* elements in the semantic system of the everyday language. Here are some examples from Mallik:

Item	Definition	Source
ghōṭ	'to swallow a stolen thing to avoid detection'	ḍhōk 'swallow'
logām	'theft in a moving goods train'	māl gāṛī 'goods train'
okhrān	'one who helps the chief operator in stealing from a goods train'	oprāno 'uproot'
bhappar	'outside disturbance at the time of a theft'	bhir bhappar 'crowd'
ulṭi	'underworld language'	ulaṭ 'turn down'
cukru	'kidnapper of a sleeping child'	curi 'theft'
bilāhalat	'serious condition of a victim in an assault'	bilā 'queer', halat 'condition' (Hindi)

Item	Definition	Source
bidhobā	'boy without girlfriend'	bidhobā 'widow'
ruṭihā	'to share bread secretly with a convict detained in a prison'	ruṭi 'bread'
bastā	'person promised employment but cheated'	bastā 'sack'
pancabāj	'one who leaves victim at crossroads after a snatch'	panca 'five', bāj 'expert'
paune-āṭṭā	'boy prostitute'	paune-āṭṭā 'seven and three quarters'
khām	'thigh of a girl'	thām 'pillar'
guanā	'hidden cavity inside the throat to hide stolen goods'	gahan 'secret'
nicu-cākkā	'pick pockets by standing on footboard of train or bus'	nicu 'low', cākā 'wheel'

Intermediate between these and the straightforward variants are numerous metaphorical expressions of the type that would most readily be thought of as typical of inner city gangland speech, such as:

Item	Definition	Source
sāinborḍ-olā	'married woman'	(reference to vermilion mark on forehead of married woman; olā 'owner')
kācā-kalā	'young girl'	'unripe, banana'
sardi-khāsi	'notes and coins'	'cold, cough' (reference to noises made)
cok-khāl	'spectacles'	'eye, pocket'
ātap	'widow'	'sunbaked' (from ātap cāl 'sunbaked rice', eaten by widows)
ṭhunkā	'casual (client of prostitute)'	portmanteau of ṭhunko 'fragile', thāuko 'small-scale, retail'
ḍabal-ḍekār	'plump woman'	English *double decker*

chāmiā	'girl'	māch 'fish' (reversed to chām; + suffix −i + suffix −ā)
suṭā	'cigarette'	sukh 'happiness', ṭān 'puff'
aeṛi-mārā	'impotent'	āṛa 'testicles', mārā 'strike; dead'
obhisār-āenā	'seductive eyes'	abhisār 'tryst', āynā 'mirror'

and so on. Thomas Harman's account of the Elizabethan pelting speech contains many similar examples: *crashing-cheats* 'teeth' (*cheat* = general element for 'thing which −'); *smelling-cheat* 'nose', also 'garden, orchard'; *belly-cheat* 'apron'; *Rome-booze* 'wine'; *stalling-ken* 'house that will receive stolen ware' (*stall* 'make or ordain' i.e. 'order', *ken* 'house'); *queer-ken* 'prison-house' (*queer* 'nought', i.e. = general derogatory element, cf. Bengali *bilā*); *darkmans* 'night'; *queer cuffin* 'Justice of the Peace'.

There is no way of deciding whether such metaphorical representations 'have the same meaning' as everyday forms or not, i.e. whether they are or are not variants in Labov's definition. (To say 'same denotation, different connotation' is merely to avoid deciding; it means 'both yes and no.') Nor is there any need to decide. We can call them all 'metaphorical variants', since it is helpful to relate them to variation theory; what is most important is the fact that they are metaphorical. It is this metaphorical character that defines the antilanguage. An antilanguage is a metaphor for an everyday language; and this metaphorical quality appears all the way up and down the system. There are phonological metaphors, grammatical metaphors – morphological, lexical and perhaps syntactic – and semantic metaphors; some of these are set out in table 4 (but note that this is *not* a complete listing of the types that are to be found).

As we have pointed out already, many instances can be interpreted in more than one way, and many are complex metaphors, involving variation at more than one level.

By interpreting the total phenomenon in terms of metaphor we can relate the semantic variants to the rest of the picture. The notion of a semantic variant is apparently contradictory: how can two things be variants ('have the same meaning') if their meanings are different? But this is the wrong way of looking at it. The antisociety is, in terms of Lévi-Strauss's distinction between metaphor and metonymy, metonymic to society – it is an extension of it, within the social system; while its realizations are (predictably) metaphorical, and this applies both to its realization in social structure and to its realization in language (Lévi-Strauss 1966, ch. 7). The antisociety is, in its structure, a metaphor for the society; the two come together at the level of the social system. In the same way the antilanguage is a metaphor for the

Table 4 Types of metaphor

phonological:			alternation metathesis	sonā ≡ konā 'gold' khum ≡ mukh 'mouth'
grammatical	morphological:		suffixation compounding	koṭni (koṭan 'cotton' + i) ≡ 'bag' bilāīkhānā ('queer' + 'house') ≡ 'brothel'
	lexical:		alternation	billī ('cat') ≡ 'prostitute'
	syntactic:		expansion	chappar khāoā ≡ lukāno 'hide' (cf. Engl. bing a waste ≡ 'depart')
semantic:				ghoṭ ('swallow stolen object') ≡ nicu-cakkā ('pick pockets from footboard of tram') ≡ ?

language, and the two come together at the level of the social semiotic. So there is no great difficulty in assimilating the 'second life' social hierarchy to existing internalized representations of social structure; nor in assimilating concepts like 'hidden cavity inside the throat to receive stolen goods', or 'to share bread secretly with a convict', to the existing semiotic that is realized through the language. Semantic variants 'come together' (i.e. are interpretable) at the higher level, that of the culture as an information system.

The phenomenon of metaphor itself is, of course, not an 'antilinguistic' one; metaphor is a feature of *languages*, not just antilanguages (although one could express the same point another way by saying that metaphor constitutes the element of antilanguage that is present in all langues). Much of everyday language is metaphorical in origin, though the origins are often forgotten, or unknown. What distinguishes an antilanguage is that it is itself a metaphorical entity, and hence metaphorical modes of expression are the norm; we should *expect* metaphorical compounding, metatheses, rhyming alternations and the like to be among its regular patterns of realization.

We know much less about its modes of meaning, its semantic styles. Harman gives a dialogue in Elizabethan antilanguage, but it is almost certainly one he has made up himself to illustrate the use of the words in his glossary (1567, 148–50). Mallik includes no dialogue, although he does quote a number of complete sentences, which are very helpful (1972, 83–4, 109–10). It is not at all easy to record spontaneous conversation (especially in an antilanguage!). But, as Berger and Luckmann rightly point out, the reality-generating power of language lies in conversation; furthermore it is cumulative, and depends for its effectiveness on continuous reinforcement in interaction. To be able to interpret the real significance of an antilanguage, we need to have access to its conversational patterns: texts will have to be collected, and edited, and subjected to an exegesis that relates them to the semantic system and the social context. Only in this way can we hope to gain insight into the characterology (to use a Prague School term) of an antilanguage – the meaning styles and coding orientations that embody its characteristic countercultural version of the social system.

Meanwhile, the easiest way in to an antilanguage is probably through another class of languages that we could call 'music-hall languages' (or, in American, 'vaudeville languages'). It is worth speculating (but speculation is no substitute for finding out) whether Gobbledygook – in its original sense as a 'secret language' of Victorian working class humour, not its metaphorical sense as the language of bureaucrats – is, in origin, a descendant of the Elizabethan antilanguage, with its teeth drawn once the social conditions in which the antilanguage emerged and flourished had ceased to exist. Gobbledygook has some distinctively antilanguage features: one brief example, *erectify a luxurimole flackoblots* 'erect a luxurious block of flats', contains metathesis, suffixation, and compounding with a common morph – all totally vacuous, hence the comic effect. The banner of Gobbledygook was borne aloft (and raised to semantic heights) in England in the 1950s by Spike Milligan, who created an antilanguage of his own – a 'kind of mental slapstick', in the words of HRH The Prince of Wales – known as Goonery. Here is a specimen of conversation (Milligan, 1973):

> *Quartermess*: Listen, someone's screaming in agony – fortunately I speak it fluently.
> *Willium*: Oh sir. Ohh me krills are plurned.
> *Quartermess*: Sergeant Fertangg, what's up? Your boots have gone grey with worry.
> *Willium*: I was inside the thing, pickin' up prehistoric fag-ends, when I spots a creature crawling up the wall. It was a weasel, suddenly it went . . .
> *(sound effects)* POP
> *Quartermess*: What a strange and horrible death.
> *Willium*: Then I hears a 'issing sound and a voice say . . . 'minardor'
> *Quartermess*: Minardor? We must keep our ears, nose and throat open for anything that goes Minardor.
> *Henry*: Be forewarned Sir, the Minardor is an ancient word, that can be read in the West of Ministers Library.
> *Quartermess*: It so happens I have Westminster Library on me and, Gad, look there I am inside examining an occult dictionary.
> *(sound effects)* THUMBING PAGES

But when we reach this point, it is high time to ask: why the interest in antilanguages? They are entertaining; but have they any importance, or are they just collectors' pieces? I think if we take them seriously – though not solemnly! – there are two ways in which antilanguages are of significance for the understanding of the social semiotic.

1 In the first place, the phenomenon of the antilanguage throws light on the difficult concept of social dialect, by providing an opposite pole, the second of two idealized extremes to which we can relate the facts as we actually find them.

Let us postulate an ideally homogenous society, with no division of labour, or at least no form of social hierarchy, whose members (therefore) speak an ideally homogeneous language, without dialectal variation. There probably never has been such a human group, but that does not matter; this is an ideal construct serving as a thesis for deductive argument. At the other end of the scale, we postulate an ideally dichotomized society, consisting of two distinct and mutually hostile groups, society and antisociety; the members of these speak two totally distinct tongues, a language and an antilanguage. Again, there has probably never been such a thing – it reminds us of the Eloi and the Morlocks imagined by H. G. Wells in *The time machine*. But it serves as the antithesis, the idealized opposite pole.

What we do find in real life are types of sociolinguistic order that are interpretable as lying somewhere along this cline. The distinction between standard and nonstandard dialects is one of language versus antilanguage, although taking a relatively benign and moderate form. Popular usage opposes *dialect*, as 'anti-', to *(standard) language*, as the established norm. A nonstandard dialect that is consciously used for strategic purposes, defensively to maintain a particular social reality or offensively for resistance and protest, lies further in the direction of an antilanguage; this is what we know as a 'ghetto language' (cf. Kochman's (1972) account of Black English in the United States).

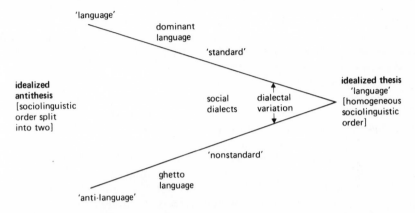

Fig. 10 Types of sociolinguistic order

Social dialects are not necessarily associated with caste or class; they may be religious, generational, sexual, economic (urban/rural) and perhaps other things too. What distinguishes them is their hierarchical character. The social function of dialect variation is to express, symbolize and maintain the social order; and the social order is an essentially hierarchic one. An antilanguage is, at one and the same time, *both* the limiting case of a social dialect (and hence the realization of one component in the hierarchy of a wider social order that includes both society and antisociety), *and* a language (and hence the realization of a social order that is constituted by the antisociety itself); in the latter role, it embodies its own hierarchy, and so displays internal variation of a systematic kind – Mallik, for example, refers to the different groups existing within the antisociety, each with its own social status and each having its own distinctive speech forms   (29–9).

The perspective of the antilanguage is one in which we can clearly see the meaning of variability in language: in brief, the function of alternative language is to create alternative reality. A social dialect is the embodiment of a mildly but distinctly different world view – one which is therefore potentially threatening, if it does not coincide with one's own. This is undoubtedly the explanation of the violent attitudes to nonstandard speech commonly held by speakers of a standard dialect: the conscious motif of 'I don't like their vowels' symbolizes an underlying motif of 'I don't like their values.' The significance for the social semiotic, of the kind of variation *in the linguistic system* that we call social dialect, becomes very much clearer when we take into account the nature and functions of antilanguages.

2 In the second place, there is antilanguage as *text*. A central problem for linguistics is that of relating text to system, and of relating modes of text description that are applicable to conversation (Mitchell 1957; Sacks *et al.* 1974) to a theory of the linguistic system. I have been suggesting, for example in chapter 7, that this problem can be usefully approached through a functional interpretation of the semantic system, an interpretation in terms of its major functional components which are relatable (i) to the text, as an ongoing process of selection in meaning; (ii) to the linguistic system; and (iii) to the situation, as a semiotic construct derivable from the 'social semiotic' (the culture considered as an information system). It is beyond the scope of the discussion to develop this further here; but one point may be made which emerges specifically with reference to the description of antilanguages.

Conversation, as Berger and Luckmann point out, depends for its reality-generating power on being casual; that is to say, it *typically* makes use of *highly coded* areas of the *system* to produce *text* that is *congruent* – though once coding and congruence have been established as the norm, it can tolerate and indeed thrives on a reasonable quantity of matter that is incongruent or uncoded. 'Uncoded' means 'not (yet) fully incorporated into the system'; 'incongruent' means 'not expressed through the most typical (and highly coded) form of representation'; and both concepts are of a 'more or less' kind, not 'all or nothing'. Now, certain types of social context typically engender text in which the coding process, and the congruence relation, tend to be foregrounded and brought under attention. An example is the language of young children (and of others interacting with them), since children are simultaneously both interacting and constructing the system that underlies the text.

Other examples are provided by verbal contest and display. Here the foregrounding is not a sign of the system coming into being, but an effect of the particular functional orientation within the system, and the special features that arise in a context where a speaker is using language just in order to secure for himself the rewards that accrue to prowess in the use of language.

An antilanguage has something of both these elements in it. Anti-languages are typically used for contest and display, with consequent fore-grounding of interpersonal elements of all kinds. At the same time, the speakers of an antilanguage are constantly striving to maintain a counter-reality that is under pressure from the established world. This is why the language is constantly renewing itself – to sustain the vitality that it needs if it is to function at all. Such is the most likely explanation of the rapid turnover of words and modes of expression that is always remarked on by commentators on underworld language. But there is more to it than that. Within the experiential mode of meaning, an antilanguage may take into itself – may encode at the semantic level – structures and collocations that are selfconsciously opposed to the norms of the established language. This can be seen clearly in texts in the more intellectual antilanguages such as those of mysticism (and cf. some of the Escher-like semantic sleights of Goonery, e.g.

I have Westminster Library on me and, Gad, look there I am inside). But it is almost certainly present also in the typical conversation of the underworld and the 'second life'.

The result is that conversation in an antilanguage is likely to display in sharper outline the systematic relations between the text and the linguistic system. The modes of expression of the antilanguage, when seen from the standpoint of the established language, appear oblique, diffuse, metaphorical; and so they are, *from that angle*. But seen in their own terms, they appear directed, as powerful manifestations of the linguistic system in the service of the construction of reality. It is the reality that is oblique, since we see it as a metaphorical transformation of the 'true' reality; but the function of the text with respect to that reality is a reinforcing one, all the more direct because it is a reality which needs more reinforcement.

An antilanguage is not something that we shall always be able to recognize by inspection of a text. It is likely to be characterized by some or all of the various features mentioned, and hence to be recognizable by its phonological or lexicogrammatical shape as a metaphoric alternant to the everyday language. But in the last resort these features are not necessary to an antilanguage. We have interpreted antilanguage as the limiting case of social dialect, and this is a valid perspective; but it is an extreme, not a typical case because it is not primarily defined by variation – or, rather, the variation by which it could be defined would be variation in a special sense. A social dialect is a cluster of associated variants – that is, a systematic pattern of tendencies in the selection of values of phonological and lexicogrammatical variables under specified conditions. Attention is on variation rather than on the meanings that are exchanged. An antilanguage, while it may display such variation, is to be defined, on the other hand, as a systematic pattern of tendencies in the selection of meanings to be exchanged. (We left open the question whether or not this could be brought under the rubric of variation.) In this respect, therefore, it is more like Bernstein's (1974) concept of a code, or coding orientation. A code may be defined just in this way: as a systematic pattern of tendencies in the selection of meanings to be exchanged under specified conditions. (Note that the 'specified conditions' are in the sociolinguistic environment. They may be social or linguistic, the tendency being, naturally, that the higher the level of the variation, the more likely it is that the relevant context will be social rather than linguistic. Hence in the definition of code we could say 'in specified social contexts'.) So now we can interpret an antilanguage as the limiting case of a code. Again it is an extreme, not a typical case, but this time for a different reason: because the subjective reality that is realized by it is a conscious counter-reality, not just a subcultural variant of, or angle on, a reality that is accepted by all. Still this is a relative matter: an antilanguage is not a clearly distinct category – it is a category to which any given instance approximates more or less.

An antilanguage of the kind presented at the start brings into sharp relief the role of language as a realization of the power structure of society. The antilanguages of prison and criminal countercultures are the most clearly defined because they have specific reference to alternative social structures, as well as the additional attributes of secret languages and professional jargons; and hence they are full of overt markers of their antilanguage status. The obliqueness of meaning and form that makes them so effective as bearers of an alternative reality also makes them inherently comic – so reflecting another aspect of the same reality, as seen by its speakers. In any case not all antilanguages are languages of social resistance and protest. The 'arcane languages' of sorcery and mysticism are of the same order (hence some of Castaneda's (1971) difficulties in understanding Don Juan). An antilanguage may be 'high' as well as 'low' on the diglossic spectrum. The languages of literature are in a certain sense antilanguages – or rather, literature is both language and antilanguage at the same time. It is typical of a poetic genre that one or other mode of meaning is foregrounded. At times the effect comes close to that of an antilanguage in the social sense, for example in competitive genres such as the Elizabethan sonnet; at other times the generic mode has little or nothing of the antilanguage about it, leaving the individual poet free to impart his own subjective reality, if he so wishes, by creating an antilanguage of his own. (And the listener, or reader, is free to *interpret* the text as antilanguage if *he* so wishes.) The antilinguistic aspect of literature is sometimes well to the fore; at other times and places it recedes into insignificance. A work of literature is its author's contribution to the reality-generating conversation of society – irrespective of whether it offers an alternative reality or reinforces the received model – and its language reflects this status that it has in the sociosemiotic scheme. But that is another topic.

10

An interpretation of the functional relationship between language and social structure

In this chapter I shall summarize what has been said or implied earlier about how language expresses the social system. In the course of the discussion I shall move towards the view that the relation of language to the social system is not simply one of expression, but a more complex natural dialectic in which language actively symbolizes the social system, thus creating as well as being created by it. This, it is hoped, will clarify my interpretation of language within the framework of the culture as an information system, and give some indication of what I understand by the concept of 'language as social semiotic'.

As an underlying conceptual framework, I shall distinguish between (i) *language as system* and (ii) *language as institution*. The salient facts about language as *system* are (a) that it is *stratified* (it is a three-level coding system consisting of a semantics, a lexicogrammar and a phonology) and (b) that its semantic system is organized into *functional* components (ideational, including experiential and logical; interpersonal; textual). The salient fact about language as *institution* is that it is *variable*; there are two kinds of variation, (a) *dialect* (variation according to the *user*), and (b) *register* (variation according to the *use*). This is, of course, an idealized construct; there are no such clearcut boundaries in the facts themselves.

1 Language as institution

1.1 Dialect
Classical dialectology, as developed in Europe, rests on certain implicit assumptions about speakers and speech communities. A speech community is assumed to be a social unit whose members (i) communicate with each other, (ii) speak in a consistent way and (iii) all speak alike. This is obviously, again, an idealized picture; but in the type of settled rural community for which dialect studies were first developed, it is near enough reality to serve as a theoretical norm.

Dialectal variation, in such a model, is essentially variation *between* speech communities. We may recognize some variation also within the community – squire and parson, or landlord and priest, probably speak differently from other people – but this is at the most a minor theme; and we do not envisage variation as something that arises *within* the speech of an individual speaker.

When dialectology moved into an urban setting, with Labov's monumental New York city studies, variation took on a new meaning. Labov showed that, within a typical North American urban community, the speech varies (i) *between* the members according to social class (low to high), and (ii) *within* each member according to 'style scale' (amount of monitoring or attention paid to one's own speech, casual to formal). The effect of each of these factors is quantitative (hence probabilistic in origin), but the picture is clear: when single dialect variables are isolated for intensive investigation, some of them turn out to be socially stratified. The forms of the variable ('variants') are *ranked* in an order such that the 'high' variant is associated with higher social status *or* a more formal context of speech, and the 'low' with lower social status *or* a more casual context of speech.

1.2 Social dialect

As long as dialect variation is geographically determined, it can be explained away: one group stays on this side of the mountain, the other group moves to the other side of the mountain, and they no longer talk to each other. But there are no mountains dividing social classes; the members of different social classes do talk to each other, at least transactionally. What is the explanation of this socially determined variation? How do 'social dialects' arise?

One of the most significant of Labov's findings was the remarkable uniformity shown by people of all social groups in their attutudes towards variation in the speech of others. This uniformity of attitude means that the members are highly sensitive to the social meaning of dialectal variation, a form of sensitivity that is apparently achieved during the crucial years of adolescence, in the age range about 13–18.

We acquire this sensitivity as a part of growing up in society, because dialect variation is functional with respect to the social structure. And this is why it does not disappear. It was confidently predicted in the period after World War II that, with the steadily increasing dominance of the mass media, dialects would disappear and we should soon all be speaking alike. Sure enough, the *regionally* based dialects of rural areas *are* disappearing, as least in industrial societies. But with the urban dialects the opposite has happened: diversity is increasing. We can explain this by showing that the diversity is socially functional. It expresses the structure of society.

It would be a mistake to think of social structure simply in terms of some particular index of social class. The essential characteristic of social structure as we know it is that it is hierarchical; and linguistic variation is what expresses its hierarchical character, whether in terms of age, generation, sex, provenance or any other of its manifestations, including caste and class.

Let us postulate a perfectly homogeneous society, one without any of these forms of social hierarchy. The members of such a society would presumably speak a perfectly homogeneous language, one without any dialectal variation. Now consider the hypothetical antithesis of this: a society split into two conflicting groups, a society and an antisociety. Here we shall expect to find some form of matching linguistic order: two mutually opposed lingustic varieties, a language and an antilanguage. These are, once again, idealized constructs; but phenomena approximating to them have arisen at various times and places. For example, the social conditions of sixteenth-century England generated an antisociety of 'vagabonds', who lived by extorting wealth from the established society; and this society had its anti-language, fragments of which are reported in contemporary documents. The antilanguage is a language of social conflict – of passive resistance or active opposition; but at the same time, like any other language, it is a means of expressing and maintaining the social structure – in this case, the structure of the antisociety.

Most of the time what we find in real life are dialect hierarchies, patterns of dialectal variation in which a 'standard' (representing the power base of society) is opposed by nonstandard varieties (which the members refer to as 'dialects'). The nonstandard dialects may become languages of opposition and protest; periods of explicit class conflict tend to be characterized by the development of such protest languages, sometimes in the form of 'ghetto languages', which are coming closer to the antilanguage end of the scale. Here dialect becomes a means of expression of class consciousness and political awareness. We can recognize a category of 'oppressed languages', languages of groups that are subjected to social or political oppression. It is characteristic of oppressed languages that their speakers tend to excel at verbal contest and verbal display. Meaning is often the most effective form of social action that is available to them.

1.3 Register

Dialects, in the usual sense of that term, are different ways of saying the same thing. In other words, the dialects of a language differ from each other phonologically and lexicogrammatically, but not, in principle, semantically.

In this respect, dialectal variation contrasts with variation of another kind, that of *register*. Registers are ways of saying different things.

Registers differ semantically. They also differ lexicogrammatically, because that is how meanings are *expressed*; but lexicogrammatical differences among registers are, by and large, the automatic consequence of semantic differences. In principle, registers are configurations of meanings that are typically exchanged – that are 'at risk', so to speak – under given conditions of use.

A dialect is 'what you speak' (habitually); this is determined by 'who you are', your regional and/or social place of origin and/or adoption. A register is 'what you are speaking' (at the given time), determined by 'what you are doing', the nature of the ongoing social activity. Whereas dialect variation reflects the social order in the special sense of *the hierarchy of social structure*, register variation also reflects the social order but in the special sense of *the diversity of social processes*. We are not doing the same things all the time; so we speak now in one register, now in another. But the total *range* of the social processes in which any member will typically engage is a function of the structure of society. We each have our own repertory of social actions, reflecting our place at the intersection of a whole complex of social hierarchies. There is a division of labour.

Since the division of labour is *social*, the two kinds of language variety, register and dialect, are closely interconnected. The structure of society determines who, in terms of the various social hierarchies of class, generation, age, sex, provenance and so on, will have access to which aspects of the social process – and hence, to which registers. (In most societies today there is considerable scope for individual discretion, though this has not always been the case.) This means, in turn, that a particular register tends to have a particular dialect associated with it: the registers of bureaucracy, for example, demand the 'standard' (national) dialect, whereas fishing and farming demand rural (local) varieties. Hence the dialect comes to symbolize the register; when we hear a local dialect, we unconsciously switch off a large part of our register range.

In this way, in a typical hierarchical social structure, dialect becomes the means by which a member gains, or is denied, access to certain registers.

So if we say that linguistic structure 'reflects' social structure, we are really assigning to language a role that is too passive. (I am formulating it in this way in order to keep the parallel between the two expressions 'linguistic structure' and 'social structure'. In fact, what is meant is the linguistic *system*; elsewhere I have not used 'structure' in this general sense of the organization of language, but have reserved it for the specialized sense of constituent structure.) Rather we should say that linguistic structure is *the realization of* social structure, actively symbolizing it in a process of mutual creativity. Because it stands as a metaphor for society, language has the property of not only transmitting the social order but also maintaining and potentially modifying it. (This is undoubtedly the explanation of the violent attitudes that under certain social conditions come to be held by one group towards the speech of others. A different set of *vowels* is perceived as the symbol of a different set of *values*, and hence takes on the character of a threat.) Variation in language is the symbolic expression of variation in society: it is created by society, and helps to create society in its turn. Of the two kinds of variation in language, that of dialect expresses the diversity of social structure, that of register expresses the diversity of social process. The interaction of dialect and register in language expresses the interaction of structure and process in society.

2 Language as system

2.1 Function
We have considered how variation in language is socially functional. We must now consider how the linguistic *system* is socially functional.

The most important fact about language as system is its organization *into functional components.*

It is obvious that language is used in a multitude of different ways, for a multitude of different purposes. It is not possible to enumerate them; nor is it necessary to try: there would be no way of preferring one list over another. These various ways of using language are sometimes referred to as 'functions of language'. But to say language has many 'functions', in this sense, is to say no more than that people engage in a variety of social actions – that they do different things together.

We are considering 'functions' in a more fundamental sense, as a necessary element in the interpretation of the linguistic system. The linguistic system is orchestrated into different modes of meaning, and these represent its most general functional orientations. No doubt language has evolved in this way because of the ways in which it is used; the two concepts of function are certainly interrelated. But if we seek to explain the internal workings of language we are forced to take into consideration its external relation to the social context.

The point is a substantive one, and we can approach it from this angle. Considered in relation to the social order, language is a resource, a meaning potential. Formally, language has this property: that it is a coding system *on three levels*. Most coding systems are on two levels: a *content*, and an *expression*: for example, traffic signals, with content 'stop/go' coded into expression 'red/green'. But language has evolved a third, abstract level of *form* intermediate between the two; it consists of content, form and expression, or, in linguistic terms, of semantics, lexicogrammar and phonology. Now, when we analyse the content side, the semantic system and its representation in the grammar, we find that it has an internal organization in which the social functions of language are clearly reflected.

2.2 Functional components
The semantic system is organized into a small number of components – three or four depending on how one looks at them – such that *within* one component there is a high degree of interdependence and mutual constraint, whereas *between* components there is very little: each one is relatively independent of the others.

The components can be identified as follows:

1 ideational (language as reflection), comprising
    (a) experiential
    (b) logical
2 interpersonal (language as action)
3 textual (language as texture, in relation to the environment)

When we say that these components are relatively independent of one another, we mean that the choices that are made within any one component, while strongly affected by other choices within the same component, have no effect, or only a very weak effect, on choices made within the others. For example, given the meaning potential of the interpersonal component, out of the innumerable choices that are available to me I might choose (i) to offer a proposition, (ii) pitched in a particular key (e.g. contradictory-defensive), (iii) with a particular intent towards you (e.g. of convincing you), (iv) with a particular assessment of its probability (e.g. certain), and (v) with indication of a particular attitude (e.g. regretful). Now, all these choices are strongly interdetermining; if we use a network mode of representation, as in systemic theory, they can be seen as complex patterns of internal constraint among the various sub-networks. But they have almost no effect on the ideational meanings, on the *content* of what you are to be convinced of, which may be that the earth is flat, that Mozart was a great musician, or that I am hungry. Similarly, the ideational meanings do not determine the interpersonal ones; but there is a high degree of interdetermination *within* the ideational component: the kind of process I choose to refer to, the participants in the process, the taxonomies of things and properties, the circumstances of time and space, and the natural logic that links all these together.

2.3 Functional components and grammatical structure

So far, I have been looking at the matter from a semantic point of view, taking as the problem the interpretation of the semantic system. Suppose now we take a second approach, from a lexicogrammatical point of view – 'from below', as it were. In the interpretation of the lexicogrammatical system we find ourselves faced with a different problem, namely that of explaining the different *kinds of structure* that are found at this level. Consideration of this problem is beyond our scope here; but when we look into it, we find that the various types of grammatical structure are related to these semantic components in a systematic way. Each kind of meaning tends to be realized as a particular kind of structure. Hence in the encoding of a text each component of meaning makes its contribution to the structural output; but it is a contribution which has on it the stamp of that particular mode of meaning. We would summarize this as follows (see Halliday 1977):

Semantic component	Type of grammatical structure by which typically realized
1 ideational:	
(a) experiential	constituent (segmental)
(b) logical	recursive
2 interpersonal	prosodic
3 textual	culminative

2.4 Functional components and social context

Thirdly, we may approach the question 'from above', from the perspective of language and the social order – at what I have called the 'social semiotic' level. When we come to investigate the relation of language to social context we find that the functional components of the semantic system once again provide the key. We saw that they were related to the different types of grammatical structure. There is also a systematic relationship between them and the semiotic structure of the speech situation. It is this, in part, that validates the notion of a speech situation.

Let us assume that the social system (or the 'culture') can be represented as a construction of meanings – as a semiotic system. The meanings that constitute the social system are exchanged through a variety of modes or channels, of which language is one; but not, of course, the only one – there are many other semiotic modes besides. Given this social-semiotic perspective, a *social context* (or 'situation', in the terms of situation theory) is a temporary construct or instantiation of meanings from the social system. A social context is a semiotic structure which we may interpret in terms of three variables: a 'field' of social process (what is going on), a 'tenor' of social relationships (who are taking part) and a 'mode' of symbolic interaction (how are the meanings exchanged). If we are focusing on language, this last category of 'mode' refers to what part the language is playing in the situation under consideration.

As said above, these components of the context are systematically related to the components of the semantic system; and once again, given that the context is a semiotic construct, this relation can be seen as one of realization. The meanings that constitute the social context are *realized* through selections in the meaning potential of language. To summarize:

Component of social context	Functional-semantic component through which typically realized
1 field (social process)	experiential
2 tenor (social relationship)	interpersonal
3 mode (symbolic mode)	textual

The linguistic system, in other words, is organized in such a way that the social context is predictive of the text. This is what makes it possible for a member to make the necessary predictions about the meanings that are being exchanged in any situation which he encounters. If we drop in on a gathering, we are able to tune in very quickly, because we size up the field, tenor and mode of the situation and at once form an idea of what is likely to be being meant. In this way we know what semantic configurations – what register – will probably be required if we are to take part. If we did not do this, there would be no communication, since only a part of the meanings we have to understand are explicitly realized in the wordings. The rest are unrealized; they are left out – or rather (a more satisfactory metaphor) they are out of focus. We succeed in the exchange of meanings because we have access to the semiotic structure of the situation from other sources.

3 Language as social semiotic

3.1 Variation and social meaning

The distinction between language as system and language as institution is an important one for the investigation of problems of language and society. But these are really two aspects of a more general set of phenomena, and in any interpretation of the 'sociolinguistic order' we need to bring them together again.

A significant step in this direction is taken by variation theory. We have said that a feature of language as *institution* is that it is variable: different groups of speakers, or the same speakers in different task-roles, use different dialects or registers. But this is not to imply that there is no variation in the *system*. Some linguists would deny this, and would explain all variation institutionally. Others (myself among them) would argue that this is to make too rigid a distinction between the system and the institution, and would contend that a major achievement of social dialectology has been to show that dialect-like variation is a normal feature of the speech of the individual, at least in some but possibly in all communities. At certain contexts in the language a speaker will select, with a certain probability, one among a small set of variants all of which are equivalent in the sense that they are alternative realizations of the same higher-level configuration. The conditions determining this probability may be linguistic or social or some combination of the two. To know the probability of a particular speaker pronouncing a certain variant (say [t], glottal stop or zero) at a certain point in the speech chain (say word-final), we take the product of the conditioning effects of a set of variables such as: is the word lexical or structural? does the following word begin with a vowel? is the phrase thematic? is the speaker angry? and is his father a member of the working class? (This is, of course, a caricature, but it gives a fair representation of the way these things are.)

So variation, which we first recognize as a property of language as institution (in the form of variation *between* speakers, of a dialectal kind), begins to appear as an extension of variation which is a property of the system. A 'dialect' is then just a sum of variants having a strong tendency to cooccur. In this perspective, dialectal variation is made out to be not so much a consequence of the social structure as an outcome of the inherent nature of language itself.

But this is one-sided. In the last analysis, the linguistic system is the product of the social system; and seen from that angle, dialect-like variation *within* an individual is a special case of variation *between* individuals, not the other way round. The significant point, however, is that there is no sharp line between this externally conditioned, so-called 'sociolinguistic', variation that is found in the speech of an individual *because* it is a property of language as institution, and the purely internally conditioned variation that occurs within a particular part of the linguistic system (e.g. morpho-phonemic alternation). Conditioning environments may be of any kind; there is ultimately no discontinuity between such apparently diverse phenomena as (i) select [ʔ] not [t] before a consonant and (ii) select [ʔ] not [t] before a king. This explains how it comes about that all variation is potentially meaningful; any set of alternants may (but need not) become the bearer of social information and social value.

3.2 Language and social reality

Above and beyond 'language as system' and 'language as institution' lies the more general, unifying concept that I have labelled 'language as social semiotic': language in the context of the culture as a semiotic system.

Consider the way a child constructs his social reality. Through language as system – its organization into levels of coding and functional components – he builds up a model of the exchange of meanings, and learns to construe the interpersonal relationships, the experiential phenomena, the forms of natural logic and the modes of symbolic interaction into coherent patterns of social context. He does this very young; this is in fact what makes it possible for him to learn the language successfully – the two processes go hand in hand.

Through language as institution – its variation into dialects and registers – he builds up a model of the social system. This follows a little way behind his learning of grammar and semantics (compare the interesting suggestion by Sankoff (1974) that some patterns at first learnt as categorical are later modified to become variable), though it is essentially part of a single unitary process of language development. In broadest terms, from dialectal variation he learns to construe the patterns of social hierarchy, and from variation of the 'register' kind he gains an insight into the structure of knowledge.

So language, while it represents reality *referentially*, through its words and structures, also represents reality *metaphorically* through its own internal and external form. (1) The functional organization of the semantics symbolizes the structure of human interaction (the semiotics of social contexts, as we expressed it earlier). (2) Dialectal and 'diatypic' (register) variation symbolize respectively the structure of society and the structure of human knowledge.

But as language becomes a metaphor of reality, so by the same process reality becomes a metaphor of language. Since reality is a social construct, it can be constructed only through an exchange of meanings. Hence meanings are seen as constitutive of reality. This, at least, is the natural conclusion for the present era, when the exchange of information tends to replace the exchange of goods-and-services as the primary mode of social action. With a sociological linguistics we should be able to stand back from this perspective, and arrive at an interpretation of language through understanding its place in the long-term evolution of the social system.

3.3 Methodological considerations

It has been customary among linguists in recent years to represent language in terms of rules.

In investigating language and the social system, it is important to transcend this limitation and to interpret language not as a set of rules but as a *resource*. I have used the term 'meaning potential' to characterize language in this way.

When we focus attention on the processes of human interaction, we are seeing this meaning potential at work. In the microsemiotic encounters of daily life, we find people making creative use of their resources of meaning, and continously modifying these resources in the process.

Hence in the interpretation of language, the organizing concept that we need is not structure but *system*. Most recent linguistics has been structure-bound (since structure is what is described by rules). With the notion of system we can represent language as a resource, in terms of the choices that are available, the interconnection of these choices, and the conditions affecting their access. We can then relate these choices to recognizable and significant social contexts, using sociosemantic networks; and investigate questions such as the influence of various social factors on the meanings exchanged by parents and children. The data are the observed facts of 'text-in-situation': what people say in real life, not discounting what they think they might say and what they think they ought to say. (Or rather, what they *mean*, since saying is only one way of meaning.) In order to interpret what is observed, however, we have to relate it to the system: (i) to the linguistic system, which it then helps to explain, and (ii) to the social context, and through that to the social system.

After a period of intensive study of language as an idealized philosophical construct, linguists have come round to taking account of the fact that people talk to each other. In order to solve purely internal problems of its own history and structure, language has had to be taken out of its glass case, dusted, and put back in a living environment – into a 'context of situation', in Malinowski's term. But it is one thing to have a 'socio-' (that is, real life) component in the explanation of the facts of language. It is quite another thing to seek explanations that relate the linguistic system to the social system, and so work towards some general theory of language and social structure.

V
Sociolinguistics and education

11

Sociolinguistic aspects of mathematical education

1 The development of languages

1.1 The notion of a 'developed' language
Perhaps the most remarkable aspect of human language is the range of purposes it serves, the variety of different things that people make language do for them. Casual interaction in home and family, instruction of children, activities of production and distribution like building and marketing, and more specialized functions such as those of religion, literature, law and government – all these may readily be covered by one person in one day's talk.

We can define a 'developed' language as one that is used freely in all the functions that language serves in the society in question. Correspondingly an 'undeveloped' language would be one that serves only some of these functions, but not all. This is to interpret language development as a functional concept, one which relates to the role of a language in the society in which it is spoken.

In the Caribbean island of Sint Maarten, the mother tongue of the inhabitants is English. Education and administration, however, take place in Dutch; English is not normally used in these contexts. In Sint Maarten, English is an undeveloped language. The islanders find it hard to conceive of serious intellectual and administrative processes taking place in English. They are, of course, perfectly well aware that English is used in all these functions in Britain, the USA and elsewhere. But they cannot accept that the homely English that they themselves speak (although dialectally it is of a quite 'standard' type that is readily understood by speakers from outside) is the same language as English in its national or international guise.

In the same way, English in medieval England was not a developed language, since many of the social functions of language in the community could be performed only in Latin or in French.

Not unnaturally, the members of a society tend to attach social value to their languages according to the degree of their development. A language that is 'developed', being used in all the functions that language serves in the society, tends to have a higher status, while an undeveloped language is accorded a much lower standing, even by those who speak it as their mother tongue.

1.2 The notion of a register

The notion of 'developing a language' means, therefore, adding to its range of social functions. This is achieved by developing new registers.

A register is a set of meanings that is appropriate to a particular function of language, together with the words and structures which express these meanings. We can refer to a 'mathematics register', in the sense of the meanings that belong to the language of mathematics (the mathematical use of natural language, that is: not mathematics itself), and that a language must express if it is being used for mathematical purposes.

Every language embodies some mathematical meanings in its semantic structure – ways of counting, measuring, classifying and so on. These are not by themselves sufficient to form the natural language component of mathematics in its modern disciplinary sense, or to serve the needs of mathematics education in secondary schools and colleges. But they will serve as a point of departure for the initial learning of mathematical concepts, especially if the teaching is made relevant to the social background of the learner. The development of a register of mathematics is in the last resort a matter of degree.

It is the meanings, including the styles of meaning and modes of argument, that constitute a register, rather than the words and structures as such. In order to express new meanings, it may be necessary to invent new words; but there are many different ways in which a language can add new meanings, and inventing words is only one of them. We should not think of a mathematical register as consisting solely of terminology, or of the development of a register as simply a process of adding new words.

1.3 Development of a register of mathematics

Inevitably the development of a new register of mathematics will involve the introduction of new 'thing-names': ways of referring to new objects or new processes, properties, functions and relations. There are various ways in which this can be done.

(i) Reinterpreting existing words. Examples from mathematical English are: *set*, *point*, *field*, *row*, *column*, *weight*, *stand for*, *sum*, *move through*, *even* (number), *random*.

(ii) Creating new words out of native word stock. This process has not played a very great part in the creation of technical registers in English (an early example of it is *clockwise*), but recently it has come into favour with words like *shortfall*, *feedback*, *output*.

(iii) Borrowing words from another language. This has been the method most favoured in technical English. Mathematics examples include *degree*, *series*, *exceed*, *subtract*, *multiply*, *invert*, *infinite*, *probable*.

(iv) 'Calquing': creating new words in imitation of another language. This is rare in modern English, though it is a regular feature of many languages; it was used in Old English to render Christian terms from Latin, e.g. *almighty* calqued on *omnipotens*. (Latin *omnipotens* is made up of *omni-* meaning 'all' and *potens* meaning 'mighty'; on this model was coined the English word *all-mighty*, now spelt *almighty*.)

(v) Inventing totally new words. This hardly ever happens. About the only English example is *gas*, a word coined out of nowhere by a Dutch chemist in the early eighteenth century.

(vi) Creating 'locutions'. There is no clear line between locutions, in the sense of phrases or larger structures, and compound words. Expressions like *right-angled triangle*, *square on the hypotenuse*, *lowest common multiple* are examples of technical terms in mathematics English that are to be classed as locutions rather than compound words.

vii Creating new words out of non-native word stock. This is now the most typical procedure in contemporary European languages for the creation of new technical terms. Words like *parabola*, *denominator*, *binomial*, *coefficient*, *thermodynamic*, *permutation*, *approximation*, *denumerable*, *asymptotic*, *figurate*, are not borrowed from Greek and Latin – they did not exist in these languages. They are made up in English (and in French, Russian and other languages) out of elements of the Greek and Latin word stock.

Every language creates new thing-names; but not all languages do so in the same way. Some languages (such as English and Japanese) favour borrowing; others (such as Chinese) favour calquing. But all languages have more than one mode of word-creation; often different modes are adopted for different purposes – for example, one method may be typical for technical words and another for nontechnical. There is no reason to say that one way is better than another; but it is important to find out how the speakers of a particular language in fact set about creating new terms when faced with the necessity of doing so. The Indian linguist Krishnamurthi (1962) has studied how Telugu-speaking communities of farmers, fishermen and textile workers, when confronted by new machines and new processes, made up the terms which were necessary for talking about them.

Societies are not static, and changes in material and social conditions lead to new meanings being exchanged. The most important thing about vocabulary creation by natural processes is that it is open-ended; more words can always be added. There is no limit to the number of words in a language, and there are always some registers which are expanding. Language developers have the special responsibility of creating new elements of the vocabulary which will not only be adequate in themselves but which will also point the way to the creation of others.

1.4 Structural aspects

But the introduction of new vocabulary is not the only aspect of the development of a register. Registers such as those of mathematics, or of science and technology, also involve new styles of meaning, ways of developing an argument, and of combining existing elements into new combinations.

Sometimes these processes demand new structures, and there are instances of structural innovation taking place as part of the development of a scientific register. For the most part, however, development takes place not through the creation of entirely new structures (a thing that is extremely difficult to do deliberately) but through the bringing into prominence of structures which already existed but were rather specialised or rare. Examples of this phenomenon from English can be seen in expressions like 'signal-to-noise ratio', 'the sum of the series to n terms', 'the same number of mistakes plus or minus', 'each term is one greater than the term which precedes it', 'a set of terms each of which stands in a constant mathematical relationship to that which precedes it'. We can compare these with new forms of everyday expression such as 'it was a non-event' (meaning 'nothing significant happened'), which are derived from technical registers although used in nontechnical contexts.

There is no sharp dividing line, in language, between the vocabulary and the grammar. What is expressed in one language by the choice of words may be expressed in another language (or in the same language on another occasion) by the choice of structure. The 'open-endedness' referred to earlier is a property of the lexicogrammar as a whole. There are indefinitely many meanings, and combinations of meanings, to be expressed in one way or another through the medium of the words and structures of a language; and more can always be added. This is a reflection of the total potential that every language has, each in its own way.

In the past, language development has taken place slowly, by more or less natural processes ('more or less' natural because they are, after all, the effect of social processes) taking place over a long period. It took English three or four hundred years to develop its registers of mathematics, science and technology, and they are still developing. Today, however, it is not enough for a language to move in this leisurely fashion; the process has to be speeded up. Developments that took centuries in English and French are expected to happen in ten years, or one year, or sometimes one month. This requires a high degree of planned language development. Not everyone involved in this work is always aware of the wide range of different resources by means of which language can create new meanings, or of how the language in which he himself is working has done so in the past. But there is, now, a more general understanding of the fact that *all* human languages have the potential of being developed for *all* the purposes that human society and the human brain can conceive.

2 Differences and 'distance' between languages

2.1 Languages differ in the meanings they emphasize
The principle just referred to is of fundamental importance: namely that all languages have the same potential for development as vehicles for mathematics, science and technology, or indeed for anything else.

This does not imply that all languages are identical in the meanings they express, or that 'language development' is a matter of plugging holes, of adding a fixed set of new meanings to an inventory that is already there. Languages differ in their meanings, just as they do in their words and structures and in their sounds; and the differences are found both in the basic units (of meaning, form and sound) and in the way these units are combined.

There are numerous examples of differences in meaning between languages; the ones most frequently cited tend to come from certain particular semantic areas, such as those of colour and kinship. It is important to stress, therefore, that these do not imply different modes of perception or of thought. One of the most variable apects of semantics is colour; there are innumerable ways of splitting up the colour spectrum. The fact that English has one single word *blue* covering the whole range of sky blue, royal blue, peacock blue, midnight blue, indigo, etc. does not mean that an English child cannot distinguish these colours. He may not have names for them, but that is an entirely different matter. The same applies to any other language. If a language is said 'not to distinguish between green and blue', this merely means that it has a colour term covering at least some part of the range of colour that is referred to in English by 'green' and 'blue'. It does not mean that the speakers of this language have a different colour vision.

Similarly, English has only one word 'cousin', covering a great variety of kinsfolk: mother's or father's, sister's or brother's, daughter or son, to name only the closest. This does not mean a speaker of English cannot tell his relatives apart. It means simply that the semantics of kinship, which differs widely from language to language, has little to do with biological relationships. It comes closer to reflecting the social structure, but still not with exact correspondence.

Many languages have the same word for 'yesterday' and 'tomorrow'. This does not mean that their speakers cannot distinguish between what has already happened and what is still to come.

This may be summarized as follows: languages have different patterns of meaning – different 'semantic systems', in the terminology of linguistics. These are significant for the ways their speakers interact with one another; not in the sense that they determine the ways in which the members of the community *perceive* the world around them, but in the sense that they determine what the members of the community *attend to*. Each language has its own characteristic modes of meaning, things which it brings into prominence, which it associates with one another, and which it *has to* express (under specifiable conditions) where in another language they are merely optional extras. For example, some languages (of which English is one) demand attention to the time at which an event takes place, whether it is past, present or future relative to some point of reference (initially the moment of speaking), whereas other languages (of which Chinese is one) are concerned with the completion of the event and with whether its significance lies in itself or in its consequences. Each language is perfectly capable of verbalizing the time system of the other type, but the system does not *require* it, and to do so often involves circumlocutions and relatively unusual modes of expression. Hence although speakers of both types of language have the same *perception* of events, they pay *attention* to different characteristics of them and so build up a rather different framework for the systematization of experience.

The importance of this point is that we can ask *which* mathematical ideas may be most easily conveyed when the medium of mathematics education is this or that particular language. Concepts of number, of taxonomy, of volume, weight and density, of sets and series, and so on, may be variously highlighted in the semantics of different languages, and one of the important areas of investigation in any language is finding out how best to exploit its semantic resources as a base for the teaching of mathematics.

2.2 Some remarks about 'distance'

The concept of language 'distance' – the notion of how far apart any pair of languages is said to be – depends partly on linguistic considerations ('language as system') and partly on sociolinguistic ones ('language as institution'). Sociolinguistically, in terms of status and functions, we can recognize a series beginning with the neighbourhood language, through local, regional and national languages, to an international language, and it is obvious that the greatest sociolinguistic distance is that which separates a neighbourhood language from an international one.

Linguistically, the 'distance' is harder to measure; it is a concept that up to the present has remained largely intuitive, although almost universally recognized. There is a general principle whereby languages that belong to the same cultural region tend to be alike in the meanings (and often also in the sounds) they employ. This similarity is not dependent on any historical, genetic relationship between the languages concerned. East Africa, India and Southeast Asia all provide examples of the phenomenon, which is known as 'areal affinity'.

The significance of this for educators is that it is generally easier to transfer from the mother tongue to a language from the same culture area than to one that is culturally very remote, since the former is likely to be much closer in its ways of meaning. (It may also be closer in its structures, but that is by no means so generally the case.) A person is more likely to attain a high degree of competence in a language areally related to his mother tongue than in one that does not share such affinity.

2.3 The uniqueness of the mother tongue

Opinions differ regarding the uniqueness of the mother tongue. It is certainly true that many people acquire a second and even a third or fourth language to a level of competence that is indistinguishable from that attained in their mother tongue, particularly when these languages are from the same culture area.

On the other hand, it is true that for very many people, even those who regularly use more than one language, no language ever completely replaces the mother tongue. Certain kinds of ability seem to be particularly difficult to acquire in a second language. Among these, the following are perhaps most important in an educational context:

(i) Saying the same thing in different ways. One of the great resources of a teacher is to be able to alter the wording of what he says while keeping the meaning as close as possible. Very often a pupil who has found it difficult to grasp a point will see it readily when it is expressed in a different way. All too often the teacher who is forced to teach in a language other than his mother tongue has at his command only one way of saying something.

(ii) Hesitating, and saying nothing very much. Hesitating is a way of keeping the channel of communication open while thinking what to say next; closely related to it is what we might call 'waffling' (if this may be allowed to function as a technical term), which is keeping the words going while saying practically nothing. Both of these have important social functions, not least in the classroom; they are remarkably difficult to achieve in a second language.

(iii) Predicting what the other person is going to say. This is very much easier in one's own language; yet it is an essential of successful learning that the pupil should at any given moment be able to predict a large part of what the teacher is going to say next. The fact that people are able to communicate and exchange meanings at all depends on this ability.

(iv) Adding new verbal skills (learning new words and new meanings) while talking and listening. All the time, as we talk and listen, we are hearing new meanings, things that we have never heard before. In our mother tongue, we process these new elements all the time, without thinking. In a second language, it is often very difficult to continue interacting (talking and listening) while at the same time learning new things; each of these types of activity tends to demand the whole of one's attention.

It is not being suggested that we can never learn to do these things in a second language. Plenty of people the world over do so with complete success. Nevertheless there are vast numbers of children being educated through the medium of a second language – and of teachers trying to teach them – who have not mastered these essential abilities.

3 The relation between mathematics and natural language

3.1 Mathematical concepts and their names
How do we set about learning mathematical concepts and their names? A child begins forming mathematical concepts very early in life. Here is an illustration from one English-speaking child, Nigel. At 20 months Nigel had learnt the number-name *two*, which he could use quite correctly in expressions such as 'two books', 'two cars' and so on.

One day, he held up a toy bus in one hand and a toy train in the other. 'Two chuffa,' he said hopefully, using his baby word for train. It didn't seem quite right, so he tried again. 'Two ... two ... two ...' he went on, trying to find the right words. But the problem was beyond him, so he gave up. This was an early attempt at classifying, at finding a higher class to which both the objects belonged. It failed, frustrated by the English language, which has no everyday word for the class of wheeled vehicles; but the fact that he had attempted it, and realized he had failed, showed that he had grasped the essential principle.

He had a posting box, with a number of holes in the lid to each of which corresponded a piece of a particular shape – star, triangle, circle, and so on. He soon learnt to post them all correctly, and then demanded names for all the shapes. He was not satisfied until he had names for each of them.

At his second birthday he was given a wooden train and a set of grooved pieces, some straight and some curved, which could be fitted together to make a railway track. When he had learnt to fit them together, he experimented with various layouts, which gradually increased in complexity over the next two years. For these figures, too, he demanded names, but finding that in this case there were none (or none known to his parents) he began inventing the names for himself. These names had forms such as 'cruse-way', 'shockle-way', 'dee-way' and the like, showing that he had mastered one of the principles on which names are constructed in English.

These examples show that a child has a natural tendency to organize his environment in systematic ways (which is essentially a mathematical operation), and to make use of language for doing so, even if he has to create the necessary language for himself. Of course, children differ considerably in what aspects of their environment interest them most, and it is obvious that some children are at an advantage because of the wide range of experience that is available to them. But most children grow up in environments in which there is plenty for their brains to work on, and it would be a mistake to suppose that a rural life with few manmade artefacts provides no basis for systematic learning. For example, the environment may contain few simple geometric shapes, but judging distance and terrain may be extremely important.

What matters most to a child is how much talking goes on around him, and how much he is allowed and encouraged to join in. There is strong evidence that the more adults talk to a child and listen to him and answer his questions, the more quickly and effectively he is able to learn.

3.2 Different levels of technicality

Robert Morris (1975) remarked that 'the language of modern mathematics is borrowed to a very large extent from the commonplace language of ordinary folk'; and it is true that, in English at least, modern mathematics has tended to redefine simple words rather than coining new ones for its technical terms. This in fact is part of the difficulty; the fact that a concept such as 'set' has a precise mathematical definition may be obscured by the simplicity of the word itself.

Be that as it may, 'modern' mathematics does make greater demands on language than 'traditional', partly because it is relatively non-numerical, but perhaps even more because its relations with other aspects of life are emphasized more explicitly, whereas in earlier days, mathematics tended to remain quite separate from the rest of a child's experience.

However, it would be a mistake to suppose that the language of mathematics (by which is meant the mathematical register, that form of natural language used in mathematics, rather than mathematical symbolism) is entirely impersonal, formal and exact. On the contrary, it has a great deal of metaphor and even poetry in it, and it is precisely here that the difficulties often reside. Expressions such as 'four from six leaves two' represent essentially concrete modes of meaning that take on a metaphorical guise when used to express abstract, formal relations (i.e. when interpreted as '6 − 4 = 2').

There are many different levels of technicality within mathematical language. Mathematical and scientific language has however a number of features which are *not* in themselves technical, but which relate to the nature of the subject-matter and the activities associated with it. Mathematical and scientific English, for example, shows a high degree of nominalization. Consider the sentence 'The conversion of hydrogen to helium in the interiors of stars is the source of energy for their immense output of light and heat.' This could be reworded as 'Inside stars hydrogen is converted into helium, and from this (process? result?) they get the energy to put out an immense amount of light and heat.' The second version corresponds more closely to modes of expression in a number of other languages. It is not easy to say whether there is any *general* reason, independent of which language is being used, why mathematical and scientific registers should prefer nominal modes of expression. In English, at any rate, there are good reasons for it, despite the fact that teachers of English tend to object to it (see Halliday 1967a and c). In English, locutions with nominals in them have a greater semantic and syntactic potential for different emphases and different information structures, e.g. 'It is the conversion of hydrogen to helium that is . . ', 'What the conversion of hydrogen to helium does is to . . .', and so on. At the same time, nominalization does sometimes obscure ambiguities; for example, in the above sentence it is not clear whether it is the conversion *process*, or the helium that *results* from that process, that provides the energy. The non-nominalized form of the sentence forces us to make this explicit.

3.3 Language is a natural human creation

Verbalizing does not necessarily imply naming. One may use language to introduce a concept, or to help children towards an understanding of it, without at any time in the process referring to the concept by name.

We are readily aware that there is no need to *name* a concept at the outset. This does not mean that we keep silent while manipulating objects or doing whatever else is being done to facilitate learning. On the contrary, the more *informal* talk goes on between teacher and learner *around* the concept, relating to it obliquely through all the modes of learning that are available in the context, the more help the learner is getting in mastering it.

Language, unlike mathematics, is not clearcut or precise. It is a natural human creation, and, like many other natural human creations, it is inherently messy. Anyone who formalizes natural language does so at the cost of idealizing it to such an extent that it is hardly recognizable as language any more, and bears little likeness to the way people actually interact with one another by talking.

The consequence of this is that a term for a mathematical concept may also exist as an element in natural language, and so carry with it the whole semantic load that this implies. This is one of the difficulties faced by those who are creating mathematical terminology in a language not previously used for formal mathematical purposes. The process of word *creation* can be speeded up by planning and by the work of commissions on terminology. By contrast, the process by which layers of meaning *accrue* is a natural process and it takes time. Only gradually as the new words become familiar, and come to be used in broader and broader ranges of verbal environments – in new structures, and particularly in new collocations, and new arguments – will they be fully domesticated in the language, and acquire a wide range of associations. Eventually they will acquire the meanings that are 'in the air', and this will be the case even for speakers of that language who do not know their exact meanings as technical terms.

4 Postscript

Our experience of reality is never neutral. Observing means interpreting; experience is interpreted through the patterns of knowledge and the value systems that are embodied in cultures and in languages.

To the extent that any field of experience is pattern-free and value-free, to that extent it must seem odd, and unlike other forms of experience. Presumably mathematics approaches as closely to this point as we ever get. Even mathematical reality, however, is far from being free of superimposed patterns and values. On the one hand, the concepts of organized mathematics are mediated through the mathematical meanings that are built into the everyday language, meanings which are in turn ultimately derived from the actions and events of daily life. On the other hand, mathematical idealizations are themselves the bearers of social value (the two senses of 'ideal' are closely related); moreover, mathematics involves talk, and it is impossible to talk about things without conveying attitudes and interpersonal judgements.

Perhaps for these reasons there is a feeling shared by many teachers, and others concerned with education, that learning ought to be made less dependent on language; and teachers of mathematics, in particular, emphasise the importance of learning through concrete operations on objects. This is a very positive move. At the same time, there is no point in trying to eliminate language from the learning process altogether. Rather than engage in any such vain attempt, we should seek equally positive ways of advancing those aspects of the learning process which are, essentially, linguistic. We need not deplore the tendency of language to impose patterns and values on reality; on the contrary, it is a tendency that a learner can put to his advantage, once he, and his teachers, are aware of how language functions (and how his particular language functions) in these respects.

Table 5 presents a 'checklist' of possible sources of linguistic difficulty facing a learner of mathematics. The entries under each heading can be seen either as possible difficulties for the learner, or as factors of concern to the educator. The headings under 'linguistic' are the different *kinds* of possible misunderstanding by a learner; they are also the components of the mathematical register. A language that is being used for mathematical purposes has to develop the appropriate meanings, together with the words and structures to express them, and also to express the meanings that are represented in the mathematical notation. No language is inherently 'more mathematical' than any other. All languages have the potential of developing mathematical registers; but since languages differ in their meanings, and in their structure and vocabulary, they may also differ in their paths towards mathematics, and in the ways in which mathematical concepts can most effectively be taught.

Table 5 Linguistic factors in mathematical education

---

1 *Linguistic ('language as system')*
  a meanings ('semantics'):
    i arguments
    ii single items
  b words and structures ('lexicogrammar'):
    i sentence and phrase structure ('syntax')
    ii words ('vocabulary')
    iii word structures ('morphology')
  c symbols: degree and kind of 'fit' between verbal expression and mathematical notation

2 *Sociolinguistics ('language as institution')*
  a functional status of language being used as medium of education:
    i general: how widely used in the society in question
    ii special: how far mathematical registers are developed
  b if language being used is *other than* mother tongue, whether:
    i international language
    ii national language
    iii regional language
    iv standard dialect, then:
  c 'distance' from mother tongue:
    i in functions and status
    ii in world view and meaning styles
    iii in internal structure

12

Breakthrough to literacy:
Foreword to the American edition*

Since the programme that produced *Breakthrough to literacy* was called 'Programme in Linguistics and English Teaching', and since some of us in it were linguists, it was not unreasonable to assume that what we were trying to develop there was a 'linguistic approach'. We would accept this label if we could interpret it to mean what we ourselves understand by a linguistic approach. But there have been several 'linguistic approaches' to reading and writing that are so different from what we have in mind that we hesitate to subscribe to this designation. In what sense, then, is *Breakthrough* 'linguistic' in its conception? It is linguistic in the sense that it is founded on an understanding and interpretation of what language is and what part it plays in our lives: on the notion of language as a system, and how it works – or, to put the same thing in another way, of language as a 'meaning potential', a resource that men and women develop in the course of, and for the purpose of, significant and meaningful interaction with one another. This enables us to place language in a perspective, a perspective that we can share with a child. A child who is learning his mother tongue is learning how to mean. He is building up a potential, a potential for symbolic action which in large measure is going to determine the kind of life he leads.

The *Breakthrough* approach is 'linguistic', then, not in the sense that it derives from this or that particular conception of linguistics – a subject whose academic boundaries have tended to be drawn much too narowly for most educational purposes – but in the sense that it is based on a serious consideration of the nature and functions of language. We start from what children can do with language, which is already a great deal by the time they come to school; and from what they cannot yet do but are learning to do with language, as well as what they will need to learn to do with it in order to succeed in school and in life.

We all use language for many different purposes, in a wide variety of contexts. And some of these purposes are such that they cannot be adequately served by language in its spoken form; they need writing. The impetus for reading and writing is a functional one, just as was the impetus for learning to speak and listen in the first place. We learn to speak because we want to do things that we cannot do otherwise; and we learn to read and write for the same reason. This does not mean simply attending to the

* David Mackay, Brian Thompson and Pamela Schaub, *Breakthrough to literacy* (Glendale, California 1973).

practical things of life, like getting fed and clothed and amused. Human beings are interested in the world around them not only as a source of material satisfaction but also as something to explore, reflect on and understand – and to sing about and celebrate in story and in rhyme. For this they need to talk, and sooner or later to write.

This was true in the history of the human race, and it is true also in the history of the individual. From his first year of life a child is learning to speak, and to understand others speaking; he is already beginning to exchange meanings with the people around him. There comes a time when what he wants to be able to do with language, the acts of meaning he wants to perform, can no longer be achieved by speaking and listening alone; and from this point on, reading and writing will make sense to him. But if the reading and writing are unrelated to what he wants to mean, to the functional demands that he is coming to make of language, then they will make very little sense to him. They will remain, as they do for so many children, isolated and meaningless exercises. If we want to talk about 'reading readiness', we should really interpret it in these social-functional terms. A child is 'ready' for the written medium when he begins to use language in the ecological settings to which writing is appropriate.

There are some people who say that books are on the way out, and that the written language is no longer important. As this stands they are certainly wrong; but they are making a valid point. The spoken language is once more coming into its own, assuming once again in our own society the honourable place that it had in all of human history until the European renaissance, and that in many societies it has never lost. This is slowly coming to be reflected in educational thinking and practice; teachers are more and more willing to take the spoken language seriously. But the changes that are taking place, far from relegating the written language to a position of unimportance, are providing a new and healthy environment for the written language to function in. It is a rather different environment from that in which many of us ourselves learnt to read and write, and we have to be prepared to reappraise the significance of reading and writing in a world of television, tape recorders and a resurgence of oral literature. But these things do not destroy the need for reading and writing; rather they create new contexts for them, with new dimensions of significance. Illiteracy is still a form of servitude – because our total demands on language, both spoken and written, go on increasing. It is not at all surprising that developing countries give top priority to the attainment of literacy among children and adults.

For the same reason it is also not surprising, when one thinks about it, that experience with *Breakthrough* has demonstrated very clearly the value of our continued insistence on seeing reading and writing in the broader context of the learning of language as a whole. There is still a tendency to isolate reading and writing as if they had nothing to do with the mother tongue; as if they were totally separate skills for which the child had no relevant prior knowledge. But the most important thing about written language is that it is language; and the most important thing about written

English is that it is English. It is when reading and writing become divorced from the rest of the child's language experience, and his language-learning experience, that they become empty and meaningless chores.

I am often asked by teachers if it is possible to give a succinct account of the essential nature of language in terms that are truly relevant to the educational process. It is not easy to do this, because it means departing very radically from the images of language that are presented in our schoolbooks and in the classroom: not only from the older image, which was focused on the marginalia of language and gave about as good a picture of what language is really like as a book of etiquette would give of what life is really like, but also from the newer one, which is focused on the mechanisms of language and reduces it to a set of formal operations. We have to build up an image of language which enables us to look at how people actually do communicate with one another, and how they are all the time exchanging meanings and interacting in meaningful ways. To a certain extent each one of us has to do this for himself by his own efforts, and by reference to his own personal experience. But we can get some help, perhaps, from the notions about language that we unconsciously subscribe to because they are embedded in the informal ways in which we talk about it, which is something we do all the time.

We are always talking about talking, saying things like 'I didn't mean that', 'You haven't answered my question' and 'Were those his exact words?'; and such 'language about language' embodies volumes of insights into the nature and function of language. These insights, which are known in the trade as 'folk linguistics', are absorbed at an unconscious level in the course of learning the language and learning the culture. Folk linguistic notions, like other folk ideas enshrined in our semantic system, can be wildly wrong. But they are often right, and sometimes contain significant truths which in our more contrived wisdom we have lost sight of.

If we examine the preconceptions that are implicit in our everyday talk about language we get a picture that is in some respects surprisingly accurate, and in ways that are quite relevant to the processes of education. Think of the concept that is expressed by the word to *mean*, in its ordinary everyday use. It can be used of people, and of language: 'what does he mean?', 'what does that notice mean?'. But it cannot be used of most *things*. We do not ask 'what does your watch mean?' – even though we readily ask 'what does your watch say?'. The formal properties of a symbolic system are not specifically human, but the semantic ones are. Only people can mean. But they can do it in other ways than through language, for example by dancing or painting; and they can invest symbols with meanings, as in 'red means stop'. On the other hand, even people do not mean as a conscious act, so there is no usual way of expressing an *intention* to mean; we say 'what shall I say?', but not 'what shall I mean?'.

Now our meanings are encoded, or in folk terminology 'expressed', in what we refer to as 'wordings'. A wording, translated into linguistic terms, is a sentence structure or clause structure or some other grammatical structure with lexical items ('words') occupying the functional roles that that structure defines. And we are well aware, not because we are linguists but because we are people who have language, that this encoding of meanings in wordings is not just a simple matching process. You can 'keep the meaning but change the wording' – although, in fact, you never quite 'keep the meaning' when you do this. What happens is that you keep one kind of meaning, but vary another.

The wording is still not what we hear; it has to be encoded all over again. But this time there are two possible codes, a phonic and a graphic, or a spoken and a written. Again there is a rich folk linguistic terminology: sounds and letters, pronouncing and spelling (in traditional English linguistics, the word *letter* meant 'speech sound' as well as 'letter'). 'How do you pronounce it?' and 'how do you spell it?' are both questions that can be asked about a word, or about any piece of wording – a word is simply the chunk of wording we are most readily aware of.

So our folk linguistic has, built into it, a clear conception of language as a three-level phenomenon, which is exactly what it is. It consists of meaning, wording, and sounding or writing. We could represent the folk linguistic model like this:

When linguists talk about 'the semantic system', 'the lexicogrammatical (or syntactic) system' and 'the phonological system', they are simply referring to the meaning, the wording and the sounding; but considering them, not as sets of isolated instances, as we usually are when we talk about these things in daily life, but as a total potential. This is the main difference between the folk linguistic and the professional linguistic perspectives: a linguist is interested not just in what is said or written on a particular occasion, but also in what can be said or written (the language as a system) and what is likely to be said or written under given conditions of use.

Language is a system of meanings: an open-ended range of semantic choices that relate closely to the social contexts in which language is used. Meaning is encoded as wording; and wording, in turn, as speaking or writing. This is a very abstract conception; but it is exactly the conception of language that a child internalizes in the course of learning his mother tongue, because it is so faithfully represented in our ordinary ways of talking about language. Moreover the child is still working hard at building up the system, all the time adding to the potential that he already has. Of course he does not 'know' what language is in the sense of being able to give a lecture on it; but he is conscious of what he can do with it, and often more intuitively aware of what it is like than is an adult, who has long forgotten the efforts that he himself put into learning it. A child's understanding about language can be seen in the ways in which he himself talks about it, using over and over again such words as *question* and *answer* and *word* and *mean* and *say*, and expressions like 'what's this called?' and 'that's not what I meant.'

Teachers to whom we have made these points, when we have stressed the importance of what a child already knows about language, have sometimes reacted by saying in effect 'What you say is fine for the clever ones, those who have every advantage and are going to learn anyway. But it won't do for those that I work with. They haven't got these insights; in fact I sometimes wonder if they know any language at all.' But this is to misunderstand the burden of what we are saying. This is not the place to take up the complex questions of 'deficiency' theory, compensatory language programmes and the like; *Breakthrough* does not assume, or preclude, any particular standpoint on these issues (though the authors have their own views). But it is precisely the children most likely to fail, whatever the reason, who have the most to gain from building upon what they already know – and this includes what they already know about language.

It is not always easy to avoid getting lost in a maze of social and linguistic preconceptions which lead one imperceptibly to the assumption that children who have a different accent or a different grammar from one's own therefore have a speech potential that is narrower in range and an understanding of language that is less deep. But this is a false assumption. Where children are likely to suffer is where there is a relative lack of continuity between their native culture and that of the school, because the values of the school, and the meanings that are typically exchanged, may be remote from and in certain ways opposed to the values and the habits of meaning that are familiar to them. But this makes it all the more important to emphasize what continuity there is, by starting from what is common knowledge to all. It is reasonable to suppose that the greater the cultural gap (as things are) between the out-of-school and the in-school environment of a child, the more important it is to make explicit the positive qualities of the out-of-school environment and to build on them in the teaching process; if this is true in general, then nowhere is it more particularly applicable than in the realm of language.

There are many children, typically though not exclusively urban children, in English-speaking countries, whose soundings, wordings and even meanings are often markedly different from those of the people who teach them. But they have the same linguistic system, and the same intuitive knowledge of what the system is like. They have constructed the same edifice, although the contents of the rooms may be different. In this context *Breakthrough* has much to offer, because while it places a high value on *language* it does not insist on this or that particular *kind* of language. *Breakthrough* takes no sides on the issue of 'dialect primers or not?' – because it has no primers. The children's reading material is what they have written themselves: not what the teacher has written at their dictation, in a praiseworthy but misguided attempt to put the child at the centre of the picture, but what they have constructed out of their own linguistic resources. Hence, *Breakthrough* does not make knowledge of the standard language a *precondition* of success in reading and writing. But neither does it shelve the problem. Rather, it makes the learning of the standard language a concomitant, a natural *consequence* of the process of learning to read and write. It assumes, in other words, that one of the aims of language education may be to develop a child's control over the standard language – without in any way downgrading his own form of the mother tongue.

In discussing *Breakthrough* with teachers, we have sometimes found ourselves uncomfortably facing two directions at once, caught as it were in the crossfire between two extreme positions. On one side are those who favour an extreme of structure: the rigid structuring of the teaching situation, in which classroom interaction is closely regulated and the options are 'closed'. These strict pedagogical principles may be what lie behind the equally strict linguistic principles according to which language is treated as a set of rules to be imparted and obeyed. (This is the philosophy of those editors and secretaries who rewrite my English according to their rules of grammar, giving me endless trouble changing it all back into my own language with my own preferred forms of expression.) But the one does not always imply the other: some people who are educational doves are the fiercest of hawks in their attitudes to language.

On the other side are those who favour an extreme of non-structure: the educational principle that I have referred to as 'benevolent inertia', according to which, provided the teacher does not actually interfere in any way in what is going on, then learning will somehow take place. *Breakthrough* is not really at home in a situation of either of these extremes. It thrives best in a milieu that is child-centred but in which the teacher functions as a guide, creating structure with the help of the students themselves. But it does not depend on the adoption of any one set of pedagogical techniques or of any particular body of methodological principles for the teaching of reading and writing.

There is no doubt that many of our problems in literacy education are of our own making: not just ourselves as individuals, or even educators as a profession, but ourselves as a whole – society, if you like. In part the problems stem from our cultural attitudes to language. We take language all too solemnly – and yet not seriously enough. If we (and this includes teachers) can learn to be a lot more serious about language, and at the same time a great deal less solemn about it, then we might be more ready to recognize linguistic success for what it is when we see it, and so do more to bring it about where it would otherwise fail to appear.

13

Language and social man
(Part 2)

In this final chapter I shall suggest some topics for exploration by linguists of all ages. These are topics which can be followed up in various ways in an educational context: not only through further reading, but also by observations on the part of an individual or in study groups. In many instances, pupils in the class can be enlisted to help in the inquiry, for example by keeping a language diary, or by noting down things they hear said by a small brother or sister; in this way language becomes an exciting area for classroom research. The issues are ones which teachers have found to be relevant to their own work, and which can be investigated in the course of one's daily life, through observation and questioning, without the need for a year's leave of absence and a research foundation grant. The suggested topics are the following:

1 Language development in young children
2 Language and socialization
3 Neighbourhood language profile
4 Language in the life of the individual
5 Language and situation
6 Language and institutions
7 Language attitudes

In the succeeding sections I discuss these topics and put forward some ideas for questions that might be pursued. Many more could of course be added. The ideas that lie behind them, the basic conception of language as a resource for living and of its central place in the educational process, have been developed, enriched and made accessible to teachers by Doughty, Pearce and Thornton in their outstanding programme of materials *Language in use* (1971).

1 Language development in young children

Anyone with a young child in the family can make himself a positive nuisance trying to record its speech, not only by cluttering up the house with concealed microphones and other equipment but also by accumulating vast quantities of unprocessed tape. (It takes ten hours to listen to ten hours of tape, and anything up to five hundred hours to transcribe it.) The most useful piece of research equipment is a notebook and pencil; and the most important research qualification (as in many other areas) is the ability to *listen to language*, which is not difficult to acquire and yet is surprisingly seldom developed. This means the ability to attend to the actual words that are being spoken, as distinct from the usual kind of listening which involves the automatic decoding and processing of what is said. To put it another way, 'listening to language' means listening to the wording, or else the sounding (if the interest is in the phonetics), instead of only fastening on the meaning. The surprising thing is that by learning to do this one becomes a better listener all round: in attending to his language, one gains a more accurate impression of what the speaker meant.

Skulking behind the furniture and writing down what a small child says, and also what is said to and around him, with a brief note on what he is doing at the time (this is essential), is a useful source of insight – provided it is not carried to extremes. Pupils who have small brothers and sisters can do some valuable research here; the older ones can keep accurate records, while the younger ones, though they cannot be expected to do very much field work, will make up for this by virtue of the intrinsic interest of their own glosses and their interpretative comments.

What are we looking for? There are various kinds of understanding to be gained from listening to a child; not in the romantic sense, as a fount of intuitive wisdom – we shall never know whether he possesses such wisdom or not, because whatever he has disappears in the process of his learning to communicate it to us – but as a young human being struggling to grow up, linguistically as in other ways. We can see what are the functions for which he is building up a linguistic system, and how these functions relate to his survival and his social wellbeing. There is no need for an exact phonetic record – that is something to be left to the specialist – and no need to wait until we hear complete sentences or even recognizable words of English. The child of nine to eighteen months will have a range of vocal signals that are meaningful and understandable to those around him, such as Nigel's *nànànànà* meaning 'give me that!'; in other words, he will have a range of *meanings*, which define what he can do in the various spheres of action to which his vocal resources are applied (see the set of initial functions in chapter 1, pp. 19–20).

What the child does with language, at this early stage, is all the time shaping his own image of what language is. At a certain point, round about eighteen months old, he will abandon his laborious attempt to work through half a million years of human evolution creating his own language, and shortcircuit the process by 'going adult' and taking over the language he hears around him. The impetus for this move is still a functional one; the demands he makes on language are rapidly increasing, and his own 'do-it-yourself' system can no longer meet them. His language is now further strengthened and enriched as a resource for living and learning, by the addition of a whole new range of semantic choices; and his image of what language is, and what it can do, is enriched correspondingly. With this image he comes ready equipped to school; and the sad thing is that so few teachers in the past have either shared the image or even sought to understand what, in fact, the child can already do with language when he comes to them, which is a very great deal. To look into the functional origins of language, at the beginning of the development process, is to go a long way towards a sympathetic appreciation of what language means to a child when he first sets foot in school.

Points to consider
a Very young children:

> What are the functions for which the very young child first begins to learn language?
> What meanings does he learn to express, within these functions? What sort of meanings can he *respond to* (e.g. 'Do you want . . .')?
> Who does he (a) talk to (b) listen to? In what types of situation?
> What kind of reinforcement does he get for his efforts? Who understands him most readily? Has he an interpreter (e.g. an older brother or sister)?

b Children nearer school age:

> What are the functions for which the child is now using language?
> Is it possible, in fact, to recognize from among the mass of particular instances any general types of use that might be significant: learning about the material environment, learning about social relations and cultural values, controlling behaviour, responding emotionally and so on?
> What sort of difficulties does he encounter? Are there things he cannot make language do for him?
> What are the functions for which he is now beginning to need the *written* language, and writing as a medium? This is the key question for the child first coming into school. Will learning to read and write make sense to him, matching his experience of what language is and what it is for, so that he sees it as a means of enlarging that experience; or will it seem to be a meaningless exercise which is unrelated to any of his own uses of language?

2 Language and socialization

This topic is closely related to the last; but here the focus of attention is shifted away from the learning of language as a whole onto the role of language in relation to the child as 'social man', and the ways in which language serves to initiate the child into the social order.

Every child is brought up in a culture, and he has to learn the patterns of that culture in the process of becoming a member of it. The principal means whereby the culture is made available to him is through language: language is not the only channel, but it is the most significant one. Even the most intimate of personal relationships, that of the child with its mother, is from an early age mediated through language; and language plays some part in practically all his social learning.

Bernstein's work has provided the key to an understanding not merely of the part played by language in the home life and the school life of the child but, more significantly, of *how* language comes to play this central part; and hence of how it happens that some children fail to meet the demands that are made by the school on their linguistic capacities, not because these capacities are lacking but because they have typically been deployed in certain ways rather than in others.

The types of social context which Bernstein identifies as critical to the process of the child's socialization were mentioned in chapter 1, p. 30: the regulative, the instructional, the imaginative or innovative, and the interpersonal. These are clearly related to the developmental functions of language as I outlined them: instrumental, regulatory and so on. But whereas I was asking 'what are the key linguistic functions through which the child first *learns language*?', the underlying question being about language development and the nature of language itself, Bernstein is asking 'what are the key linguistic contexts through which the child *learns the culture*?', with the emphasis on social development and cultural transmission. For example, the ways in which a parent controls the behaviour of a child reveal for the child a great deal about statuses and roles, the structure of authority, and moral and other values in the culture.

There are various possible lines of approach if one is inquiring into the part played by language in significant social contexts. One interesting type of investigation was devised and carried out by Bernstein and Henderson (1973), who took a number of specific tasks involved in bringing up a child, for example 'teaching children everyday tasks such as dressing or using a knife and fork', 'showing them how things work', 'disciplining them', and 'dealing with them when they are unhappy', and asked mothers how much more difficulty they thought parents would have in carrying out these tasks if they had no language with which to do it – imagining, for example, that they were deaf and dumb. The answers do not, of course, tell us what the mothers actually say to their children on these occasions; but they give an idea of their orientation towards different functions of language, and there turn out to be certain significant differences which go with social class.

It is not impossible to examine actual samples of the language used in particular instances of the types of situation that are significant for the child's socialization; and to ask what the child might have learnt about the culture from the things that were said to him. For example, a form of control such as 'you mustn't touch things that don't belong to you' carries a great deal of potential information about private property and ownership. Naturally one or two such remarks by themselves would not tell him very much; but from their constant varied repetition and reinforcement he would learn a lot about the culture of which he had involuntarily taken out membership. And the interesting point is that this learning would have taken place not only without instruction, but without organized knowledge behind it, through the most ordinary everyday uses of language in ordinary everyday kinds of situation.

For a teacher there is the additional question of the role of language in the classroom – or rather roles, since the school is a complex institution and language has many different parts to play in it. The key question, perhaps, is this: to the extent that the school is a new culture into which the child has been socialized (and, as we have seen, this makes greater demands on some children than it does on others), is the actual pattern of language use in the daily life of the school adequate to the socializing task? If it is not – and in many instances at present it almost certainly is not – what can be done to remedy this situation?

A study of the use of language in the classroom may reveal some of the assumptions that are made by the teacher about the school as a social institution – assumptions about the nature of educational processes, about teacher-pupil relationships, about the values accorded to objects, their schemes of classification, and the like – while at the same time showing that the children get little help in becoming aware of these things, or in learning the relevant schemes of social relations and social values. Or, on the other hand, it might turn out that the school provides very adequate means for making such matters explicit: again, not by *teaching* them, but by encouraging and developing a use of language that is culturally rich and socially enlightened. Either way, there is much to be gained from watching language at work in the socializing process.

Points to consider
a What part does language play in the socialization of the child?

What types of situation are likely to be significant at the pre-school stage (e.g. listening to stories, having meals, playing with other children)? Can these be seen as concrete instances of Bernstein's four 'critical contexts for socialization'?
What might the child learn from these situations, about social relations, social values, the structure of knowledge and the like?
How would he learn these things – from what kinds of use of language (for example, in games with adults, *my turn . . . your turn*, leading to a concept of a particular kind of role relation, with a privilege that is shared and exercised by turns)?
What demands on his own linguistic abilities, in terms of the development functions of language, are made by these situations (e.g. verbal games, teasing, helping mother in the kitchen, going shopping, competing with other children)?

b How do the forms of the child's socialization find linguistic expression in his modes of behaving and learning?

What differences appear between children from different cultures, such as British, West Indian, Pakistani? Between children from different sub-cultures, such as social class groups within the native British population? How are these expressed in language? (For example, different concepts of family relationships, expressed partly by different modes of address.) (The point is not that such groups speak different languages or dialects; the emphasis should be on the way they *use* language, on the meanings that are expressed.)

What is the significance for the school of the child's preschool experience, seen in terms of patterns of language use? Are certain ways of using language in school likely to be less familiar to him, and if so can they be made explicit in a manner that is likely to help?

3 Neighbourhood language profile

There has never been any lack of interest in the local varieties of English speech, and numerous accounts of the vocabulary and pronunciation of different dialects have appeared since the Elizabethan period.

Systematic linguistic study of rural dialects began about a hundred years ago, in France, Germany and Switzerland; since that time dialect surveys have been undertaken in many countries ranging from China to the United States. These are designed to show the particular characteristics of the speech in each locality, and to trace its derivation from an earlier stage of the language.

Dialect studies are based on the assumption, which is largely borne out in practice, that there are homogeneous speech communities: the people of one locality all speak alike. The notion of a 'dialect' is defined on this assumption; 'the dialect of Littleby' means the speech that one learns by virtue of growing up as an inhabitant of Littleby. The researcher typically searches out the oldest inhabitant, among those who have lived in the village all their lives, and takes his speech as representative, rather than that of younger people or of those who have moved into the area from outside, whose speech will probably not be 'pure Littleby'.

Recently, and particularly in the United States, attention has turned to urban dialects; and it has been found out that the traditional concepts of dialectology do not hold good for large industrial cities. In one respect, of course, this is obvious: everyone knows that the inhabitants of a city like London do not all speak alike. There is not only geographical variation, distinguishing the speech of one *locality* from that of another – south-east London, north London and so on – but also social variation, distinguishing the speed of one *social class* from that of another. But the pattern of urban dialects is much more complex that this. Our understanding of the nature of city speech is largely due to the work of William Labov, whose pioneer studies of New York speech gave a radically different picture of the dialect structure of an industrial community.

Labov showed up the extraordinary complexity of the social stratification: not only in the sense that there are some very minute distinctions separating different speech varieties, but also, more importantly, that such distinctions may have great social significance in the community. The interesting finding is that, while the typical New Yorker is very inconsistent in his own speech habits, switching from one pronunciation to another according to the situation, and particularly according to the degree of conscious attention to speech that is involved, he is almost entirely consistent in his judgement of the speech of other people, and can be extremely sensitive to the slightest variation in what he *hears*. He is quite unaware that such variation occurs within his own speech, although he may be subconsciously troubled by the fact; but he responds to subtle differences and changes in the speech of others, and uses the information to identify their social status. Labov found, for instance, that if he played a taperecording of just one sentence to a sample of New Yorkers, not only would those who heard it agree in large measure about what sort of employment the speaker they were listening to would be best fitted for, but also, if he 'doctored' the tape at just one point – altering it in a way which would be equivalent, in London terms, to dropping just one *h* – the subjects rated the same speaker one notch lower on their employment scale. Labov concluded from these investigations that an urban speech community (unlike a rural one) is not so much a group of people who speak in a certain way, but rather a group of people who share the same prejudices about how others speak.

If the townsman does vary in his speech habits, the variation is normally not random, but relates to the context of situation. He may switch between a neighbourhood dialect and some form of standard speech, perhaps with some intermediate degrees; but the choice, though probably entirely subconscious, is likely to depend on who he is speaking to, what sort of occasion it is and what kind of environment they are in – in other words, on the field, mode and tenor of discourse, as we defined these earlier. That is to say, his dialect switching is actually an expression of register variation. This phenomenon is by no means confined to urban communities; in fact it was first studied in detail in villages and small towns, for example by John Gumperz, who worked in countries as different from each other as India and Norway. But it is characteristic of the city dweller that he does not keep to one constant set of speech habits. His pronunciation, at least, is likely to vary according to circumstances; and even those who, as adults, do not display any noticeable variation in their speech have almost certainly moved away in certain respects from the neighbourhood dialect they learnt as children.

Neighbourhood speech patterns in the city are always liable to be complicated by movements of population, as is happening in English cities with the arrival of large groups of immigrants, so that even the neighbourhood is not always a homogeneous speech unit. Nevertheless neighbourhood speech has a very powerful influence among children, in their own peer group; it is remarkable that children coming into a neighbourhood from outside, even if they outnumber those from the locality, tend to grow up speaking the local language, so that the concept of a neighbourhood dialect is a valid and important one. It is the language of the children's peer group, in the street, the park and later on in the school playground; and it serves for the child as his badge of membership in the culture. It should be added that we still know very little about the linguistic characteristics of children's peer group dialects, which show a number of special peculiarities some of which are highly significant for an understanding of how languages change.

Points to consider
a Is it possible to identify a neighbourhood dialect in your area?

> Would there be general agreement on what is the characteristic speech of the neighbourhood?
> How specifically can it be tied to a particular area? Is it, for example, Home counties? London? South-east London? Catford? Brownhill Road area?
> Taking some such locality, perhaps intermediate in size, what is noticeable and distinctive about the speech habits, in terms of grammar, vocabulary or pronunciation? (The best way to find out is to listen to yourself imitating the neighbourhood speech. In doing so you probably produce a caricature rather than a photographic likeness; but a caricature exaggerates precisely the features that we in fact find distinctive. Do you find yourself saying 'a cuppa tᵉea', 'in the pᶠark', with *t* and *p* affricated at the beginning of a stressed syllable? If so this is obviously a noticeable feature of the dialect, though probably less pronounced than you yourself make it appear.)
> How widespread is each of the particular features that enter into the picture? (Some will be confined to the immediate locality, others will be characteristic of the whole city or region.)

b Are there noticeable differences of speech within the neighbourhood? If so: Are there social class differences? Other subcultural differences (e.g. between native and immigrant groups)? Generational differences? Institutional differences (e.g. between one school and another)?

> Do all children begin by learning the same type of speech? (If so, this is probably the most markedly differentiated type, the variety that is most specific to the locality in question; and it is this to which the term 'neighbourhood dialect' is most strictly applicable.)
> Do adult and adolescent speakers typically use more than one variety? If so, under what circumstances? When do they switch from one to another, and why?
> Can the 'language profile' of the neighbourhood be related to the social structure?

c What is the relation of the neighbourhood speech to 'standard English'?
> Is the neighbourhood speech itself a form of standard English, an 'accent' rather than a dialect in the strict sense of the term?
> What are its limits of tolerance? Is it acceptable in school?
> Do adults (a) recognize the desirability of using, and (b) themselves actually use, a form of speech that is closer to standard English? If so,

when do they use it? How do they learn it? Are there speakers who do not
learn it, and if so what are the consequences for them?

4 Language in the life of the individual

It is surprisingly difficult to get any clear impression of what we actually do
with language in the course of our daily lives. If we were asked to make up
out of our heads a linguistic record for the day, most of us would be at a
complete loss to reconstruct what was actually said to us and what we
ourselves said – let alone *why* we said some of the things we did say.

Yet the day's language makes up a significant part of the total experience
of a typical human being, whether adult or child. It can be a useful as well as
entertaining exercise to investigate how a child spends a typical day, as far as
using language is concerned: what he says, what is said to and around him,
and also what he reads and what he writes, if these are applicable. (It can also
be illuminating to look into how one spends one's own linguistic day.)

One technique that has been used is that of the 'language diary'. This is
exactly what the name implies: an account of the day's linguistic doings, in
which are recorded in as much detail as possible the language activities of the
day, showing the time span, the type of language event and some observations on the language used. The record might contain no more than entries
like: 8:30–8:35 At the newsagent's: buying newspaper, transactional dialogue, self and newsagent; structure of language events: (a) greeting, (b)
transaction, (c) comment on weather, (d) valediction. The actual text might
have been something like the following:

Morning, Tom!
Good morning to you, sir!
Have you got a *Guardian* left this morning?
You're lucky; it's the last one. Bit brighter today, by the looks of it.
Yes, we could do with a bit of a dry spell. You got change for a pound?
Yes, plenty of change; here you are. Anything else today?
No, that's all just now, Tom. Be seeing you.
Mind how you go.

Children can be asked to keep language diaries, noting down instances of
language use at home and in school. The kind of observation they can make
will, of course, depend on the age group; but once the concept has been
understood it does not much matter what the format is – any form of
record-keeping is appropriate. From accumulated samples of this kind one
builds up a picture of types of interaction among individuals; and this, in
turn, brings out something of the complex patterns of daily life as lived in a
particular community in a particular culture.

In a community where there is dialect switching, the diary can record the
circumstances under which different varieties of speech are employed, using
categories such as 'neighbourhood' and 'standard'. Language diaries have in
fact mainly been used in multilingual situations, to show how the different

languages figure in the lives of individual members of the community: which language do they hear on radio or in the cinema, in which language does one speak to one's wife or husband, consult the doctor, fill up official forms, do the shopping, and so on. But the same principle applies in 'multidialectal' communities, where the language diary helps to make one aware of some of the social complexities of everyday activities. (It is easier to start by noting examples of other people's language behaviour before attempting to be one's own diarist.)

There are various ways of recording language behaviour, which essentially resolve themselves into four: one can record sounds, wordings, meanings or registers. Recording sounds, that is, giving accurate accounts of pronunciation, is a task for the specialist, although we are all amateur phoneticians when it comes to reacting to other people's accents, and a few key features can often be identified as indices of dialect variation. Recording wordings means taking down in full the actual words that are used; this can be done with a notebook and pencil, especially with the aid of shorthand, but also, given sufficient practice, in longhand. Recording meanings means paraphrasing and précis-ing what is said as one notes it down. These three ways of recording language correspond to the three levels of language itself, the levels of sound, of form (grammar and vocabulary) and of meaning; hence each of the three is concerned with a different aspect of linguistic reality. With a taperecorder, of course, one can obtain a 'photographic' image of the whole, and process it at any level one likes; but working with a taperecorder tends to restrict one to the less interesting uses of language, those where the participants remain relatively static, and it is also liable to become somewhat obsessive, so on the whole in linguistic journalism it is probably better to rely on a notebook and pencil, combined with one's own intuition about what is important and what can be left out – an intuition that is notably lacking in taperecorders.

For certain purposes it is very useful to record the actual wordings, particularly in studying the part played by language in the life of a child. Here is an extract from an account of a linguistic 'day in the life of' Nigel at two and a half years old: the dramatis personae here are Nigel, his mother, his father and his aunt:

N You want a **bìscuít** <u><2></u>
A Do you want a **bìscuít**? <u><2></u>
N Yḛ [*very high level tone*]
M Have you washed your **hánds**? <2>
A **Còme**, <1> I'll **hèlp** you <1>
N You want **Mùmmy** to **hélp** you <u><2></u>
A Mummy's **bùsy** <1>
N You want **Dàddy** to **hélp** you <u><2></u>
A Shall I . . . ?
F **Nò** <1> it's all **rīght**, <3> I'll go **wīth** him <3> [*They go*]
N [*Suiting actions to words*] More **wáter** <2> . . . turn the **tàp ón** <u><2></u> . . .

pull the **plùg óut** <<u>2</u>> [*returning*] ... you want to have half of Daddy's
biscuit and Daddy have the **òther hálf** <<u>2</u>> ... oh you didn't roll your
sleèves down <1>

F   Oh you didn't roll your **sleèves** down! <1>

N   You **ròll thém** <<u>2</u>> [*does so*] ... where's the **bìscuít** <<u>2</u>> [*takes it and
eats*] ... the train picture you tore **ùp** <1> ... that was very **bàd** <1> ...
you want **anòther bíscuit** <<u>2</u>> .... want to have half of **Dàddy's bíscuit**
<<u>2</u>> ... want to **bréak it** <2>

F   All **ríght**, <3> ... this is the last **òne** <1>

The numbers in angle brackets show the intonation patterns, which in
English, as it happens, are an important element in the wording, though they
are not shown in our orthography; those occurring here are <1> falling
tone, <2> rising tone, <<u>2</u>> falling-rising tone, and <3> half-rising tone.
The bold type indicates the word or words on which the tone is made
prominent. The conversation is quite trivial in itself, but it reveals a number
of things about the child's use of language. Nigel happens at this stage to
refer to himself as *you*; also, he uses a tone ending on a rise, <2> or <<u>2</u>>,
when the language function is pragmatic (instrumental or regulatory), and a
falling tone otherwise. The passage happens to illustrate all the three main
types of pragmatic function: instrumental *you want a biscuit*, regulatory *you
want Mummy to help you*, and regulatory in the special sense of asking
permission *turn the tap on* ('may I?', though in fact permission is assumed
and the pattern comes to mean simply 'I'm going to'). Interposed with the
dominant motive of obtaining the biscuit are various nonpragmatic elements
with their own functions, heuristic (rehearsing a moral judgement) and
personal-informative. When one examines the wording closely, there is a
great deal to be learnt from a simple exchange of this kind, about the very
essential part that is played by ordinary everyday language in the socialization of the child.

However, for many purposes it is enough to record the 'register' that is
being used; and here the concepts of 'field', 'tenor' and 'mode' provide a
valuable framework for giving information about language use in as succinct
a way as possible.

1   *Field.* The kind of language we use varies, as we should expect, according to what we are doing. In differing contexts, we tend to select different
words and different grammatical patterns – simply because we are expressing different kinds of meaning. All we need add to this, in order to clarify
the notion of register, is that the 'meanings' that are involved are a part of
what we are doing; or rather, they are part of the expression of what we are
doing. In other words, one aspect of the field of discourse is simply the
subject matter; we talk *about* different things, and therefore use different
words for doing so. If this was all there was to it, and the field of discourse
was *only* a question of subject matter, it would hardly need saying; but, in
fact, 'what we are talking about' has to be seen as a special case of a more
general concept, that of 'what we are doing', or 'what is going on, within

which the language is playing a part.' It is this broader concept that is referred to as the 'field of discourse'. If, for example, the field of discourse is football, then no matter whether we are playing it or discussing it around a table we are likely to use certain linguistic forms which reflect the football context. But the two are essentially different kinds of activity, and this is clearly reflected in the language: if we are actually playing we are unlikely to waste our breath referring explicitly to the persons and objects in the game. This difference, between the language of playing football and the language of discussing football, is also a reflection of the 'mode of discourse'; see below.

The 'field', therefore, refers to what the participants in the context of situation are actually engaged in doing, like 'buying-selling a newspaper' in our example above. This is a more general concept than that of subject matter, and a more useful one in the present context since we may not actually be *talking about* either buying and selling or newspapers. We may be talking about the weather; but that does not mean that the field of discourse is meteorology – talking about the weather is part of the strategy of buying and selling.

2 *Tenor.* The language we use varies according to the level of formality, of technicality, and so on. What is the variable underlying this type of distinction? Essentially, it is the role relationships in the situation in question: who the participants in the communication group are, and in what relationship they stand to each other.

This is what, following Spencer and Gregory (1964), we called the 'tenor of discourse'. Examples of role relationships, that would be reflected in the language used, are teacher/pupil, parent/child, child/child in peer group, doctor/patient, customer/salesman, casual acquaintances on a train, and so on. It is the role relationships, including the indirect relationship between a writer and his audience, that determine such things as the level of technicality and degree of formality. Contexts of situation, or settings, such as a public lecture, playground at playtime, church service, cocktail party and so on can be regarded as institutionalized role relationships and hence as stabilized patterns of the tenor of discourse.

3 *Mode.* The language we use differs according to the channel or wavelength we have selected. Sometimes we find ourselves, especially those of us who teach, in a didactic mode, at other times the mode may be fanciful, or commercial, or imperative: we may choose to behave as teacher, or poet, or advertiser, or commanding officer: Essentially, this is a question of what function language is being made to serve in the context of situation; this is what underlies the selection of the particular rhetorical channel.

This is what we call the 'mode of discourse'; and fundamental to it is the distinction between speaking and writing. This distinction partly cuts across the rhetorical modes, but it also significantly determines them: although certain modes can be realized through either medium, they tend to take quite different forms according to whether spoken or written – written advertising, for example, does not say the same things as sales talk. This is because the two media represent, essentially, different *functions* of language, and therefore embody selections of different kinds. The question underlying the concept of the mode of discourse is, what function is language being used for, what is its specific role in the goings-on to which it is contributing? To persuade? to soothe? to sell? to control? to explain? or just to oil the works, as in what Malinowski called 'phatic communion', exemplified above by the talk about the weather, which merely helps the situation along? Here the distinction between the language of *playing* a game, such as bridge or football, and the language of *discussing* a game becomes clear. In the former situation, the language is functioning as a part of the game, as a pragmatic expression of play behaviour; whereas in the latter, it is part of a very different kind of activity, and may be informative, didactic, argumentative, or any one of a number of rhetorical modes of discourse.

It will be seen from the foregoing that the categories of 'field of discourse', 'tenor of discourse', and 'mode of discourse' are not themselves kinds or varieties of language. They are the backdrop, the features of the context of situation which determine the kind of language used. In other words, they determine what is often referred to as the register: that is, the types of meaning that are selected, and their expression in grammar and vocabulary. And they determine the register collectively, not piecemeal. There is not a great deal that one can predict about the language that will be used if one knows *only* the field of discourse or *only* the tenor or the mode. But if we know all three, we can predict quite a lot; and, of course, the more detailed the information we have, the more linguistic features of the text we shall be able to predict.

It is possible, nevertheless, to make some broad generalization about each of these three variables separately, in terms of its probable linguistic consequences.

The field of discourse, since it largely determines the 'content' of what is being said, is likely to have the major influence on the selection of vocabulary, and also on the selection of those grammatical patterns which express our experience of the world that is around us and inside us: the types of process, the classes of object, qualities and quantities, abstract relations and so on.

The tenor of discourse, since it refers to the participants in the speech situation, and how they relate to each other both permanently and temporarily, influences the speaker's selection of mood (his choice of speech role: making statements, asking questions and so on) and of modality (his assessment of the validity of what he is saying); it also helps to determine the key in which he pitches his assertions (forceful, hesitant, gnomic, qualified and so on) and the attitudes and feelings he expresses.

The mode of discourse, which covers both the channel of communication, written or spoken, and the particular rhetorical mode selected by the speaker or writer, tends to determine the way the language hangs together – the 'texture', to use a literary term: including both the internal organization of each sentence as a thematic construct and the cohesive relations linking one sentence with another.

The difference between speech and writing has an important effect on the whole pattern of lexicogrammatical organization, because it tends to influence the lexical density of the discourse. In general, written language is more highly 'lexicalized' than spoken language; it has a more complex vocabulary. This does not necessarily mean that written language uses words that are more unusual, though this may be true too; but it means that it has a greater lexical *density*, packing more content words into each phrase or clause or sentence. To express this in another way, written language contains more lexical information per unit of grammar. By the same token, written language also tends to be simpler than spoken language in its grammatical organization; speech, especially informal speech such as casual conversation, displays complexities of sentence structure that would be intolerable (because they would be unintelligible) in writing. Naturally, there is considerable variety within both the written and the spoken modes: there are forms of writing that are more like speech, and forms of spoken language that are very close to the written ('he talks like a book'). But this kind of variation also largely depends on the rhetorical channel or genre, so it is still a function of the mode of discourse. Jean Ure remarks, for example, that the lexical density is determined by the extent to which the language is what she calls 'language-in-action' (1971).

There is a close interaction between tenor and mode, and Gregory prefers to identify a separate subheading which he calls 'functional tenor' to account for the variation in the rhetorical genre, included here under mode (see Gregory 1967 and table 6 below; Benson and Greaves 1973). The combination of the medium, the rhetorical channel and the social relationship of speaker and hearers, or writer and readers (and such a relationship is presumed to exist even if a writer is writing for an unknown public – this is often a big factor in his success), tend to influence the level of formality and technicality at which the speaker or writer is operating, and hence lead him to prefer certain words over others and to pitch his discourse at a certain point on the 'style scale'. This concept of a single scale of formality of 'style' varying across a range of qualities such as intimate, casual, consultative, formal and frozen (Joos 1962), can be applied in some instances; but it is important to recognize that it is a complex notion encompassing a variety of rather different linguistic features. Furthermore the term 'formality' (or 'level of formality') is the source of some confusion in discussions of language, because it is used in two different senses. On the one hand it refers to the use of forms of the language – words, or grammatical structures – that are conventionally associated with certain modes: with impersonal letters or memoranda, various types of interview and the like. On the other hand it is used to refer to the degree of respect that is shown linguistically to the person who is being addressed: languages differ rather widely as regards how (and also as regards how much) they incorporate the expression of respect, but there are ways of addressing parents and elders, social and occupational superiors, and so on, that are recognized as the marks of the social relationship involved. Although there is some overlap between these two senses of 'formality', they are in principle rather distinct and have different manifestations in grammar and vocabulary.

Table 6 Suggested categories of (1) dialectal and (2) diatypic variety differentiation. (From Gregory 1967.)

1 Dialectal

	situational categories	*contextual categories*	*examples of English varieties (descriptive contextual categories)*	
user's	individuality	idiolect	Mr X's English, Miss Y's English	*dialectal varieties:* the linguistic reflection of reasonably permanent characteristics of the *user* in language situations
	temporal provenance	temporal dialect	Old English, modern English	
	geographical provenance	geographical dialect	British English, American English	
	social provenance	social dialect	Upper-class English, Middle-class English	
	range of intelligibility	standard/non-standard	Standard English, non-standard English	

2 Diatypic

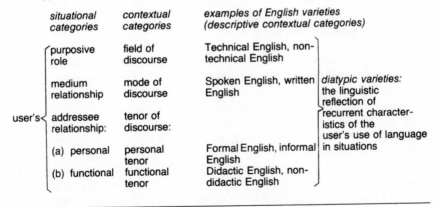

	situational categories	*contextual categories*	*examples of English varieties (descriptive contextual categories)*	
user's	purposive role	field of discourse	Technical English, non-technical English	*diatypic varieties:* the linguistic reflection of recurrent characteristics of the user's use of language in situations
	medium relationship	mode of discourse	Spoken English, written English	
	addressee relationship:	tenor of discourse:		
	(a) personal	personal tenor	Formal English, informal English	
	(b) functional	functional tenor	Didactic English, non-didactic English	

So there is some tendency for the field of discourse to determine the content of what is said or written, for the tenor to determine the tone of it, and for the mode to determine the texture. But this is only an approximation. In the first place, we cannot really separate what is said from how it is said, and this is just as true of everyday language as it is of myth and poetry.

In the second place, the field, tenor and mode of discourse make their impact as a whole, not in isolation from each other; the linguistic reflection of any one of them depends on its combination with the other two. There is not a great deal that one can say about the language of football, taken as a rubric just by itself (field of discourse), or the language of public lectures (mode), or the language of teacher and pupil (tenor). These are certainly meaningful concepts, as is proved by the fact that if we hear a recording or read a passage out of context we can usually identify it in precisely such terms as these; but we often do so by means of linguistic clues which are themselves rather trivial, like the lecturer's voice quality or the urgent 'sir!' of the schoolboy. In order to be able to predict the interesting and important features of the language that is used, we need to characterize the situation in terms of all three variables in interaction with each other.

Suppose we have the setting described in some such terms as these:

Field: Instruction: the instruction of a novice
            – in a board game (e.g. Monopoly) with equipment present
            – for the purpose of enabling him to participate
Tenor: Equal and intimate: three young adult males; acquainted
            – but with hierarchy in the situation (2 experts, 1 novice)
            – leading to superior-inferior role relationship
Mode: Spoken: unrehearsed
            Didactic and explanatory, with undertone of non-seriousness
            – with feedback: question-and-answer, correction of error

Here we can predict quite a lot about the language that will be used, in respect of the meanings and the significant grammatical and lexical features through which they are expressed. If the entries under field, tenor and mode are filled out carefully and thoughtfully, it is surprising how many features of the language turn out to be relatable to the context of situation. This is not to claim that we know what the participants are going to say; it merely shows that we can make sensible and informed guesses about certain aspects of what they might say, with a reasonable probability of being right. There is always, in language, the freedom to act untypically – but that in itself serves to confirm the reality of the concept of what is typical.

There is an experiment well known to students of linguistics in which the subject listens to a recording that is 'noisy' in the technical sense (badly distorted or jammed), so much so that he cannot understand anything of what is being said. He is then given a simple clue as to the register; and next time he listens he understands practically the whole text. We always listen and read with expectations, and the notion of register is really a theory about these expectations, providing a way of making them explicit.

To gain some impression of 'language in the life of the individual', it is hardly necessary, or possible, to keep detailed records of who says what, to whom, when, and why. But it is not too difficult to take note of information about register, with entries for field, tenor and mode in the language diary. This can give valuable insights into what language means to the individual. It will also effectively demolish any suspicion that there are social groups whose language is impoverished or deficient, since it goes straight to language as behaviour potential, to the semantic system that lies behind the wordings and the 'soundings' which are so often ridiculed or dismissed from serious attention.

Points to consider
a What does the language profile of an individual's daily life look like?
   What roles has he adopted, that have been expressed through language? What forms of interaction have these involved (e.g. the role of 'eldest daughter' implies interaction with parent(s) on the one hand and with younger brother(s) or sister(s) on the other; that of 'teacher' suggests interaction with pupils and also, perhaps, with school principal)?
   In what language events (types of linguistic situation) has he participated? Has he made use of different variants (dialect switching), and if so, with what kind of linguistic variation and under what circumstances?
b What is the pattern of register variation?
   Can we specify the relevant background features for particular instances of language use?
       field of discourse: the nature of the activity, and subject-matter
       tenor of discourse: the role relationships among the participants
       mode of discourse: the channel, and the part played by language in the total event.
   Where are the properties of the field, tenor and mode revealed in the language, spoken or written? How far could the eavesdropper fill in the situational background; and conversely, what features of the language could have been predicted from the situational information?
c How much more difficult would it have been for the individual to survive *without* language?

5 Language and the context of situation

Like all the headings in our list, this is closely related to the others; in particular, it overlaps with the previous one, that of language in the life of the individual. But there is a difference of perspective: here we are focusing attention on the generalized contexts of language use and the function of language within these contexts, rather than on the linguistic profile of an individual speaker. The question that is raised is not so much what language means to an individual in his daily life as what the typical social contexts are in which he participates as an articulate being.

   As in the last section, there is no difficulty in understanding the general principle: it is obvious that we use language in contexts of situation, and that these can be described in various ways. The problem here has always been how best to describe the various kinds of setting, and especially how to bring out what is significant and distinguish it from all the irrelevant particularities that are associated with specific instances.

This already arises in the treatment of register, as a problem of what Ellis calls 'delicacy of focus'. Suppose, to take a trivial example, that the field of discourse is shopping: do we characterize this as simply 'transaction', or as 'buying' (as distinct from, say, borrowing), or as 'buying in a shop' (as distinct from in the market), or as 'buying in a chemist's shop' (as distinct from a grocer's) or as 'buying a toothbrush' (as distinct from a cake of soap)? And since the criterion is bound to be our assessment, in some form or other, of whether it matters or not, we may as well ask whether we are likely to take any interest in a situation of this kind in the first place.

One way of deciding whether a particular type of situation is of interest or not is to consider, in terms of the second of the headings above, whether it is of any significance for the socialization of a child. For example, it is a good working hypothesis to assume that any type of situation in which a parent is controlling the child's behaviour is potentially important for linguistic and social development; and this suggests not only that these situations are of interest to us, but also that a certain amount of information needs to be given about them, specifically information about what aspect of the child's behaviour it is that is being regulated: whether, for example, attention is being focused on his personal relationships ('don't talk to Granny like that!') or on his behaviour towards objects ('don't tear it').

Generally speaking, the concept of social man provides the grounds for assessing the importance of a given class of context. The fact that a particular type of language use is relevant to the socialization of the child is one guarantee of significance; but it is not the only one – there are other ways in which it may be of importance in the culture. We might for example think of a linguistic setting such as 'teacher-parent consultation', subdivided into individual contact, parents' association meeting, exchange of letters and so on; this may be assumed to be of some significance in an educational context, and therefore the forms of linguistic interaction between teacher and parent might well be worth looking into. Even more interesting are the forms of linguistic interaction between teacher and pupil in the classroom, and in other school settings. There have now been a number of useful studies of classroom language, and these all depend on some notion of the relevant contexts of situation.

Another quite different reason for thinking about 'language and situation' is the fact that the pupil, in the course of his education, is expected to become sensitive to the use of language in different situation types, and to be able to vary his own linguistic behaviour in response to them. The move, in schools, away from a total preoccupation with formal composition towards an awareness of the many different types of language use involved a fairly drastic redefinition of the educationally relevant contexts of situation – a redefinition which was not without its dangers and difficulties, as subsequent debate revealed, but which was very necessary nevertheless. Both *Breakthrough to literacy* and *Language in use* demand an enlightened and imaginative view of language and situation; because of this, they are an excellent source of insight into questions of relevance. As we have stressed all along, there is no difference between knowing language and knowing how to use it; success in the mother tongue is success in developing a linguistic potential for all the types of context that are engendered by the culture. From this point of view, if we think that a pupil when he leaves school should be able to use language adequately in this or that particular range of contexts, then those contexts are important even if they do not seem to provide any great scope for linguistic virtuosity or the exercise of the creative imagination. And there is some value to be gained from an occasional glance at those types of language use which are not normally regarded as the responsibility of the school. An example is the language of technical instructions: if one looks carefully (and sympathetically) at the leaflets issued by the manufacturers of appliances, not to the general public but to those responsible for the installation and maintenance of these appliances, one can get a very clear picture of how language is related to the context of situation in which it is functioning – or rather that in which it is *intended* to function: one should always remember that a leaflet of this kind is as out of context in the classroom as would be the gas boiler itself, or whatever other object it is designed to accompany.

These are very clearly questions of register, and we almost inevitably use concepts relating to field, tenor or mode of discourse when we talk about language in relation to the situation. Formulations like 'the language of the classroom', 'the language of technical instructions', are all characterizations of this kind, sometimes relating to just one of the three dimensions, often combining features of more than one. It is, in fact, very revealing to analyse some of the formulations that are commonly used, and taken for granted as meaningful descriptions of types of language use, in order to see what information they provide which might enable us to make predictions about the text; and we can do this by relating them to field, tenor and mode. Anthropologists often use terms like 'pragmatic speech', 'ritual language' or Malinowski's 'phatic communion'; the question is what we can gather from these about the field of activity. the participant roles and role relationships involved, and the part played by language in the process.

Some of the terms that typically figure in discussions of language in the context of English teaching are worth considering from this point of view, terms such as 'creative writing', 'imaginative language', 'jargon', 'ordinary language'. These are rarely as objective and precise as they are made to seem. Jargon, for instance, often means no more than technical terms which the speaker personally dislikes, perhaps because he is not sure how to use them. If we try to interpret these labels in terms of field, tenor and mode, we find that it is not easy to see what they really imply about the kind of language used. It is not that they are not meaningful; but there is no consensus as to *what* they mean, so we have very little clue as to what would be generally regarded as a specimen of such language. What is creative in one type of situation (or in one person's opinion) would not be so in another.

The term 'situation' is sometimes misleading, since it conjures up the idea of 'props', the specific and concrete surroundings of a particular speech event such as might appear in a photograph of the scene. But this image is much too particular; what is significant is the situation *type*, the configuration of environmental factors that typically fashions our ways of speaking and writing.

Points to consider

a   What are examples of socially significant situation types, considered from an educational point of view?
How accurately and specifically do we define them? What is the 'delicacy of focus', e.g. school–classroom–English class – 'creative writing' session? In what ways are such situation types significant for the pupils' success in school (as distinct from those that are critical for the child's 'socialization' in general, as in section 2 above)? What do we expect to learn from an imaginative inquiry into the use of language in these contexts?

b   What are the generalized functions of language within these situation types?
What do we mean when we talk of 'creative', 'transactional', 'practical', 'expressive' (etc.) language? How far is an interpretation of language in these terms dependent on our awareness of the situation?
Can we relate the use of language to the interaction of social roles within these situation types? (The notion that the type of language used – expressive, creative, etc. – is solely governed by the free choice or whim of the individual is very much oversimplified, and leads to some highly artificial and unrealistic classroom exercises.)
Are there 'pure' types of language use, or do real situations always generate some kind of mixed type? (This is a vast topic in its own right. Probably most use of language is neither rigidly pure nor hopelessly mixed, but involves a dominant register and one or two subsidiary motifs. *Language in use* provides opportunities for exploring this notion further.)

6 Language and institutions

Again, this is related to the previous headings; it suggests a further angle on the general theme of language and social interaction. In section 4 the focus of attention was on the individual; it was the individual who supplied the common thread linking one language event with another. In section 5 we took the situation as the basic construct and used that as the means of relating language events. Here we focus attention on social institutions, such as a family, a school or a factory; these provide continuity of yet another kind, such as is implied by expressions like 'language in the home' or 'language in school'.

We can think of any social institution, from the linguistic point of view, as a communication network. Its very existence implies that communication takes place within it; there will be sharing of experience, expression of social solidarity, decision-making and planning, and, if it is a hierarchical institution, forms of verbal control, transmission of orders and the like. The structure of the institution will be enshrined in the language, in the different types of interaction that take place and the linguistic registers associated with them.

An obvious example is a school, which is examined from this point of view by Peter Doughty in chapter 6 of *Exploring Languages*:

> In the sense that a school functions as a social group within a discernible social context, it is a speech community: there will be patterns of interaction peculiar to the school, and consequently, there will also be patterns of language in use peculiar to it, and those who work together in the school develop common responses to them (pp. 100–101).

The school is a communication network, composed of many smaller networks that crisscross each other and may be relatively fixed and constant or fluid and shifting. Consider for example the question of how decisions are transmitted. One communication network is formed by the chain of command, which might run from principal to head of department to member of staff to pupil. The detailed pattern is modified and varied from one instance to another; but the mechanisms are usually linguistic, and can be described (again, on the theoretical basis of field, tenor and mode) in terms of a few recognized situation types: formal interview, tête-à-tête, assembly, noticeboard and so on. It is interesting to follow what happens in the case of a particular policy decision, from its original discussion (if any) and adoption to its eventual putting into effect, seeing how language is used at each stage and how it signals the social relationships involved. As Doughty puts it, there are 'ways of operating through which one individual indicates to another his understanding of their mutual status and relationship.'

There are also the linguistic aspects of the processes whereby a decision is made, as distinct from those by which it is transmitted. Suppose it is initiated from a level some way *below* the level of authority required for its adoption; for example, a suggestion from the class for a visit to the docks. How is this formulated for the purpose of being referred upward for decision, from the class to the teacher, or from the teacher to the principal?

The making and implementing of decisions is only one of the aspects of the life of an institution that can be considered from this point of view, taking the institution as a communication network.

The characteristics of one type of institution, and the features that set it off from others, are likely to be revealed in unexpected ways in the language. For example, certain institutions, of which the school is one, are distinguished by the existence of a clientele, a group for whom the institution is originally designed but who are distinct from the members of it, the professionals who, typically, earn their living from the institution. The school has pupils; similarly, a hotel has guests, a hospital has patients, an airline has passengers. (These contrast with institutions such as a family, a club, or a union branch, which have only members; and with those which have a 'general public' with whom they communicate only indirectly and through special channels, such as an industrial enterprise, or a government department.) Here the status of the clientele is largely revealed by the nature of the communication that takes place between it and the members. There is a recognized class of jokes about institutions which lose sight of the interests of the clientele who constitute the sole reason for their existence, centring round the basic theme of 'this would be a splendid place to work in if it wasn't for the . . . (pupils, guests, etc.).' The reality behind this form of humour, the rather natural tendency on the part of the professionals to regard the customers as an unnecessary intrusion in the smooth running of the institution, is again most clearly revealed through the language.

The school itself, therefore, is only one of many institutions that are of interest from this point of view, as a communication *network*, a nexus of interpersonal contexts for the use of language. But in one respect it differs from the others mentioned above. Most other institutions of this general type – those with a clientele – serve their clientele in nonlinguistic ways. The hospital treats their ailments, the airline moves them from place to place, the hotel feeds and entertains them. In a school, the relation between staff and pupils is essentially one of talk. The whole function of the school is to be a communication network joining professional and client. (Perhaps the nearest type of institution to it in this respect is a church.) Hence an understanding of the institutional use of language is even more fundamental in the school than elsewhere.

Recently we have begun to see some penetrating accounts of the use of language in the classroom (e.g. Sinclair *et al.* 1972; *Five to Nine* 1972), and these will no doubt shed a rather new light on the nature of the school as an institution, and therefore on the educational process. This refers not only to the teacher's own use of language, but also to the sort of language he gets, as well as the sort of language he expects, from the pupils. The latter are no longer enjoined to silence, as they were once; the communication channels are now two-way. But at the same time there are restraints, and only certain types of linguistic behaviour on the part of the pupils are normally regarded as acceptable – depending, of course, on the context: forms of speech which are not acceptable in the classroom or corridor would pass unnoticed on the sportsfield. This is another instance of variation in register.

Finally there is also the external aspect of the communication patterns: communication between the school and the outside world. We have already referred to teacher-parent interaction; but there are many other aspects to this, which taken together reflect the place of the school in the community as a whole. This also is best seen through attention to the language, which is likely to show up many of the assumptions that are made, by the school on the one hand and the community on the other, about the role of the school in the life of social man.

Points to consider
a What do we mean by an institution, from a linguistic point of view? In other words, can we define it by reference to the concept of a communication network?

Who talks to whom, and who writes to whom, as an essential part of the fabric of the institution?
Who talks or writes to whom as a means of contact between the institution and the outside world?

b   What is the special nature of the school as a communication network? How does it differ, in this regard, from other institutions of a comparable nature?
How are decisions made, and how are they transmitted? What are the *linguistic* features of the decision processes?
What types of communication are necessary to, and characteristic of, the life of the school? (These again can be seen in terms of field, tenor and mode: what significant kinds of activity are carried on through language, what is the specific channel of communication in each case, and what are the role relationships involved?)

c   Where are the *breakdowns* in communication, and why?

7 Language attitudes

The subject of attitudes to language has been discussed frequently over the past ten years. One of the early treatments of it in an educational context was in Halliday *et al.* (1964), *The linguistic sciences and language teaching* (ch. 4), where it was stressed that the reason for insisting on public discussion of attitudes to language was that these can be, and have been, extremely harmful in their effects on educational practice (cf. Trudgill 1975).

We referred in chapter 1 to the 'stereotype hypothesis', and to the fact that teachers often base their initial judgement of a child, and their expectations of his performance, very largely upon his accent. This is already very damaging, since a child – like an adult – tends to behave as he is expected to do: if he is stereotyped as a failure, he will fail. But it is not only in their initial expectations that teachers have discriminated in this way. They have often totally rejected the child's mother tongue, and tried to stamp it out with the full force of their diapproval and scorn. It is unlikely that a child will come out of this sort of ordeal unscathed. When the authors of *The linguistic sciences and language teaching* wrote that 'A speaker who is made ashamed of his own language habits suffers a basic injury as a human being: to make anyone, especially a child, feel so ashamed is as indefensible as to make him feel ashamed of the colour of his skin' (105), they were actually taken to task in the columns of a women's magazine, on the grounds that whereas a child cannot change the colour of his skin, he can learn to change his language. This seems to imply that if Catholics are discriminated against, the best way to help them is by forcible conversion to Protestantism.

To reject this is not to argue that a teacher ought to learn to talk to the children in their neighbourhood dialect, a gesture which by itself serves little purpose. But he should be prepared to recognize both his own and other people's folk-linguistic attitudes; and, ideally, to explore these attitudes, taking the pupils into his confidence. The pupils' own experience will tell them that language is one of the many aspects of human behaviour that is judged by others as 'good' or 'bad'; they can be encouraged to try and find out why this is, and can be guided by the teacher towards an understanding which enables them to see through and behind these judgements. (It is not unknown for the pupils to guide the teacher, in the first instance.) This puts questions of dialect and accent, standard and nonstandard, into a perspective. We all need to learn some form of the standard language – it does not matter much with what accent, and there is little chance of the teacher's influencing this anyway – but if the standard differs from our mother tongue, we do not throw the mother tongue away. There are functions of language to which the one is appropriate but not the other. Learning standard English, in fact, is more a matter of learning new registers than of learning a new dialect.

Social man is, inevitably, his own ethnographer; he has his own model of himself, his society, and his language. This model contains a great deal of useful insight; but it is cluttered up with attitudes which may originally have been protective to the individual himself but which no longer serve him any purpose and become harmful if he is in a position to influence others. Such attitudes are difficult to recognize because they are disguised and legitimized as statements of fact. This is why one of the most far-reaching trends of the past decade has been the trend, in education, towards a much greater social and linguistic objectivity and understanding; the approach to language is now on the whole constructive and positive, instead of being largely negative as it was before.

In exploring language, we are very naturally led to explore the folk linguistic that goes with it. An important part of this, as Peter Doughty points out, is derived from experience at school; and the school is a good place in which to explore it. The class can collect cuttings about language from letters to the press, columns in popular magazines and so on, to see what sort of ideas people have; they can note the words that are used to pass judgement on language (*good, correct, wrong, lazy, ugly, etc.*), the explanations that are offered for these judgements, if any (why is something said to be *wrong* or *sloppy*?), and the particular aspects of language that are brought up for discussion (accent, grammar, vocabulary). It is easy to assume that there must be a general consensus about all such matters, but this is largely illusory: apart from the prescriptive rules that were codified in the English textbooks of the previous generation, which have a very strong power of survival, the consensus consists in little more than a general agreement that there must be a right and a wrong in language somewhere.

It is perhaps worth adding a note about phonetics, especially at a point in history when educated Britons are once again becoming linguists, in the other sense of the term (speakers of foreign languages), as they used to be not so very long ago. In any class where some or all of the pupils 'speak with an accent' – which means the vast majority of the schools in the country – it will be easy to show that for learning French or German or Italian or Russian some of the sounds in their own speech are much more helpful that those of

RP (= 'received pronunciation', not 'royal pronunciation', although it could be roughly defined as the Queen's English). In learning foreign languages, the child who speaks RP has no advantages; and it is very disheartening – though not uncommon – to hear children struggling hard to pronounce foreign sounds badly, in good English, when if they had not been taught to disvalue their own native speech they could have used this as a model and pronounced the foreign sounds well and with ease.

The ability to make observations on the speech of the pupils in accurate phonetic terms is, naturally, something that requires training. But one part of this is a training in listening objectively to speech sounds, and in seeing through the folk-linguistic jargon of 'pure', 'harsh', 'grating', 'rich', and other such terminological obstacles to clear thinking; and this one can achieve on one's own, given a reasonable dash of curiosity and open-mindedness. A teacher who is interested in this aspect of language can then try out the 'stereotype hypothesis' on himself, and see how far his own expectations of an individual pupil's performance do in fact correlate with how that pupil pronounces English. In the long run, we may find that the advantage lies with the child who has mastered a variety of different speech forms, although this would have more to do with register than with dialect. At the very least we can show that questions of accent and dialect can be the subject of rational and tolerant discussion, instead of being used as a means of typecasting human beings into readymade categories and labelling them with badges of inferiority and shame. We tend to treat language all too solemnly, yet without taking it seriously; if we could learn to be rather more serious about it, and at the same time a lot less solemn, we should come nearer to exploiting its full potential as the cornerstone of the educational process.

Points to consider

a What are the most familiar attitudes towards linguistic norms and cor-
   rectness?
   What linguistic opinions are held by (i) the children, (ii) their parents, (iii)
   your colleagues, (iv) you?
   How are these attitudes manifested and expressed?
   Are the value judgements concerned mainly with grammar? with vocabulary? with dialect and accent? Is a distinction made between *grammar* (= 'what should be') and *usage* (= 'what is')?

b What is the effect of these attitudes on the relationship between teacher
   and pupil?
   Do they provide a clue to (i) the teacher's expectations, (ii) the teacher's
   assessments of the pupil's performance?
   What is the effect of these attitudes on the child's own expectations of the
   school, and on his feelings about his chances of success?
   What is the effect on his actual performance?

References

Abdulaziz, M. H. 1971: 'Tanzania's national language policy and the rise of Swahili political culture'. In Whiteley 1971.

Baratz, Joan C. 1969: 'A bi-dialectal task for determining language proficiency in economically disadvantaged Negro children'. *Child Development* **40**.
— 1970: 'Teaching reading in an urban Negro school system'. In Williams 1970a.
Baratz, Joan C. and Shuy, Roger W. (eds.): *Teaching Black children to read.* Washington, DC: Center for Applied Linguistics.
Barthes, Roland 1970: 'L'ancienne rhétorique'. *Communications* **16**.
Basso, Keith H. 1967: 'Semantic aspects of linguistic acculturation'. *American Anthropologist* **69**.
Bellack, A. A., Dliebard, H. M., Hyman, R. T. and Smith, F. L. Jr 1966: *The language of the classroom.* New York: Teachers College Press.
Benson, James D. and Greaves, William S. 1973: *The language people really use.* Agincourt, Ontario: The Book Society of Canada.
Berger, Peter L. and Kellner, Hansfried 1970: 'Marriage and the construction of reality'. In Hans Peter Dreitzel (ed.), *Recent sociology 2: patterns of communicative behavior.* New York: Macmillan.
Berger, Peter L. and Luckmann, Thomas 1966: *The social construction of reality: a treatise in the sociology of knowledge.* New York: Doubleday. London: Allen Lane (Penguin Press) 1967.
Bernstein, Basil 1971: *Class, codes and control 1: theoretical studies towards a sociology of language.* (Primary Socialization, Language and Education.) London: Routledge & Kegan Paul.
—(ed.) 1973: *Class, codes and control 2: applied studies towards a sociology of language.* (Primary Socialization, Language and Education.) London: Routledge & Kegan Paul.
—1974: 'A brief account of the theory of codes'. Appendix to Bernstein 1971. London: Paladin.
—1975: *Class, codes and control 3: towards a theory of educational transmissions.* (Primary Socialization, Language and Education.) London: Routledge & Kegan Paul.
Bickerton, Derek 1971: 'Inherent variability and variable rules'. *Foundations of Language* **7**.
Blom, J. P. and Gumperz, John J. 1972: 'Some social determinants of verbal behavior'. In Gumperz and Hymes 1972.
Bourdieu, Pierre 1971: 'The Berber house, or the world reversed'. In *Echanges et*

communications: mélanges offerts à Claude Lévi-Strauss à l'occasion de son 60e anniversaire. The Hague: Mouton. Also in Douglas 1973.

Bright, William (ed.) 1966: *Sociolinguistics: proceedings of the UCLA Sociolinguistics Conference, 1964.* (Janua Linguarum Series Maior 20.) The Hague: Mouton.

Britton, James N. 1970: *Language and learning.* London: Allen Lane (Penguin Press).

Brown, Roger and Gilman, Albert 1960: 'The pronouns of power and solidarity'. In Thomas A. Sebeok (ed.), *Style in language.* Cambridge, Mass. and New York: MIT Press and Wiley. Also in Fishman 1968; Giglioli 1972.

Bühler, Karl 1934: *Sprachtheorie: die Darstellungsfunktion der Sprache.* Jena: Fischer.

Castaneda, Carlos 1971: *A separate reality: further conversations with Don Juan.* New York: Simon & Schuster. (Pocket Books 1972.)

Cedergren, Henrietta and Sankoff, David 1974: 'Variable rules: performance as a statistical reflection of competence'. *Language* **50**.

Chabrol, C. and Marin, L. (eds.) 1971: *Sémiotique narrative: récits bibliques.* (Langages 22.) Paris: Didier/Larousse.

Cicourel, Aaron V. 1969: 'Generative semantics and the structure of social interaction'. In *International days of sociolinguistics.*

Clark, Eve V. 1973: 'What's in a word? On the child's acquisition of semantics in his first language'. In T. E. Moore (ed.), *Cognitive development and the acquisition of language.* New York: Academic Press.

Conklin, Harold C. 1968: 'Lexicographical treatment of folk taxonomies'. In Fishman 1968.

Coulthard, R. M., Sinclair, J. McH., Forsyth, I. J. and Ashby, M. C. 1972: 'Discourse in the classroom'. London: Centre for Information on Language Teaching and Research. (Mimeo.)

Daneš, František (ed.) 1974: *Papers on functional sentence perspective.* Prague: Academia (Czechoslovak Academy of Sciences).

Dixon, Robert M. W. 1965: *What is language? a new approach to linguistic description.* (Longman Linguistics Library.) London: Longman.

— 1970: *The Dyirbal language of North Queensland.* Cambridge: Cambridge University Press.

Doughty, Peter S., Pearce, John J. and Thornton, Geoffrey M. 1971: *Language in use.* (Schools Council Programme in Linguistics and English Teaching.) London: Edward Arnold.

— 1972: *Exploring language.* (Explorations in Language Study.) London: Edward Arnold.

Douglas, Mary 1971: 'Do dogs laugh? a cross-cultural approach to body symbolism'. *Journal of Psychosomatic Research* **15**.

— 1972: 'Speech, class and Basil Bernstein'. London: *The Listener* **2241** (9 March).

— (ed.) 1973: *Rules and meanings: the anthropology of everyday knowledge.* (Penguin Modern Sociology Readings.) Harmondsworth: Penguin.

Dumont, Louis 1970: *Homo hierarchicus: the caste system and its implications.* London: Weidenfeld & Nicolson. (London: Granada (Paladin) 1972.)

Ellis, Jeffrey 1965: 'Linguistic sociology and institutional linguistics'. *Linguistics* **19**.
— 1966: 'On contextual meaning'. In C. E. Bazell et al. (eds.), *In memory of J. R. Firth*. (Longman Linguistics Library.) London: Longman.
Elmenoufy, Afaf 1969: *A study of the role of intonation in the grammar of English*. University of London PhD thesis.
Enkvist, Nils Erik, Spencer, John and Gregory, Michael J. 1964: *Linguistics and style*. (Language and Language Learning 6.) London: Oxford University Press.
Ervin-Tripp, Susan M. 1969: 'Sociolinguistics'. *Advances in Experimental Social Psychology* **4**. Also in Fishman 1971b.
— 1972: 'Children's sociolinguistic competence and dialect diversity'. In *Early childhood education*. Chicago: National Society for the Study of Education. (71st Yearbook)
— 1973: *Language acquisition and communicative choice: essays selected and introduced by Anwar S. Dil*. Stanford, California: Stanford University Press.

Fasold, Ralph W. 1970: 'Two modes of socially significant linguistic variation'. *Language* **46**.
Ferguson, Charles A. 1968: 'Language development'. In Joshua A. Fishman, J. Das Gupta and Charles A. Ferguson (eds.), *Language problems of developing nations*. New York: Wiley.
— 1971a: 'Absence of copula and the notion of simplicity'. In Hymes 1971b.
— 1971b: *Language structure and language use: essays selected and introduced by Anwar S. Dil*. Stanford, California: Stanford University Press.
Ferguson, Charles A. and Farwell, Carol B. 1973: 'Words and sounds in early language acquisition: English initial consonants in the first fifty words'. *Papers and Reports on Child Language Development* **7**. Stanford, California: Stanford University Committee on Linguistics.
Firbas, Jan 1964: 'On defining the theme in functional sentence analysis'. *Travaux Linguistiques de Prague* **1**.
— 1968: 'On the prosodic features of the Modern English finite verb as means of functional sentence perspective'. *Brno Studies in English* **7**.
Firth, J. R. 1935: 'The technique of semantics'. *Transactions of the Philological Society*. Also in Firth 1957.
— 1950: 'Personality and language in society'. *The Sociological Review* **42**. Also in Firth 1957.
— 1957: *Papers in linguistics 1934–1951*. London: Oxford University Press.
Fishman, Joshua A. (ed.) 1968: *Readings in the sociology of language*. The Hague: Mouton.
— 1971a: 'The sociology of language: an interdisciplinary social science approach to language in society'. In Fishman 1971b.
— (ed.) 1971b: *Advances in the sociology of language* **1**. The Hague: Mouton.
Fishman, Joshua A. and Lueders-Salmon, Erika 1972: 'What has the sociology of language to say to the teacher? On teaching the standard variety to speakers of dialectal or sociolectal varieties'. In Courtney Cazden, Vera P. John and Dell H. Hymes (eds.), *Functions of language in the classroom*. New York: Teachers College Press.
Five to nine: aspects of function and structure in the spoken language of elementary

school children. Toronto 1972: York University and Board of Education for the Borough of North York (English Department)

Flavell, J. H., Botkin, P. T., Fry, C. C., Jr., Wright, J. W. and Jarvis, P. E. 1968: *The development of role-taking and communication skills in children*. New York: Wiley.

Frake, Charles O. 1961: 'The diagnosis of disease among the Subanun of Mindanao'. *American Anthropologist* **63**. Also in Hymes 1964.

Friedrich, Paul 1966: 'Structural implications of Russian pronominal usage'. In Bright 1966.

Garfinkel, Harold 1967: *Studies in ethnomethodology*. Englewood Cliffs, NJ: Prentice-Hall.

Garvin, Paul and Mathiot, Madeleine 1956: 'The urbanization of the Guarani language: a problem in language and culture'. In A. F. C. Wallace (ed.), *Men and cultures: selected papers of the 5th International Congress of Anthropological and Ethnological Sciences*. Philadelphia: University of Pennsylvania Press.

Giglioli, Pier Paolo (ed.) 1972: *Language and social context*. (Penguin Modern Sociology Readings.) Harmondsworth: Penguin.

Goffman, Erving 1963: *Stigma: notes on the management of spoiled identity*. Englewood Cliffs, NJ: Prentice-Hall.

Gorman, T. P. 1971: 'Sociolinguistic implications of a choice of media of instruction'. In Whiteley 1971.

Greenberg, Joseph 1963: *Essays in linguistics*. Chicago and London: University of Chicago Press. (Phoenix Books.)

Gregory, Michael 1967: 'Aspects of varieties differentiation'. *Journal of Linguistics* **3**.

Greimas, A. J. 1969: 'Des modèles théoriques en sociolinguistique'. In *International days of sociolinguistics*.

— 1971: 'Narrative grammar: units and levels'. *Modern Language Notes* **86(6)**.

Grimshaw, Allen 1971: 'Sociolinguistics'. In Fishman 1971b.

Gumperz, John J. 1968: 'The speech community'. In *International encyclopedia of the social sciences*. New York: Macmillan.

— 1971: *Language in social groups: essays selected and introduced by Anwar S. Dil*. Stanford, California: Stanford University Press.

Gumperz, John J. and Hymes, Dell H. (eds.) 1972: *Directions in sociolinguistics*. New York: Holt, Rinehart & Winston.

Gumperz, John J. and Wilson, Robert 1971: 'Convergence and creolization: a case from the Indo-Aryan/Dravidian border'. In Hymes 1971b.

Halliday, M. A. K. 1967a: *Grammar, society and the noun*. London: H. K. Lewis (for University College London).

— 1967b: *Intonation and grammar in British English*. (Janua Linguarum Series Practica 48.) The Hague: Mouton.

— 1967c: 'Notes on transitivity and theme in English, Part 2'. *Journal of Linguistics* **3**.

— 1969: 'Functional diversity in language, as seen from a consideration of modality and mood in English'. *Foundations of Language* **6**. Excerpt in Halliday 1976.

— 1970: *A course in spoken English: intonation.* London: Oxford University Press. Excerpt in Halliday 1976.

— 1971: 'Linguistic function and literary style: an inquiry into the language of William Golding's *The Inheritors'.* In Seymour Chatman (ed.), *Literary style: a symposium.* New York: Oxford University Press. Also in Halliday 1973.

— 1972: *Towards a sociological semantics.* (Working Papers and Prepublications, Series C, 14.) Università di Urbino, Centro Internazionale di Semiotica e di Linguistica. Also in Halliday 1973.

— 1973: *Explorations in the functions of language.* (Explorations in Language Study.) London: Edward Arnold.

— 1975a: *Learning how to mean: explorations in the development of language.* (Explorations in Language Study.) London: Edward Arnold.

— 1975b: 'Learning how to mean'. In Eric and Elizabeth Lenneberg (eds.), *Foundations of language development: a multidisciplinary approach.* New York: Academic Press/Paris: UNESCO Press. .

— 1975c: 'Talking one's way in: a sociolinguistic perspective on language and learning'. In Alan Davies (ed.), *Problems of language and learning.* London: Heinemann, in association with the SSRC and SsRE.

— 1976: *System and function in language: selected papers,* ed. Gunther Kress. London: Oxford University Press.

— 1977: 'Types of linguistic structure, and their functional origins'. (Mimeo.)

Halliday, M. A. K. and Hasan, Ruqaiya 1976: *Cohesion in English.* (English Language Series 9.) London: Longman.

Halliday, M. A. K., McIntosh, Angus and Strevens, Peter 1964: *The linguistic sciences and language teaching.* (Longman Linguistics Library.) London: Longman. (Bloomington, Indiana: Indiana University Press 1966.)

Harman, Thomas 1567: *A Caveat or Warening for Commen Cursetores vulgarely called Vagabones.* London: Wylliam Gryffith. Included as 'A caveat for common cursitors' in Gāmini Salgādo (ed.), *Cony-Catchers and Bawdy Baskets: an anthology of Elizabethan low life.* (Penguin English Library.) Harmondsworth: Penguin 1972.

Hasan, Ruqaiya 1971: 'Rime and reason in literature'. In Seymour Chatman (ed.), *Literary style: a symposium.* New York: Oxford University Press.

— 1973: 'Code, register and social dialect'. In Bernstein 1973.

Haugen, Einar 1966: 'Dialect, language, nation'. *American Anthropologist* **68**. Also in Anwar S. Dil (ed.), *The ecology of language: essays by Einar Haugen.* Stanford, California: Stanford University Press 1972.

Hawkins, Peter R. 1969: 'Social class, the nominal group and reference'.*'Language and Speech* **12**. Also in Bernstein 1973.

Hill, Trevor 1958: 'Institutional Linguistics'. *Orbis* **7**.

Hjelmslev, Louis 1961: *Prolegomena to a theory of language.* Revised English edition, tr. Francis J. Whitfield, Madison: University of Wisconsin Press. (Original Danish version 1943.)

Hoenigswald, Henry 1971: 'Language history and creole studies'. In Hymes 1971b.

Huddleston, Rodney D. 1965: 'Rank and depth'. *Language* **41**.

Hudson, Richard A. 1967: 'Constituency in a systemic description of the English clause'. *Lingua* **18**.

— 1971: *English complex sentences: an introduction to systemic grammar.* (Linguistic Series 4.) Amsterdam: North Holland.

Hymes, Dell H. (ed.) 1964: *Language in culture and society: a reader in linguistics and anthropology.* New York: Harper & Row.

— 1966: 'Two types of linguistic relativity (with examples from Amerindian ethnography)'. In Bright 1966.

— 1967: 'Models of interaction of language and social setting'. *Journal of Social Issues* **23**.

— 1969: 'Linguistic theory and the functions of speech'. In *International days of sociolinguistics.*

— 1971a: Competence and performance in linguistic theory'. In Renira Huxley and Elisabeth Ingram (eds.), *Language acquisition: models and methods.* London and New York: Academic Press.

— (ed.) 1971b. *Pidginization and creolization of languages.* New York: Cambridge University Press.

International days of sociolinguistics. Rome 1969: Luigi Sturzo Institute.

Jakobson, Roman 1960: 'Closing statement: linguistics and poetics'. In Thomas A. Sebeok (ed.), *Style in language.* Cambridge, Mass. and New York: MIT Press and Wiley.

Joos, Martin 1962: *The five clocks.* Supplement 22 to *International Journal of American Linguistics* **28** (5).

Kochman, Thomas 1972: *Rappin' and stylin' out: communication in urban Black America.* Urbana, Illinois and Chicago: University of Illinois Press.

Krishnamurthi, Bhadriraju 1962: *A survey of Telugu dialect vocabulary.* Reprinted from *A Telugu dialect dictionary of occupational terms,* **1**: *Agriculture.* Hyderabad: The Andhra Pradesh Sahitya Akademi.

Labov, William 1966: *The social stratification of English in New York City.* Washington, DC: Center for Applied Linguistics.

— 1969: 'Contraction, deletion, and inherent variation of the English copula'. *Language* **45**.

— 1970a: 'The study of language in its social context'. *Studium Generale* **23**. Also in Fishman 1971; Giglioli 1972.

—1970b: 'The logic of Non-Standard English'. *Georgetown University Monograph Series on Languages and Linguistics* **22**. Also in Williams 1970; Giglioli 1972.

— 1971: 'The notion of "system" in creole languages'. In Hymes 1971b.

Labov, William and Waletzky, Joshua 1967: 'Narrative analysis: oral versions of personal experience'. In June Helm (ed.), *Essays on the verbal and visual arts.* Seattle: University of Washington Press.

Lamb, Sydney M. 1966: 'Epilegomena to a theory of language'. *Romance Philology* **19**.

— 1971: 'Linguistic and cognitive networks'. In Paul Garvin (ed.), *Cognition: a multiple view.* New York: Spartan Books.

— 1974: Discussion. In Parret 1974.

Levi-Strauss, Claude 1966: *The savage mind.* London: Weidenfeld & Nicolson. (Original French version *La pensée sauvage,* 1962.)

Loflin, Marvin D. 1969: 'Negro nonstandard and standard English: same or different deep structure?' *Orbis* **18**.

McDavid, Raven I. and McDavid, Virginia G. 1951: 'The relationship of the speech of American Negroes to the speech of whites'. In Walt Wolfram and Nona H. Clarke (eds.), *Black-white speech relationships.* Washington, DC: Center for Applied Linguistics.

McIntosh, Angus 1963: '*As You Like It:* a grammatical clue to character'. *A Review of English Literature* **4**. Also in Angus McIntosh and M. A. K. Halliday, *Patterns of language: essays in theoretical, descriptive and applied linguistics.* (Longman Linguistics Library.) London: Longman. Bloomington, Indiana: Indiana University Press 1966.

Mackay, David, Thompson, Brian and Schaub, Pamela 1970: *Breakthrough to literacy.* (Schools Council Programme in Linguistics and English Teaching.) London: Longman. Glendale, California: Bowmar 1973.

Malinowski, Bronislaw 1923: 'The problem of meaning in primitive languages'. Supplement 1 to C. K. Ogden and I. A. Richards, *The meaning of meaning.* (International Library of Psychology, Philosophy and Scientific Method.) London: Kegan Paul.

— 1935: *Coral gardens and their magic*, **2**. London: Allen & Unwin/New York: American Book Co.

Mallik, Bhaktiprasad 1972: *Language of the underworld of West Bengal.* (Research Series 76.) Calcutta: Sanskrit College.

Milligan, Spike 1973: *More Goon Show scripts: written and selected by Spike Milligan, with a foreword by HRH The Prince of Wales.* London: Sphere Books.

Mitchell, T. F. 1957: 'The language of buying and selling in Cyrenaica: a situational statement'. *Hesperis.* Also in Mitchell 1975.

— 1975: *Principles of Firthian linguistics.* (Longman Linguistics Library.) London: Longman.

Morris, Desmond 1967: *The naked ape.* London: Cape.

Morris, Robert W. 1975: 'Linguistic problems encountered by contemporary curriculum development projects in mathematics'. *Interactions between linguistics and mathematical education: final report of the symposium sponsored by UNESCO, CEDO and ICMI, Nairobi, Kenya, 1–11 September 1974.* Working Document ED–74/CONF. 808/9. Paris: UNESCO.

Nelson, Katherine 1973: *Structure and strategy for learning to talk.* Monographs of the Society for Research in Child Development 38.

Neustupný, Jiří V. 1971: 'Towards a model of linguistic distance'. *Linguistic Communcations* **5** (Monash University).

Parret, Herman 1974: *Discussing language.* (Janua Linguarum Series Maior 93.) The Hague: Mouton.

Pike, Kenneth L. 1959: 'Language as particle, wave and field'. *Texas Quarterly* **2**.

Podgórecki, Adam 1973: ' "Second life" and its implications'. (Mimeo.)

Reich, Peter A. 1970: 'Relational networks'. *Canadian Journal of Linguistics* **15**.

Reid, T. B. W. 1956: 'Linguistics, structuralism, philology'. *Archivum Linguisticum* **8**.

Rubin, Joan 1968: 'Bilingual usage in Paraguay'. In Fishman 1968.

Sacks, Harvey, Schegloff, Emanuel A. and Jefferson, Gail 1974: 'A simplest systematics for the organization of turn-taking in conversation'. *Language* **50**.

Sankoff, Gillian 1974: 'A quantitative paradigm for the study of communicative competence'. In Richard Bauman and Joel Sherzer (eds.), *Explorations in the ethnography of speaking*. Cambridge: Cambridge University Press.

Schegloff, Emanuel A. 1971: 'Notes on a conversational practice: formulating place'. In D. Sudnow (ed.), *Studies in social interaction*. Glencoe, Illinois: Free Press. Also in Giglioli 1972.

Shuy, Roger, W., Wolfram, Walter A. and Riley, William 1967: *Linguistic correlates of social stratification in Detroit speech*. US Office of Education, Cooperative Research Project 6–1347 (final report).

Sinclair, J. McH. 1972: *A course in spoken English: grammar*. London: Oxford University Press.

Sinclair, J. McH., Forsyth, I. J., Coulthard, R. M. and Ashby, M. 1972: *The English used by teachers and pupils*. University of Birmingham: Department of English Language and Literature.

Sinclair, J. McH., Jones, S. and Daley, R. 1970: *English lexical studies*. University of Birmingham: Department of English Language and Literature.

Spencer, John and Gregory, Michael J. 1964: 'An approach to the study of style'. In Enkvist *et al.* 1964.

Stewart, William 1970: 'Sociolinguistic factors in the history of American Negro dialects'. In Williams 1970.

Taber, Charles 1966: *The structure of Sango narrative*. (Hartford Studies in Linguistics 17.) Hartford, Connecticut: Hartford Seminary Foundation.

Turner, Geoffrey J. 1973: 'Social class and children's language of control at age five and age seven'. In Bernstein 1973.

— (forthcoming): 'Social class differences in the behaviour of mothers in regulative (social control) situations'. To appear in *The regulative context: a sociolinguistic enquiry*.

Ure, Jean N. 1971: 'Lexical density and register differentiation'. In G. E. Perren and J. L. M. Trim (eds.), *Applications of linguistics: selected papers of the 2nd International Congress of Applied Linguistics, Cambridge 1969*. Cambridge: Cambridge University Press.

Ure, Jean and Ellis, Jeffrey 1974: 'El registro en la lingüistica descriptiva y en la sociologia lingüistica'. In *La sociolingüistica actual: algunos de sus problemas, planteamientos y soluciones*, ed. Oscar Uribe-Villegas. Mexico: Universidad Nacional Autonoma de Mexico, 115–64. English version 'Register in descriptive linguistics and linguistic sociology'. In *Issues in sociolinguistics*, ed. Oscar Uribe-Villegas. The Hague: Mouton (in press).

Vachek, Josef 1966: *The linguistic school of Prague*. Bloomington, Indiana: Indiana University Press.

Vailland, R. 1958: *The law*. London: Cape. Excerpt in Douglas 1973.

Van Dijk, Teun A. 1972: *Some aspects of text grammars: a study in theoretical linguistics and poetics*. The Hague: Mouton.

Wegener, Philipp 1885: *Untersuchungen über die Grundfragen der Sprachlebens*. Halle.

Weinreich, Uriel, Labov, William and Herzog, Marvin J. 1968: 'Empirical foundations for a theory of language change'. In W. P. Lehmann and Y. Malkiel (eds.), *Directions for historical linguistics: a symposium*. Austin, Texas: University of Texas Press.

Wexler, P. J. 1955: *La formation du vocabulaire des chemins de fer en France (1778–1842)*. Geneva: Droz/Lille: Giard.

Whiteley, Wilfred H. (ed.) 1971: *Language use and social change: problems of multilingualism with special reference to eastern Africa*. London: Oxford University Press (for International African Institute).

Whorf, Benjamin Lee 1956: *Language, thought and reality: selected writings*, ed. John B. Carroll. Cambridge, Mass: MIT Press.

Williams, Frederick (ed.) 1970a: *Language and poverty: perspectives on a theme*. Chicago: Markham.

— 1970b: 'Language, attitude and social change'. In Williams 1970a.

Williams, Frederick and Naremore, R. C. 1969: 'On the functional analysis of social class differences in modes of speech'. *Speech Monographs* **36(2)**.

Wolfram, Walt 1971: 'Social dialects from a linguistic perspective'. In *Sociolinguistics: a crossdisciplinary perspective*. Washington, DC: Center for Applied Linguistics.

Zumthor, Paul 1972: *Poétique médiévale*. Paris: Seuil.

Index of subjects

accent 25, 26, 106, 161–2, 209, 234
acceptability 38, 51
actual, actualization 40, 51–2, 117
agent 45, 80, 84, 116, 129
ambiguity 202
anaphora, anaphoric 117
antilanguage 164–82, 185
antisociety 164, 167–8, 175, 178–9, 184
apposition 49, 129, 149
arbitrary, arbitrariness 44–5, 78
areal affinity 77–8, 199
attitudes to language 66, 94–5, 104–7, 155, 158, 161–3, 179, 184, 210, 233–5

behaviour potential 21, 39, 42, 81
behaviourism 54
borrowing 172, 195
Breakthrough to Literacy 205–10, 228

calquing 195
careful speech 156
casual:
—conversation 169–70, 180
—speech 156
Center for Applied Linguistics 93
characterology 177
choice (*see also* option) 149, 187
grammatical 113
semantic 109, 122, 137, 150, 208
classroom:
—as centre of language research 211–35

discourse, language 215, 228, 232
clause 81, 84, 113, 129, 135–6
—complex 129–30
—grammar 135
—type, *see* procces type
code (i): 25, 27, 31, 67, 86–8, 91, 98, 106, 111, 123, 125, 181
elaborated 26, 68, 86–8, 101–2
restricted 26, 68, 86–8, 101–2
code (ii):
—shift 65–6
—switching (*see also* dialect switching) 65
coding (*see also* realization) 39, 71, 173, 180, 187
cohesion 64, 117, 133–4, 144, 148. (*see also* conjunction, ellipsis, lexical collocation, lexical repetition, reference, substitution)
coining 196, 201
collocation 117, 203
colour terms 198
communication network 154, 230, 232
communicative:
—competence 32, 37–8, 61, 92, 94–5, 99
—dynamism 150
compensatory programmes 97
competence 17, 28, 38, 51, 85, 92
communicative 32, 37–8, 61, 92, 94–5, 99
complex (clause—, group—) 129–131, 132

compound, compounding 172, 177, 196
condition(al) 49, 84
congruence 156, 180
conjunction 117, 144
connotation 148, 166, 175
constituency, constituent structure (*see also* grammatical structure) 40–41, 130–31, 188
content 53,56,71,75,78,187,223
context, social context (*see also* situation type) 13, 30, 42, 79–81, 90, 109–11, 113–22, 189, 208, 214
  citational 109
  critical socializing 30, 37, 46, 88, 90–91, 105, 122, 140, 214
  imaginative/innovating 30
  instructional 30, 80–81
  interpersonal 30
  operational 108–9, 113
  regulative 30, 79, 80, 88
context:
  —of culture 65, 68–9, 109, 124, 147
  —of situation 22, 28–31, 32–5, 68,72,109,122,124,134,139, 142, 147, 150, 192, 222, 227–230
continuity:
  functional 71, 90–91
  cultural 106, 171–2, 209
control strategies 114, 214
  imperative 79, 82
  personal 79, 83, 87n
  positional 79, 83, 87n
convergence 155
conversation 134, 140, 147, 150, 169–70, 177, 180
coordination 49, 129, 148
co-text 133
creolization 78
culture, *see* social system

declarative 80,81,84,91,148,149
decreolization 96

deficit theory 16, 23, 95, 102–4, 209
deixis 64, 132
delicacy 43, 44
denotation 148, 166, 175
developmental functions 19–20, 53–5, 70–72, 121, 212–13 (*see also* heuristic, imaginative, informative, instrumental, interactional, personal, regulatory)
dialect, dialectal variety/variation 26, 33–4, 104–6, 110, 157–8, 183–5, 190–91, 225
  —primers 209
  —switching 34, 95, 217, 219
  ethnic 98
  regional (geographical) 66, 225
  rural 98, 104, 154–5, 157, 216
  social 66, 86, 93–100, 103, 113, 159, 178–9, 181, 184–5, 225
  urban 97, 104, 216–17
dialectology 10, 96, 154–5, 183, 190, 216
dialogue 71, 117, 121, 146, 177
difference theory 23–4, 95, 98, 102, 104–5
diglossia 65–6, 182
discourse (*see also* text) 109, 134 (*see also* field of discourse, mode of discourse, tenor of discourse)
distance, linguistic 78, 157, 197–9
divergence 155
diversification 44, 138
division of labour 113, 186

educational process/system 87, 101, 104, 106, 209–10, 211, 235
ellipsis 64, 117, 144
encoding (*see also* realization) 21, 39–43, 134, 140, 188, 208
endophora, endophoric 148
entry condition (to a system) 41, 128

environmentalist view 16–17
ethnic:
—dialect 98
—group 102–3
ethnography of speaking 61, 95
exchange of meanings 136, 139–141, 143, 163, 166, 171, 181, 189, 191, 196, 206
exophora, exophoric 64, 117
experiential (function, component) 48, 63, 112, 128–33, 143, 166, 180, 187–9
expression 53, 56, 71, 75, 78, 187

failure:
  educational 23–4, 68, 87, 95, 98, 101–7, 163
  language, linguistic 23, 102–7
family role system 67, 88, 91, 99, 113, 123, 125
fashions of speaking (see also semantic style) 24–5, 76, 81
fiction 145–7
field of discourse 33, 62–4, 110, 113, 115–17, 123, 125, 143–4, 146, 189, 221–2, 225
folk linguistics 21, 40, 122, 207, 235
folk taxonomies 76
foregrounding (see also prominence) 137–8, 149, 156, 169–70, 180
form, formal level 56–7, 115, 187
formality, level of 32, 74, 110, 224
functional approach 16, 72, 180, 194–5
  —to language 25, 45, 53, 63, 89, 186
  —to language development 18–21, 52–6, 212
functional components (of semantics; see also metafunctions) 27, 45, 54–6, 63, 70, 72, 90, 99, 112, 115–16, 121–5, 128–132, 135, 150, 180, 183, 186–189, 191

functional tenor 224–5
functions of language 16, 21–2, 27–31, 45–7, 53–6, 72, 94, 105–6, 121–2, 194, 213 (see also (i) developmental functions; (ii) macrofunctions; (iii) metafunctions, functional components of semantics)
behavioural 95
cognitive 95
communicative 50
conative 48
expressive 48, 49–50
referential 48, 72
representational 48, 49
social 49, 72
socio-expressive 49, 63

genre, generic 61–3, 133, 145
  —form 138
  —structure 133–4, 136
gesture 19, 37
ghetto language 179, 185
given (element) 148
glossematics 137
goal 45, 116
gobbledygook 177
good reason principle 133
Goonery 178, 180
grammar, grammatical 20, 39, 43–7, 102–3, 165 (see also lexicogrammar)
  —class 47
  —function 45, 47
  —structure (see also constituent structure) 41, 45, 56, 133, 148, 188, 196–7, 207
  —system, see lexicogrammatical system
grammaticality 38, 51

hesitating 200
heuristic function 19, 30, 55, 71, 221
hypotaxis, hypotactic 49, 84, 129

idealization in linguistics   17, 37–8, 52, 57, 192, 203
ideational (function, component) 45, 48, 56, 63, 70, 72, 112, 116–118, 123, 125, 128–33, 141, 149, 187–9
illiteracy   206
imaginative function   20, 55, 71, 90
imperative   64, 80, 81, 84
implication of utterance   133
indicative   80, 84
information:
—focus   61, 63, 132
—structure   117, 131–3, 148, 202
—system   131, 133, 144
—unit   132–3
informative function   20, 116, 221
instance, instantial   40
instrumental function   19, 55, 71
interactant (see also participant) 61–2
interaction (linguistic/verbal)   18, 38, 51, 60, 67, 97, 139, 150, 170, 200, 219
    classroom   80–81, 94
interactional function   19, 31, 55, 71, 90
international language   199, 204
inter-organism   10, 12–16, 37–8, 49, 56–7, 92
interpersonal (function, component)   46, 48, 50, 56, 63, 70, 72, 90, 112, 116–17, 119, 123, 125, 128–33, 141, 143–4, 166, 170–71, 180, 187–9
interrogative   81, 91, 148
intervention programmes   93
intonation   54–5, 64, 71, 115, 121, 131–3, 161, 171, 221
Intra-organism   10, 12–13, 37–8, 49, 56–7, 92

jargon   165, 182, 229

key (as grammatical system)   64, 144, 187
kinship terms   75, 198

language:
—as action/'doing' (see also pragmatic function)   71, 121
—as behaviour, knowledge or art   10–11
—as institution (see also institutional linguistics)   105, 162, 183–6, 199, 204
—as interaction   18, 36–8, 139, 219
—as means of learning   20–21, 30–31, 202–3
—as reflection/'thinking' (see also mathetic function)   71, 121
—as resource or rule   17, 191–2
—as system (see also linguistic system)   10–11, 39, 53, 162, 183, 186–9, 199, 204, 205
—in (of) action   32, 224
—in education   23–4, 28, 57, 101–7, 199–200
—in individual life and development   14, 200–201, 219–27 (see also language development)
—in social context   9–11, 15, 23, 27–35, 36–7, 79–84, 112, 117, 139–42, 227–33
functions of   16, 21–2, 27–31, 45–7, 53–6, 72, 94, 105–6, 121–2, 194, 213
uses of   28, 34, 46, 52–4, 99, 112, 122
language acquisition (see also language development: children)   16, 52–3
language development (children)   16–21, 52–6, 90, 115, 121–2, 135, 211–13
language development (national)   76, 194–7
language diary   219–20

language distance   199, 204
Language in Use   211, 228
language planning   76, 197
language status   194, 199, 204 (*see also* international language, local language, national language, neighbourhood language, regional language)
language teaching   57
language varieties   10, 35, 74, 110, 145, 157, 225 (*see also* dialect, register)
languages:
Bengali   172–5
Chinese   196, 198
Dutch   194
Dyirbal   165
English:
Black   93, 96, 102, 161–2, 179
Caribbean   194
Elizabethan   89, 165, 175
Old   195
Standard   94–5
Trinidad   75
French   77, 196
German   75
Greek   196
Guarani   65
Japanese   196
Kannada   77
Latin   195–6
Marathi   77
Polish   171
Russian   75, 196
Swahili   65, 77
Telugu   76, 196
Urdu   77
level, *see* stratum
lexical:
—borrowing   172, 195
—collocation   117, 203
—density   32, 148, 224
—repetition   64, 117
lexical item   32, 43, 208
lexicogrammar, lexicogrammatical system   21, 39–44, 57, 79, 121, 123, 128–31, 134–5, 173, 187–8, 208
linguistic:
—system   53, 56–7, 62–3, 67–9, 72, 75, 78, 81, 92, 97, 103, 110, 111–15, 147, 155–6, 170, 179–80, 186, 209
—units   129, 135, 198
linguistics:
autonomy of   36
branches of   10
historical   10
institutional   110
instrumentality of   36
status of   38–9, 56
listening   212
literacy   57, 100, 205
literature, literary   11, 57–8, 182
—language   157
—text   70, 137–8, 140, 147
genres of   58
local language   199, 218
location, locative   117, 129–30
locutions   196
logic (logicalness) of language   85–86
logical (function, component)   48, 63, 112, 128–33, 148–9, 187–8

macrofunctions   50, 55, 121 (*see also* mathetic, pragmatic)
mathetic function of language   54–56, 71, 90, 125
meaning (*see also* semantic(s))
act of   139, 140, 206
connotative   166, 175
denotative   166, 175
exchange of   136, 139–41, 143, 163, 166, 171, 181, 189, 191, 196, 206
referential   63
representational   162, 175
social   63
meaning potential   19, 21, 26, 28, 30, 34, 39–40, 42, 51, 55, 70, 79, 90–91, 99, 105–6, 109,

meaning potential (*contd.*)
111–12, 114–25, 139, 141,
145, 187, 205
meaning style, *see* semantic style
medium (spoken/written)   33, 110,
144, 222–4
medium (grammatical function)
84, 116
metafunctions   22, 27, 47, 50, 56,
72, 112, 121 (*see also* experiential, ideational, interpersonal,
logical, textual)
metaphor   175–7, 202
metathesis   172, 177
metonymy   175
modal element   46, 129–30
modality   64, 88, 144, 223
mode of discourse   33, 62–4, 110,
113, 115–17, 123, 125, 143–5,
189, 222–3, 225
modulation   80, 84, 117, 148, 149
mood, modal   45–6, 50, 64, 81,
113, 116–17, 129, 144, 148,
223
morphology, morphological   43–4,
161
—processes   172
mother tongue   13–14, 27, 53, 70,
121, 124, 171, 199–200, 206,
233
(/child tongue)   13–14, 27, 53, 70
(/foreign language)   199–200

names, naming   64, 195–6, 200–2
—and concepts   200, 202–3
narrative   70, 133, 145–7
national language   199, 204
native language, *see* mother tongue
nativist view   16–18
natural language   37–8
—and mathematics   195, 200–
203
negative   80, 84, 148
'Negro Nonstandard English' (*see
also* Black English)   85
neighbourhood   159

—language   199, 216–19
neologisms   195–7
network, system network   40–43,
113, 125, 128, 134, 188
relational   41
semantic   41–2, 79, 80, 82–3, 85,
114–20, 192
(*see also* communication network)
neutralization   138
new (element)   138, 148
nominal group   88, 129
nominalization   202
nonstandard dialect   102, 104–5,
161–2, 178–9, 185, 225
norm, normative   154–5, 163, 169
linguistic   154–5, 163
social   169, 171
noun, *see* nominal group
Nuffield Programme in Linguistics
and   English   Teaching,   *see*
Schools   Council . . .
numbers (= numeral system)   199,
200

option, systemic   40–43, 46, 67,
113, 128, 134
behavioural   42
semantic   44, 61, 79, 91, 109,
111, 114, 125, 133
orthography, orthographic system
21, 105

paradigmatic   40–41, 52, 128, 137
—environment   139
parataxis, paratactic   49, 84, 129
participant (in situation)   33, 61–2,
143–4
peer group   99, 123, 125, 159–60
—language   97, 126, 217
pelting speech   164–5
performance   17, 38, 51, 85
periodicity   136, 139
person   64, 116–17, 144, 149
personal function   19, 31, 55, 71,
221

personality 14–15
phonaesthesia, phonaesthetic 138
phonetic(s) 10, 156, 212, 234
phonology, phonological (system)
    21, 39, 131, 135, 172, 187,
    208
    —metaphor 175
    —processes 172
    —variation 172
polarity 91, 117
polysystemic 40, 79
pragmatic function of language
    54–6, 71, 90, 125, 221
Prague school 63, 177
predicting (the text) 62, 110, 142,
    150, 189, 199, 223
prestige form 66, 156
process (grammatical function)
    45, 129
process type 64, 117, 136
    material 64, 80, 84
    mental 148
    relational 64, 149
    verbal 148
prominence 137, 149
pronoun, personal 89
pronunciation, see accent, phonetics
propositional element, see residual
    element
protolanguage (of child) 27, 55,
    71, 121, 124, 212
psycholinguistics 17, 38, 48
psychology, psychological 11,
    38–9, 57
punctuation 148

question 91, 116, 148
quoted speech 148, 150

rank 129
    —scale 133, 135
reading, see literacy
reality:
    alternative 167–71, 179
    social 126, 167
    subjective 168–9, 172, 181

realization 39–44, 70, 79, 89, 115,
    122–5, 130, 134–5, 138, 146,
    149, 172–5, 186, 208
recursion, recursive structures 48–
    49, 130, 188
reference 117, 144, 148
region, regional:
    —dialect 66
    —language 199, 204, 218
register, diatypic variety/varia-
    tion 31–5, 62, 67–8, 110–11,
    113, 114, 123–5, 145, 150, 157,
    165, 183, 185–6, 191, 195–7,
    225, 229
    —of mathematics 195–7, 202–3
regulatory function 19, 53, 55, 71,
    121
relexicalization 165
reported speech 49, 131, 149
residual (= propositional) ele-
    ment 46, 129–30
resource, language as 17, 52, 192,
    205
rheme 46, 129–30
rhythm 160–61
Roget's Thesaurus 79, 84
role, see social role, family role
    system; also grammatical func-
    tion
rules, language as 17, 191–2

Schools Council Programme in Lin-
    guistics and English Teach-
    ing 100
second language 199–200
'second life' 167–8, 177, 181
secrecy, secret language 166, 172,
    182
semantic:
    —change 74–7, 85, 89
    —field theory 75
    —load 203
    —network 41–2, 79–85, 114–
    120, 192
    —process 150
    —structure 41, 135

semantic (*contd.*)
—style   76–7, 86, 98, 111, 113, 161, 163, 177, 195–6
—unit   70, 109, 135–6
semantic system   21, 27, 39–45, 57, 63, 72, 77, 78–81, 85–6, 89–91, 99, 109, 111–14, 123–5, 126–33, 140–42, 145, 149, 173, 187–9, 195, 198, 208
semantics:
  general   114
  generative   49, 60
sentence   109, 129, 135, 177
setting   23, 34, 65, 226
simplification   96
situation (*see also* context of situation)   13, 18, 28–31, 32–5, 61–4, 109–10, 141, 145, 189, 228–9
—as determinant of text   63, 116–17, 122, 141–50, 189, 223–4
—type   29–31, 34, 37, 46, 65, 67–8, 77, 79, 85, 89–90, 105, 109–11, 114–22, 142, 145, 230
  components of   33, 61–4, 109–110, 142–5 (*see also* field, mode, tenor of discourse)
slang   158, 165
social:
—action   143–4, 146, 186
—class   67, 80, 87–8, 94, 98–100, 102–3, 105, 158, 179, 184
—construction of reality, *see* social reality
—group   14, 154, 159–61
—hierarchy   65–6, 85, 92, 113, 123, 125, 155, 172, 178, 184, 191
—institution   230–33
—learning   106, 126, 213
—order   179
—process(es)   185–6
—reality   99, 126, 140, 167–71, 191

—role   14–15, 67, 71, 144
—structure   21–6, 66–9, 78, 86, 89, 91, 101, 105, 113–14, 125, 166–72, 184, 186, 192
—value   67, 74, 106, 141, 155–156, 160–61, 166, 191, 203
social system   36–7, 39–43, 51, 57, 67–9, 76, 78–9, 81, 92, 98, 110–11, 114–15, 123–6, 141, 147, 162, 172, 175, 183, 189
—as system of meanings   79, 99, 109, 137, 139, 141, 162, 177, 189
socialization   27, 36, 55, 99, 102, 105–6, 113, 213–16
socializing agency   68, 90, 111, 125, 159
sociolinguistic coding orientation   123, 161, 166, 181
sociolinguistics   12, 13, 32, 35, 37, 56, 62, 64, 68–9, 87, 92, 97, 108, 115, 122, 126
sociology, sociological   11, 34–5, 39, 41–2, 57, 100
—of knowledge   81
—of language   35, 65, 92, 100, 192
—semantics, *see* sociosemantics
sociosemantic(s)   25, 34, 40, 53–4, 75, 79–84, 106, 114, 121–2
sound, 'sounding'   19, 21, 122, 208, 212
speech act   15
speech community   66, 74, 154–5, 183–4, 216–17
  rural   154, 183, 216
  urban   66, 155, 159, 184, 216–217
speech situation, *see* situation
spoken language   32, 103, 110, 133, 206, 224–5
standard (dialect, language)   66, 85, 98, 102, 104, 157, 161–2, 178–9, 185, 210, 225, 234
stereotype, — hypothesis   23, 104, 233, 235

stratification theory   112
stratum, stratal organization (of language)   39, 112, 122, 128, 138, 173, 183, 187, 220
'semological',   semantic   112, 135, 173
structure, structural   40–41, 47, 128–9, 133–4
—innovation   197
—types   48–9, 129, 188
constituent   40–41, 130–31, 188
generic   133–4, 136
grammatical   41, 45, 56, 133, 148, 188, 196–7, 207
semantic   41, 135
social   21–6, 66–9, 78, 86, 89, 91, 101, 105, 113–14, 125, 166–72, 184, 186, 192
style:
—scale   66, 184, 224
—shift   66
cognitive   81
semantic   76–7, 86, 98, 111, 113, 161, 163, 177, 195–6
subculture, subcultural   24, 26, 98, 125, 158, 165, 181
—differences in language   26–7, 85–6, 160–61
subject   130, 149
subject-matter (see also field of discourse)   33, 63, 77, 110, 143–4
substitution   144
suffix, suffixing   172, 177
supersentence   109, 135
syllable   135–6
—phonology   135
synonyms   138, 165–6
syntagm   56
syntagmatic   40–41, 137
—environment   139
syntax (see also lexicogrammar)   43–4, 121, 208
system, systemic   40, 47, 92, 137, 192 (see also linguistic system, semantic system)

—network   40–43, 113, 125, 128, 134, 188
technical language   32, 76, 165, 196–7, 202–3, 229
tenor of discourse   33, 62–4, 110, 113, 115–17, 123, 125, 143–5, 146, 189, 222, 225
tense   64, 75, 80, 147
terminology   76, 195–6, 203
text   40, 57–8, 61–4, 69–70, 89, 108–9, 116, 122, 125, 133–51, 180, 192
—grammar   69, 135
textual (function, component)   46, 48, 50, 63, 70, 72, 112, 116–17, 120, 123, 125, 128–33, 136, 143–5, 166, 187–9
texture   113, 133, 136, 187, 223
theme, thematic   46, 117, 129–30, 133, 148
—structure   134, 150
—system   144
—variation   148
time system   198
tone (see also intonation)   221
—contour   133
—group   133
transitivity   45–6, 58, 64, 113, 116, 129, 136, 138, 143, 148
transmission, cultural   27, 36, 52, 89, 99, 101, 106, 114, 141

underworld language   166, 180

value (see also social value)   140
—system   162, 168
variability   96
variable   85
—rule   66, 74
variant   74, 111, 156, 158, 172–7, 181, 190
high   156, 158, 184
lexicogrammatical   175
low   156, 158, 184
metaphorical   175

variant (*contd.*)
  phonological   175
  semantic   175
variation   62–3, 66–7, 74–6, 85,
    96, 125, 155–6, 172–5, 179,
    181, 183, 220
  —theory. 172, 175, 190
  free   44
  grammatical   88, 173
variety (of language)   74, 110, 157
    (*see also* dialect, register)
  dialectal   35, 225
  diatypic   35, 145, 225
verb, verbal group   129
verbal:
  —art   146, 166
  —contest and display   140, 160,
    166, 180, 185

—play   160
—repertoire   65
vernacular, *see* local language
vocabulary   20, 39, 102–3, 148,
    160–61, 165, 195–7
  —as content   64, 148
voice   64, 144
vowel breaking   159

word (*see also* lexical item, vocabu-
    lary)   20, 32, 208
  —phonology   135
wording   21, 40, 122, 125, 135,
    150, 200, 207, 212, 220
writing system, *see* orthography
written language   32, 103, 104–5,
    110, 133, 145, 148, 157, 206

Index of names

Abdulaziz, Mohamed   77

Bailey, Charles-James N.   96
Baratz, Joan   23, 85, 94, 103
Barthes, Roland   113
Basso, Keith   76
Berger, Peter   81, 126, 169–71, 177, 180
Bernstein, Basil   24–31, 36–7, 42, 46, 67–8, 79, 86–9, 91–2, 94, 101–7, 113–14, 122, 123, 140, 161, 166, 181, 214
Benson, James   224
Bourdieu, Pierre   168
Brown, Roger   89
Bühler, Karl   48, 50

Castaneda, Carlos   182
Cazden, Courtney   93, 95, 98
Cedergren, Henrietta   172
Chabrol, C.   134
Chomsky, Noam   17, 28, 37–8, 49, 57
Cicourel, Aaron   60, 67, 109, 150
Conklin, Harold   76
Coulthard, Malcolm   80

Dixon, Robert M. W.   70, 165
Doughty, Peter   21, 26, 211, 231, 234
Douglas, Mary   25, 79, 87, 88, 114
Dumont, Louis   86, 100

Ellis, Jeffrey   33, 62, 110, 228
Elmenoufy, Afaf   133
Engelmann, Siegfried   93, 96

Ervin-Tripp, Susan   81, 93–5

Farwell, Carol   135
Fasold, Ralph   96
Ferguson, Charles   96, 110, 135
Firbas, Jan   150
Firth, J. R.   28, 35, 39, 51, 54, 61, 109
Fishman, Joshua   62, 65, 68, 92, 98
Frake, Charles   76
Friedrich, Paul   75

Garfinkel, Harold   171
Gilman, Albert   89
Goffman, Erving   172
Gorman, T. P.   65
Greaves, William   224
Gregory, Michael   33, 110, 134, 145, 222, 224–5
Greimas, A. J.   70, 81
Grimshaw, Allen   61
Gumperz, John   65, 77, 110, 154, 217

Harman, Thomas   164–5, 175, 177
Hasan, Ruqaiya   31, 68, 86, 99, 111, 134, 137
Haugen, Einar   76
Hawkins, Peter   94
Henderson, Dorothy   214
Herzog, Marvin   91
Hess, Robert   95
Hill, Trevor   110
Hjelmslev, Louis   39–40, 42, 44, 70, 136, 137
Hoenigswald, Henry   75

Huddleston, Rodney   129
Hudson, Richard   41, 129
Hymes, Dell   32, 37–8, 49–50, 61,
    63, 72, 81, 85, 92, 141

Jakobson, Roman   166
John, Vera   94
Joos, Martin   224

Kellner, Hansfried   81
Kernan, Claudia Mitchell   93
Kochman, Thomas   179
Krishnamurthi,   Bhadriraju   76,
    196

Labov, William   38, 54, 66–7, 70,
    71, 74–5, 85–7, 91, 92, 96–8,
    155, 172, 184, 216–17
Lamb, Sydney   39–41, 44, 51, 112,
    136
Lévi-Strauss, Claude   99, 168, 175
Loflin, Marvin   85
Luckmann, Thomas   126, 169–71,
    177, 180
Lueders-Salmon, Erika   98

Mackay, David   100, 205n
Malinowski, Bronislaw   28, 33, 45,
    48, 65, 68, 109, 147, 192, 223
Mallik, Bhaktiprasad   164, 172–7,
    179
Marin, L.   134
McDavid, Raven   99
McIntosh, Angus   61, 89, 159
Milligan, Spike   177–8
Mitchell, T. F.   35, 180
Morris, Robert   201

Naremore, R. C.   94
Nelson, Katherine   90
Neustupný, Jiří   78

Osser, Harry   93–4

Pearce, John   28, 33, 211

Pike, Kenneth   39, 139
Podgórecki, Adam   164, 166–8

Reich, Peter   41
Reid, T. B. W.   110
Rubin, Joan   65

Sacks, Harvey   52, 60, 134, 147,
    180
Samarin, William   96
Sankoff, David   172
Sankoff, Gillian   172, 191
Saussure, Ferdinand de   40, 44, 51
Schaub, Pamela   205n
Schegloff, Emanuel   52, 60–61
Shuy, Roger   96
Sinclair, John   80, 129, 144, 232
Spencer, John   33, 110, 222
Stewart, William   25, 96
Strevens, Peter   61

Taber, Charles   134
Taylor, Orlando   97
Thompson, Brian   205n
Thornton, Geoffrey   22, 211
Thurber, James   128n, 151
Trier, Jost   75
Trudgill, Peter   233
Turner, Geoffrey   41, 43, 79, 114

Ure, Jean   32, 62, 110, 224

Vailland, R.   160
Van Dijk, Teun A.   70

Waletzky, Joshua   70
Wegener, Philipp   109
Weinreich, Uriel   91
Wells, H. G.   178
Whorf, Benjamin Lee   25, 76
Williams, Frederick   23, 93–4, 104
Wilson, Robert   77
Wolfram, Walt   66, 93, 95–6

Zumthor, Paul   58, 70n